GREECE

Angelika Taschen

GREAT ESCAPES GREECE

THE HOTEL BOOK

TASCHEN

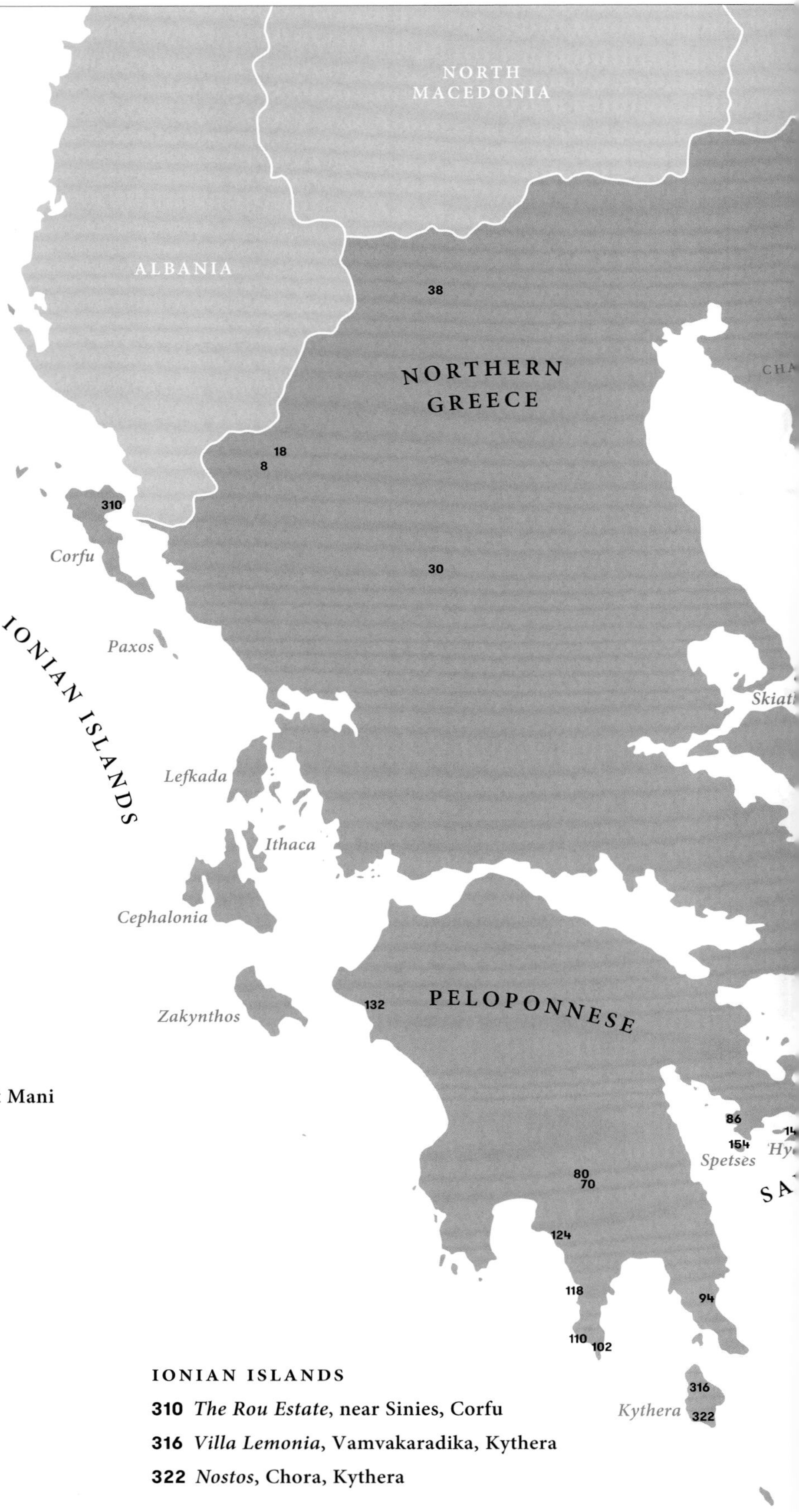

NORTH MACEDONIA
ALBANIA
NORTHERN GREECE
38
18
8
310
Corfu
30
IONIAN ISLANDS
Paxos
Lefkada
Ithaca
Cephalonia
Zakynthos
132
PELOPONNESE
86
154
Spetses
80
70
124
118
94
110
102
316
Kythera
322

NORTHERN GREECE

PELOPONNESE

SARONIC ISLANDS

IONIAN ISLANDS

CRETE

BULGARIA
TURKEY
Thassos
Samothrace
Lemnos
Lesbos
Skyros
Euboea
Psara
Chios
Andros
Tinos
Icaria
Samos
Kea
Syros
Mykonos
Patmos
Kythnos
CYCLADES
Serifos
Paros
Naxos
Leros
DODECANESE
Sifnos
Antiparos
Kimolos
Amorgos
Kos
Milos
Ios
Folegandros
Symi
Astypalaia
Santorini
Kastellorizo
Rhodes
Karpathos
CRETE
CYCLADES
162 Onar, Ahla Beach, Andros
168 Mèlisses, Paleopoli, Andros
184 The Wild Hotel by Interni, Agia Anna Beach, Mykonos
192 Soho Roc House, Paraga Beach, Mykonos
198 Boutique Hotel Ploes, Hermoupolis, Syros
210 Coco-Mat Eco Residences, Vagia Beach, Serifos
218 Beachhouse Antiparos, Apantima Beach, Antiparos
224 Verina Astra, Poulati, Sifnos
232 The Windmill Kimolos, Kimolos
240 Skinopi Lodge, Milos
248 Anemomilos, Folegandros
258 Perivolas, Oia, Santorini
264 Mystique, Oia, Santorini
DODECANESE
270 Hotel Archontiko Angelou, Alinda, Leros
276 Oku Kos, Marmari, Kos
286 The Old Markets, Symi
292 Marco Polo Mansion, Old Town, Rhodes
304 Mediterraneo Kastelorizo, Kastellorizo

ΌΔΟΣ
ΓΙΑΝΝΟΥΛΗ ΓΟΥΝΑ

CONTENTS

APEIROS CHORA

KATO PEDINA, ZAGORI, IOANNINA, EPIRUS

ΙΣ ΧΡ
ΝΙ ΚΑ
ΟΙΚΙΑΙΩΑΝΝΟΥ
Μ: ΚΟΝΤΟΥΡΗ
1861
Μηνος Σεπτεμβριου - 20

APEIROS CHORA

440 07 Kato Pedina, Zagori, Epirus
Tel. +30 26530 711 88 and +30 693 651 08 06 · apeiroschora@gmail.com
www.apeiroschora.gr and www.apeiros.gr

BEHIND THE MOUNTAIN

Zagori, which translates as "behind the mountain," is considered one of the most pristine and natural regions of Greece. Here visitors can walk through one of the world's deepest gorges in the Vikos Aoos National Park, admire age-old monasteries that cling to cliffs like birds' nests and see 46 stone villages that time seems to have passed by almost without leaving a trace. One of them is Kato Pedina, where the enchanting guesthouse Apeiros Chora is situated. Once built like a little fortress to defy the vagaries of weather, robbers and plunderers, the estate has belonged to the same family for centuries. Athina Aslanidou, Georgios Kontouris and their son are the seventh and eighth generations. They moved to the north from Athens and were able to handle the renovation of the building themselves thanks to Athina's previous occupation as a decorator and stylist. They wanted to work in an authentic and true style and therefore made rough-cut stone and wood their most important building materials, following old customs. The gentle colors of the seven bedrooms and their harmonious design also correspond to local practice – and the owners have pepped them up with urban accessories and up-to-date technology. At every turn, guests feel as if they are staying in a carefully run private house; and this also applies to the kitchen, the heart of Apeiros Chora, where a fantastic breakfast with homemade cake and bread is served every morning with jams from the proprietors' own fruit. Living areas, gardens, a library and even a spa are at guests' disposal. The hosts maintain a discreet presence, and on request help to plan customized excursions through Zagori – to the most attractive spots "behind the mountain." ◆ Book to pack: "The Quest" by Nikos Themelis

DIRECTIONS *The mountain village Kato Pedina lies at an altitude of 940 m/3,080 feet in Epirus, 34 km/17 miles from Ioannina airport (domestic flights) and 480 km/300 miles from Athens international airport* · **RATES** *€€–€€€* · **ROOMS** *6 rooms and 1 suite, named according to colors and individually furnished* · **FOOD** *Breakfast is served in the house, and the owners recommend nearby restaurants for lunch and dinner. A cook can be hired if the whole house is booked exclusively* · **HISTORY** *The oldest parts of the house date from the late sixteenth century. The present guesthouse opened in 2015* · **X-FACTOR** *Hidden rooms and underground escape routes still testify to the former defensive character of the building*

HINTER DEM BERG

Zagori, was übersetzt „hinter dem Berg" bedeutet, gilt als eine der ursprünglichsten und unberührtesten Regionen Griechenlands. Hier können Reisende im Vikos-Aoos-Nationalpark durch eine der tiefsten Schluchten der Welt wandern, uralte Klöster bestaunen, die wie Vogelnester hoch oben am Fels kleben, und 46 Steindörfer besuchen, an denen die Zeit fast spurlos vorbeigezogen zu sein scheint. Eines von ihnen ist Kato Pedina, wo das zauberhafte Gasthaus Apeiros Chora steht. Einst wie eine kleine Festung errichtet, um Wetterkapriolen, Räubern und Plünderern zu trotzen, gehört das Anwesen seit Jahrhunderten derselben Familie. Athina Aslanidou, Georgios Kontouris und ihr Sohn sind die siebte sowie achte Generation – sie zogen aus Athen in den Norden und konnten die Renovierung des Baus dank Athinas früherer Tätigkeit als Dekorateurin und Stylistin selbst leiten. Authentisch und stilgetreu wollten sie arbeiten und verwendeten daher nach altem Brauch grob behauene Steine und Holz als wichtigste Baumaterialien. Auch die sanften Farben der sieben Schlafzimmer und ihr harmonisches Design entsprechen den Gepflogenheiten der Gegend – aufgefrischt haben die Besitzer sie mit urbanen Accessoires und zeitgemäßer Technik. Überall fühlt man sich wie in einem sorgsam geführten Privathaus; auch in der Küche, wo das Herz von Apeiros Chora schlägt und jeden Morgen ein fantastisches Frühstück mit hausgemachten Kuchen und Broten sowie Marmeladen aus eigenem Obst aufgetischt wird. Zudem stehen den Gästen Wohnbereiche, Gärten, eine Bibliothek und sogar ein Spa zur Verfügung. Die Gastgeber sind stets dezent präsent und helfen auf Wunsch auch dabei, maßgeschneiderte Ausflüge durch Zagori zu planen – zu den schönsten Zielen „hinter dem Berg". ◆ Buchtipp: „Jenseits von Epirus" von Nikos Themelis

ANREISE *Das Bergdorf Kato Pedina liegt auf 940 m Höhe im Epirus, 34 km vom nationalen Flughafen Ioannina und 480 km vom internationalen Flughafen Athen entfernt* · **PREISE** *€€–€€€* · **ZIMMER** *6 nach Farben benannte und individuell eingerichtete Zimmer und 1 Suite* · **KÜCHE** *Im Haus wird Frühstück serviert, für Mittag- und Abendessen empfehlen die Besitzer nahe Restaurants. Bei Exklusivmiete kann ein Koch engagiert werden* · **GESCHICHTE** *Die ältesten Mauern stammen aus dem späten 16. Jahrhundert. 2015 wurde das heutige Gasthaus eröffnet* · **X-FAKTOR** *Vom einst wehrhaften Charakter des Baus zeugen noch immer versteckte Zimmer und unterirdische Fluchtwege*

DERRIÈRE LA MONTAGNE

Zagori, qui signifie « derrière la montagne », est considérée comme l'une des régions de Grèce ayant le mieux conservé leur caractère intact et authentique. Ici, dans le parc national de Vikos Aoos, les voyageurs peuvent se promener dans l'une des gorges les plus profondes du monde, s'émerveiller devant les anciens monastères accrochés tout en haut à la roche comme des nids d'oiseaux, et visiter 46 villages de pierre où le temps semble ne semble pas avoir laissé de traces. L'un d'eux est Kato Pedina, où se trouve la maison d'hôtes enchanteresse Apeiros Chora. Construit à l'origine comme une petite forteresse pour résister aux intempéries, aux voleurs et aux pillards, le domaine appartient à la même famille depuis des siècles. Athina Aslanidou, Georgios Kontouris et leur fils représentent la septième et la huitième génération – ils ont quitté Athènes pour le nord et ont pu superviser eux-mêmes la rénovation du bâtiment, grâce au talent d'Athina, autrefois décoratrice et styliste. Désireux de respecter l'authenticité et le style, fidèles à la tradition, ils ont utilisé comme matériaux de construction des pierres et du bois grossièrement taillés. Les couleurs douces des sept chambres et leur design harmonieux reflètent également les usages de la région – les propriétaires les ont dynamisées avec des accessoires urbains et une technologie contemporaine. Partout, vous aurez l'impression d'être dans une maison privée soigneusement gérée ; c'est le cas aussi dans la cuisine, où bat le cœur d'Apeiros Chora et où, chaque matin, un fantastique petit-déjeuner est servi avec de la pâtisserie et des pains faits maison, et des confitures provenant des fruits du jardin. Les visiteurs ont également accès à des espaces de vie, des jardins, une bibliothèque et même un spa. Toujours discrets, les hôtes vous aideront, si vous le souhaitez, à planifier des excursions sur mesure à Zagori – vers les plus belles destinations « derrière la montagne ». ◆ À lire : « The Quest » par Nikos Themelēs

ACCÈS *Le village de montagne Kato Pedina s'élève à 940 m d'altitude en Épire, à 34 km de l'aéroport national d'Ioannina et à 480 km de l'aéroport international d'Athènes* · **PRIX** *€€–€€€* · **CHAMBRES** *6 chambres et 1 suite, nommées selon leur couleur et meublées et décorées de manière individuelle* · **RESTAURATION** *Le petit-déjeuner est servi dans la maison, pour le déjeuner et le dîner les propriétaires conseillent des restaurants voisins. Un cuisinier peut être engagé en cas de location exclusive* · **HISTOIRE** *Les murs les plus anciens datent de la fin du XVI*[e] *siècle. La maison d'hôtes actuelle a été ouverte en 2015* · **LES « PLUS »** *Des pièces dissimulées et des souterrains de fuite témoignent aujourd'hui encore du caractère défensif du bâtiment*

ASTRA INN

MEGALO PAPIGO, ZAGORI, IOANNINA, EPIRUS

ASTRA INN

440 04 Megalo Papigo, Zagori, Epirus
Tel. +30 26530 421 08 · papigotsoumanis@hotmail.com
www.astra-inn.gr

A BREATHTAKING BACKDROP

The view of the "towers of Astraka" is nothing less than breathtaking: like a gigantic wall, rugged rocks rise to the sky, colored steel-gray or red-brown, depending on the time of day and the quality of the light, with forests at their feet and snow on the plateaus well into the spring. It could be a movie setting, competing with the Dolomites or the Rocky Mountains – but, as the film industry has fortunately not yet discovered it, hikers and nature lovers can still pass on the information from one insider to another. The most impressive panoramic view of Astraka is to be had from Papigo, one of the most attractive stone-built villages in Zagori and home to this pretty estate. It consists of several buildings in the local style, which Spyros and Kostas Tsoumanis have furnished comfortably in earthy and pastel shades, and with light-colored wood. Some rooms are made even more cozy by open fireplaces, and one of them boasts its own sauna. The feeling of well-being in the accommodation also extends to the restaurant, which is especially close to the hosts' hearts. Here they serve fine rustic dishes from the region: wild trout from nearby waters, meat and cheese from local farms, mushrooms and truffles from the surrounding woods, and flavorsome herbs that are gathered in the mountains. Refreshed and restored, guests can then ascend to the summits or – if they prefer to stay in the valley – go cycling, riding or rafting.
◆ Book to pack: "Eleni" by Nicholas Gage

DIRECTIONS *Papigo is in the north of Greece, 55 km/35 miles from the airport at Ioannina (domestic flights). The nearest international airports are Thessaloniki (350 km/220 miles) and Athens (500 km/310 miles)* · **RATES** *€* · **ROOMS** *3 maisonette apartments and 1 cottage (all with a kitchenette and some with a fireplace), 1 room with a fireplace, 1 room with a sauna* · **FOOD** *The restaurant is open daily for breakfast, lunch and dinner* · **HISTORY** *Opened in 2006* · **X-FACTOR** *The owners sell organic products that they produce themselves, for example herbs, tea and wines to take home*

VOR ATEMBERAUBENDER KULISSE

Wer die „Türme von Astraka" zum ersten Mal sieht, hält vor Staunen unwillkürlich eine Sekunde lang den Atem an: Wie eine mächtige Wand ragen die schroffen Felsen in den Himmel, je nach Tageszeit und Lichtverhältnissen stahlgrau oder braunrot gefärbt, Wald zu ihren Füßen und bis weit ins Frühjahr Schnee auf ihren Plateaus. Sie könnten als Kinokulisse dienen und mit den Dolomiten oder den Rocky Mountains konkurrieren – doch glücklicherweise hat die Filmbranche sie noch nicht entdeckt, sodass Wanderer und Naturliebhaber sie noch als Insidertipp untereinander weiterreichen können. Das eindrucksvollste Astraka-Panorama bietet Papigo, eines der schönsten Steindörfer von Zagori und Heimat dieses hübschen Hofs. Er besteht aus mehreren Gebäuden im lokalen Stil, die Spyros und Kostas Tsoumanis behaglich in Erd- und Pastelltönen sowie mit hellem Holz eingerichtet haben. In einigen Räumen sorgt ein offener Kamin für noch mehr Gemütlichkeit, und ein Zimmer lockt sogar mit einer eigenen Sauna. Ebenso wohl wie in den Häusern fühlt man sich im Restaurant, das den Gastgebern besonders am Herzen liegt. Hier servieren sie die feine Landküche der Region: wilde Forellen aus nahen Gewässern, Fleisch und Käse von einheimischen Bauernhöfen, Pilze und Trüffeln aus den umliegenden Wäldern sowie würzige Kräuter, die in den Bergen gesammelt wurden. Gut gestärkt kann es dann auf die Gipfel gehen oder – für alle, die lieber im Tal bleiben – zum Radfahren, Reiten oder Rafting. ◆ Buchtipp: „Eleni" von Nicholas Gage

ANREISE *Papigo liegt im Norden Griechenlands, 55 km nördlich des nationalen Flughafens Ioannina. Die nächsten internationalen Flughäfen sind Thessaloniki (350 km) und Athen (500 km)* · **PREISE** *€* · **ZIMMER** *3 Maisonette-Wohnungen sowie 1 Häuschen (alle mit Kitchenette und einige mit Kamin), 1 Zimmer mit Kamin, 1 Zimmer mit Sauna* · **KÜCHE** *Das Restaurant ist täglich für Frühstück, Mittag- und Abendessen geöffnet* · **GESCHICHTE** *2006 eröffnet* · **X-FAKTOR** *Die Besitzer verkaufen Bioprodukte aus eigener Herstellung, wie etwa Kräuter, Tees und Weine, zum Mitnehmen*

UN DÉCOR ÉPOUSTOUFLANT

Lorsque vous voyez les « Tours d'Astraka » pour la première fois, l'étonnement vous saisit et vous coupe le souffle : formant une puissante muraille, les rochers déchiquetés, de couleur gris acier ou brun-rouge selon l'heure du jour et la lumière, s'élèvent vers le ciel ; la forêt s'étend à leur pied et la neige blanchit leurs plateaux jusqu'au printemps. Ils pourraient servir de décor dans un film et rivaliser avec les Dolomites ou les montagnes Rocheuses – heureusement, l'industrie du cinéma ne les a pas encore découverts, si bien que les randonneurs et les amoureux de la nature peuvent se communiquer l'adresse entre initiés. Papigo, l'un des plus beaux villages de pierre de Zagori et le siège de cette ferme charmante, offre le panorama le plus impressionnant d'Astraka. Il est composé de plusieurs bâtiments construits dans le style local, que Spyros et Kostas Tsoumanis ont décorés dans des tons accueillants de terre et pastel et meublés de bois clair. Dans certaines chambres, des cheminées rendent la vie encore plus agréable, et une chambre possède même son propre sauna. Tout aussi confortable que les maisons, le restaurant compte beaucoup pour les hôtes qui y servent la cuisine campagnarde raffinée de la région : truites sauvages pêchées dans les eaux voisines, viande et fromage provenant de fermes locales, champignons et truffes des bois récoltés dans les environs et fines herbes savoureuses cueillies dans les montagnes. Rassasiés et satisfaits, vous pourrez vous diriger vers les sommets ou, si vous préférez rester dans la vallée, faire de la bicyclette, de l'équitation ou du rafting. ◆ À lire : « Eleni » de Nicholas Gage

ACCÈS *Papigo est situé dans le nord de la Grèce, à 55 km au nord de l'aéroport national de Ioannina. Les aéroports internationaux les plus proches sont Thessalonique (350 km) et Athènes (500 km)* · **PRIX** *€* · **CHAMBRES** *3 appartements en duplex et 1 maisonnette (tous avec kitchenette et certains avec cheminée), 1 chambre avec cheminée, 1 chambre avec sauna* · **RESTAURATION** *Ouvert tous les jours, le restaurant propose petit-déjeuner, déjeuner et dîner* · **HISTOIRE** *Ouvert en 2006* · **LES « PLUS »** *Les propriétaires vendent des produits bio de la région, par exemple des fines herbes, des tisanes et du vin, que l'on peut emporter*

BREAKFAST
8:30-10:30

HARVIA

CHATZIGAKIS MANOR

PERTOULI, PYLI, THESSALY

CHATZIGAKIS MANOR

420 32 Pertouli, Pyli, Thessaly
Tel. +30 24340 911 46 · info@chatzigaki.gr
www.chatzigaki.gr

A FAMILY AFFAIR

When the country house of the Chatzigakis family was built in the mountain village of Pertouli in 1890–1892, it was a splendid and truly international project: the architect was Swiss, and the interior furnishings came from all over the world – the silver from Asia, the porcelain from France, the carpets from Anatolia. The owners welcomed high-ranking and illustrious guests, including members of royal families and of the Filiki Eteria secret society, which was founded to end Ottoman rule over the Greeks and establish an independent state. During the Second World War, resistance fighters and the British established a headquarters here, which is why the Nazis burned the house down in 1943. With the help of historic plans, old photographs and countless family stories, in the late twentieth century Dimitris Chatzigakis succeeded in rebuilding and extending his ancestral home in the old style and using traditional construction techniques. Today, this well-tended complex consists of four areas: rooms and suites in a discreetly luxurious country style are accommodated in the main building, strictly symmetrical as in the past, in the garden residence and in the modern wing; the fourth building houses the restaurant, where local specialties are on the menu. A notable feature adorns the garden: a stone chapel that can be booked for a romantic wedding or a christening in green surroundings. Those who come to Pertouli for an active holiday rather than a family event can visit stone-built villages and bridges in the area, go hiking in the Pindos mountain range or discover the legendary rock monasteries of Meteora, which are only about 25 miles away. ◆ Book to pack: "The Angry Hills" by Leon Uris

DIRECTIONS *Pertouli lies at an altitude of about 1,200 m/3,900 feet in the Pindos mountains. The distance to Ioannina airport, for domestic flights is 130 km/80 miles, to the international airports in Thessaloniki 290 km/180 miles and Athens 390 km/240 miles* · **RATES** *€–€€€* · **ROOMS** *36 rooms and suites, in 3 buildings* · **FOOD** *Diners in the "Boudoura" restaurant have a superb view of the village and mountains. The "Marosa" café serves coffee in winter and Greek snacks by the open fire, while in summer drinks and snacks are available at the pool bar* · **HISTORY** *The estate was rebuilt between 1993 and 2000. The new wing was added in 2008* · **X-FACTOR** *The family farm supplies organic fruit and vegetables as well as eggs and traditionally produced feta and cottage cheese*

EINE FAMILIENANGELEGENHEIT

Als der Landsitz der Familie Chatzigakis 1890–1892 im Bergdorf Pertouli erbaut wurde, war er eine prachtvolle und wahrhaft internationale Angelegenheit: Der Architekt war Schweizer, und das Interieur kam aus aller Welt – das Silber aus Asien, das Porzellan aus Frankreich, die Teppiche aus Anatolien. Die Besitzer hießen hochrangige und illustre Gäste willkommen – unter ihnen Mitglieder von Königshäusern und des Geheimbundes Filiki Eteria, der die osmanische Herrschaft über die Griechen beenden und ein unabhängiges Land gründen wollte. Im Zweiten Weltkrieg schlugen Widerstandskämpfer und Briten hier ihr Hauptquartier auf, weswegen die Nazis das Haus 1943 niederbrannten. Mithilfe historischer Pläne, alter Fotos und ungezählter Familiengeschichten gelang es Dimitris Chatzigakis Ende des 20. Jahrhunderts, das Heim seiner Vorfahren im alten Stil und mit alten Techniken wiederaufzubauen und zu erweitern. Heute umfasst der gepflegte Komplex vier Bereiche: Im wie früher strikt symmetrisch gehaltenen Hauptbau, in der Gartenresidenz sowie im modernen Flügel sind Zimmer und Suiten im diskret luxuriösen Countrystil untergebracht; das vierte Haus beherbergt das Restaurant, in dem lokale Spezialitäten auf der Karte stehen. Ein besonderes Schmuckstück ziert den Garten: eine Steinkapelle, die man für eine romantische Hochzeit oder eine Taufe im Grünen buchen kann. Wer nicht für eine Familienfeier, sondern für einen Aktivurlaub nach Pertouli kommt, besichtigt die Steindörfer und -brücken der Gegend, erwandert das Pindos-Gebirge oder entdeckt die legendären Felsenklöster von Meteora, die nur rund 40 Kilometer entfernt sind. ◆ Buchtipp: „Die Berge standen auf“ von Leon Uris

ANREISE *Pertouli liegt auf ca. 1200 m Höhe im Pindos-Gebirge. Der nationale Flughafen Ioannina ist 130 km entfernt, die nächsten internationalen Flughäfen sind Thessaloniki (290 km) und Athen (390 km)* · **PREISE** *€–€€€* · **ZIMMER** *36 Zimmer und Suiten, verteilt auf 3 Gebäude* · **KÜCHE** *Gäste des Restaurants „Boudoura“ genießen einen Traumblick auf Dorf und Berge. Das Café „Marosa“ serviert im Winter Kaffee und griechisches Gebäck am Kamin, die Poolbar im Sommer Getränke und Snacks* · **GESCHICHTE** *Das Anwesen wurde zwischen 1993 und 2000 rekonstruiert. Der jüngste Flügel kam 2008 dazu* · **X-FAKTOR** *Der familieneigene Bauernhof liefert biologisch angebautes Obst und Gemüse, Eier sowie traditionell hergestellten Feta und Hüttenkäse*

UNE AFFAIRE DE FAMILLE

À l'époque de sa construction dans le village de montagne de Pertouli en 1890–1892, la maison de campagne de la famille Chatzigakis était magnifique et véritablement internationale : l'architecte était suisse, le mobilier et la déco venaient du monde entier – l'argenterie d'Asie, la porcelaine de France, les tapis d'Anatolie. Les propriétaires ont accueilli d'illustres invités, parmi lesquels des membres de familles royales et de la société secrète Filiki Eteria, qui voulait mettre fin à la domination ottomane sur les Grecs et fonder un pays indépendant. Pendant la Seconde Guerre mondiale, les résistants et les Britanniques y ont installé leur quartier général, ce pourquoi les nazis ont brûlé la maison en 1943. À l'aide de plans historiques, de photographies anciennes et d'innombrables histoires familiales, Dimitris Chatzigakis a réussi à la fin du XXe siècle à reconstruire et à agrandir la maison de ses ancêtres dans le style d'antan et en utilisant les techniques de l'époque. Aujourd'hui, le complexe bien entretenu comprend quatre constructions : le bâtiment principal, strictement symétrique comme par le passé, la résidence-jardin et l'aile moderne accueillent des chambres et des suites dans un style campagnard discrètement luxueux ; la quatrième maison abrite le restaurant qui propose des spécialités locales. Le jardin recèle un petit bijou : une chapelle en pierre, qui peut être réservée pour fêter un mariage romantique ou un baptême champêtre. Ceux qui ne viennent pas à Pertouli pour participer à une fête de famille mais pour passer des vacances actives peuvent visiter les villages et les ponts de pierre de la région, faire de la randonnée dans les montagnes du Pinde ou découvrir les légendaires monastères rupestres des Météores, qui ne sont qu'à une quarantaine de kilomètres. ◆ À lire : « Trahison à Athènes » par Leon Uris

ACCÈS *Pertouli est situé à une altitude d'environ 1200 m dans les montagnes du Pinde. L'aéroport national de Ioannina est à 130 km, les aéroports internationaux les plus proches sont ceux de Thessalonique (290 km) et d'Athènes (390 km)* · **PRIX** *€–€€€* · **CHAMBRES** *36 chambres et suites dans 3 bâtiments* · **RESTAURATION** *Les clients du restaurant « Boudoura » ont une vue imprenable sur le village et les montagnes. L'hiver, le café « Marosa » sert du café et des pâtisseries grecques près de la cheminée, l'été le bar de la piscine propose des boissons et des snacks* · **HISTOIRE** *La propriété a été reconstruite entre 1993 et 2000. L'aile la plus récente a été ajoutée en 2008* · **LES « PLUS »** *La ferme familiale fournit des fruits et des légumes issus de l'agriculture biologique, des œufs ainsi que de la feta préparée à l'ancienne et du cottage*

NYMFAIO RETREATS

AMYNTAIO, WESTERN MACEDONIA

NYMFAIO RETREATS

530 78 Nymfaio, Amyntaio, Western Macedonia
info@nymfaioretreats.com
www.nymfaioretreats.com

A WORK OF ART

When sculptor Nikomachi and wine maker Mihalis spent five years in China, where she worked as a creative director and studied calligraphy while he expanded his wine export business, this house was their anchor in Greece. They often came home from Shanghai to Nymfaio to see family and friends, to relax and to recharge their batteries. Nikomachi herself restored the family property, sited in the mountains of Western Macedonia and built in 1925 from stone, mortar and wood. She left only the walls and floors intact. Everything else was newly designed and constructed within a year – and nevertheless looks today as if it had always been there. Designed with a sure touch, the house is an act of homage to the history of the region, while providing every contemporary comfort at the same time. Wrought-iron window grilles and balcony railings, partitions of wood and glass, and the open fireplaces are reminders of bygone days. They are combined with antique and new furniture in a romantic country-house style, with wonderful wall colors and invisible modern luxury. An energetic local couple vigorously take care of the food and all necessary housework, and the owners, based in Athens, play their part in ensuring guests' well-being: Nikomachi makes her first-floor studio available to amateur artists on request, and Mihalis curates wine seminars. The region, just like the house, is calming and simultaneously inspiring: in idyllic Nymfaio there stands a superbly restored Greek Orthodox church, in the nearby woods wild berries, mushrooms and truffles wait to be gathered, depending on the season of the year, and the surrounding mountains are a challenging terrain for walkers and mountain bikers.
◆ Book to pack: "The Secret Sister" by Fotini Tsalikoglou

DIRECTIONS *The village of Nymfaio lies in Western Macedonia at an altitude of 1,350 m/4,400 ft. The distance to Kastoria airport, for domestic flights, is 60 km/37 miles, while the nearest international airports are Thessaloniki (175 km/110 miles) and Athens (545 km/340 miles)* · **RATES** *€€–€€€ (3 nights minimum stay in the main season)* · **ROOMS** *5 rooms (not all with their own bathroom) for up to 12 persons; bookings are taken for the whole house only* · **FOOD** *Breakfast and one homemade northern Greek meal daily are including in the price. Real gems are stored in the wine cellar* · **HISTORY** *Renovated in 2011, a retreat for guests since 2019* · **X-FACTOR** *An unusually lovely refuge*

EIN KUNSTWERK

Als die Bildhauerin Nikomachi und der Winzer Mihalis für fünf Jahre nach China zogen, wo sie als Kreativdirektorin arbeitete und Kalligrafie studierte, während er seinen Weinexport ausbaute, war dieses Haus ihr Anker in Griechenland. Immer wieder kamen sie aus Schanghai nach Nymfaio, um ihre Familie und Freunde zu sehen, zu entspannen und neue Energie zu tanken. Nikomachi hatte den Familienbesitz in den Bergen Westmakedoniens, der 1925 aus Stein, Schlammmörtel und Holz erbaut worden war, selbst renoviert. Nur Wände und Böden ließ sie stehen, alles andere wurde innerhalb eines Jahres neu entworfen und errichtet – und sieht heute trotzdem so aus, als wäre es der ursprüngliche Zustand. Das stilsicher designte Haus ist eine Hommage an die Geschichte der Region und bietet zugleich allen Komfort der Gegenwart. So erinnern schmiedeeiserne Fenster- und Balkongitter, Raumteiler aus Holz und Glas sowie offene Kamine an vergangene Zeiten, sie werden mit antiken und neuen Möbeln im romantischen Landhausstil, wunderbaren Wandfarben und unsichtbarem modernem Luxus kombiniert. Ein rühriges Ehepaar aus dem Ort kümmert sich resolut um die Küche und alle anfallenden Hausarbeiten, und die Besitzer tragen von Athen aus zum Wohl ihrer Gäste bei – so stellt Nikomachi Hobbykünstlern auf Wunsch ihr Atelier im ersten Stock zur Verfügung, und Mihalis kuratiert Weinseminare. Wie das Haus, so ist auch die Region beruhigend und inspirierend zugleich: Im idyllischen Nymfaio steht eine hervorragend restaurierte griechisch-orthodoxe Kirche, im nahen Wald warten je nach Jahreszeit Wildbeeren, Pilze oder Trüffeln auf Sammler, und die umliegenden Berge sind ein anspruchsvolles Revier für Wanderer und Mountainbiker. ◆ Buchtipp: „Die verlorene kleine Schwester" von Fotini Tsalikoglou

ANREISE *Das Dorf Nymfaio liegt auf 1350 m Höhe in Westmakedonien. Der nationale Flughafen in Kastoria ist 60 km entfernt, die nächsten internationalen Flughäfen sind Thessaloniki (175 km) und Athen (545 km)* · **PREISE** *€€–€€€ (in der Hochsaison 3 Nächte Mindestaufenthalt)* · **ZIMMER** *5 Zimmer (nicht alle mit eigenem Bad) für bis zu 12 Personen; das Haus wird nur exklusiv vermietet* · **KÜCHE** *Frühstück und eine hausgemachte nordgriechische Mahlzeit täglich sind im Preis inbegriffen. Im Weinkeller lagern wahre Schätze* · **GESCHICHTE** *2011 renoviert und seit 2019 ein Retreat für Gäste* · **X-FAKTOR** *Ein selten schönes Refugium*

UNE ŒUVRE D'ART

Lorsque la sculptrice Nikomachi et le vigneron Mihalis étaient en Chine – ils y sont restés cinq ans, elle travaillait comme directrice de création et a étudié la calligraphie tandis qu'il développait l'exportation de son vin –, cette maison a été leur point d'ancrage en Grèce. Ils sont venus de Shanghai à Nymfaio à maintes reprises pour voir leur famille et leurs amis, pour se détendre et se ressourcer. Nikomachi elle-même avait rénové la propriété familiale construite en 1925 en pierre, en mortier de terre et en bois dans les montagnes de la Macédoine occidentale. Elle n'a conservé que les murs et les sols, tout le reste a été redessiné et reconstruit en l'espace d'un an ; pourtant, aujourd'hui encore, on dirait que tout a toujours été là. La maison au design accompli est un hommage à l'histoire de la région et offre en même temps tout le confort du présent. Les grilles des fenêtres et des balcons en fer forgé, les cloisons des pièces en bois et en verre et les cheminées ouvertes rappellent le passé, elles sont associées à des meubles anciens et neufs dans un style de maison de campagne romantique, à des couleurs murales superbes et à un luxe moderne invisible. Un couple du village s'occupe résolument de la cuisine et de toutes les tâches ménagères, et les propriétaires contribuent d'Athènes au bien-être de leurs hôtes – Nikomachi met par exemple sur demande son studio du premier étage à la disposition d'artistes amateurs, et Mihalis organise des séminaires sur le vin. Comme la maison, la région est à la fois apaisante et inspirante : dans l'idyllique Nymfaio se dresse une église grecque orthodoxe parfaitement restaurée, dans la forêt voisine des baies sauvages, des champignons ou des truffes attendent les cueilleurs selon la saison, et les montagnes environnantes offrent un terrain exigeant aux randonneurs et aux vététistes. ◆ À lire : « The Secret Sister » par Fotini Tsalikoglou

ACCÈS *Le village de Nymfaio est situé à 1350 m d'altitude en Macédoine occidentale. L'aéroport national de Kastoria est à 60 km, les aéroports internationaux les plus proches sont Thessalonique (175 km) et Athènes (545 km)* · **PRIX** *€€–€€€ (pendant la haute-saison séjour de 3 nuits minimum)* · **CHAMBRES** *5 chambres (pas toutes avec salle de bains) pour jusqu'à 12 personnes; location exclusive uniquement* · **RESTAURATION** *Le petit-déjeuner et un repas maison (cuisine de la Grèce du Nord) tous les jours, sont compris dans le prix. La cave à vins recèle des trésors* · **HISTOIRE** *Restaurée en 2011 et depuis 2019 un lieu de retraite pour ses hôtes* · **LES « PLUS »** *Un refuge d'une beauté rare*

GRAFFITI
SCRABBLE
MASTERMIND
CHALLENGE

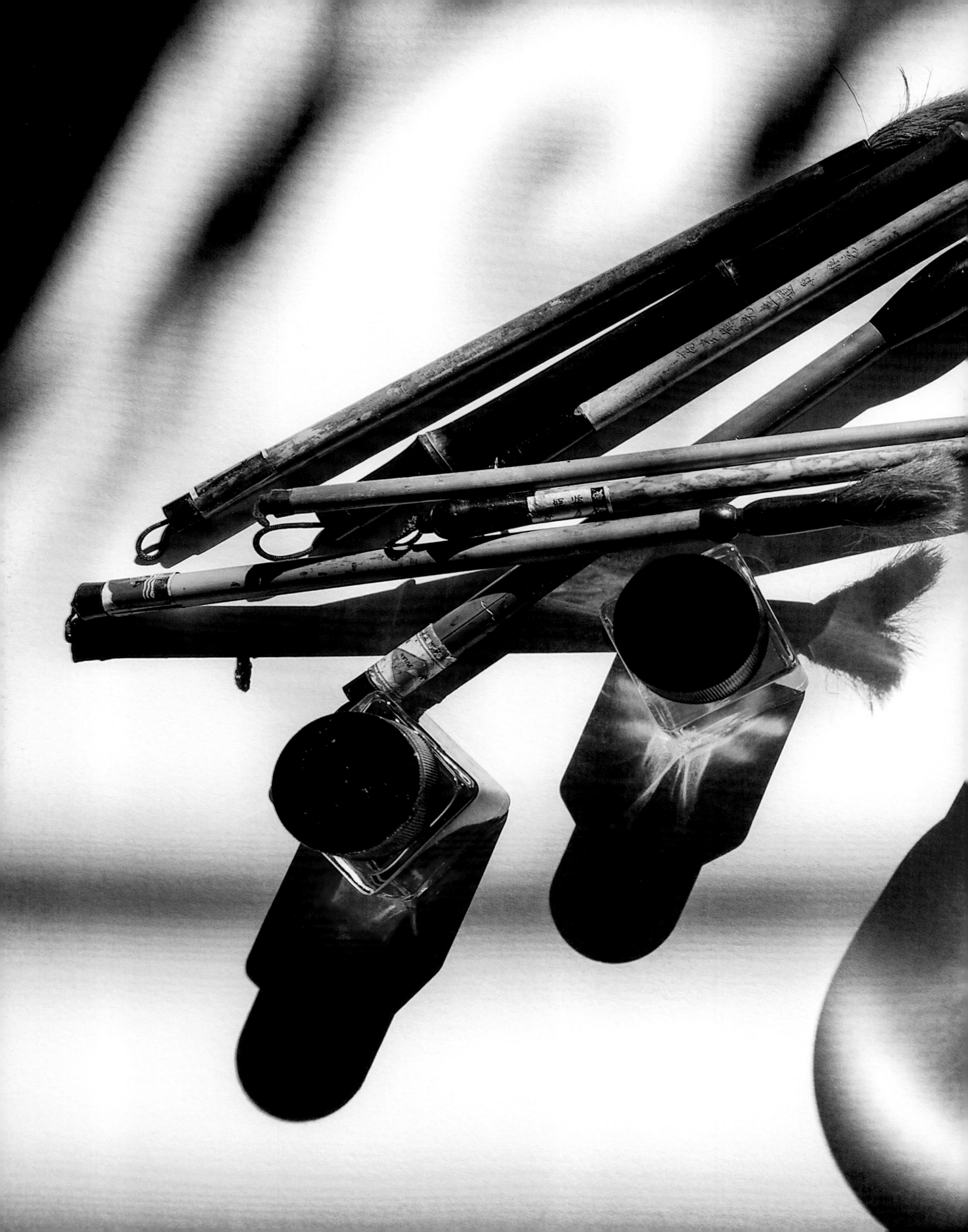

IMARET

KAVALA, EASTERN MACEDONIA

IMARET

Th. Poulidou Street 30–32, 652 01 Kavala, Eastern Macedonia
Tel. +30 2510 620 151 · info@imaret.gr
www.imaret.gr

A RICH LEGACY

He was born in Kavala, the son of a tobacco merchant, and when he died in Alexandria he had become the founding father of modern Egypt: Muhammad Ali Pasha (1769–1849) is still revered in the land on the Nile and has not been forgotten in his home town. In the early nineteenth century he established one of the most renowned Islamic places of education far and wide – an ensemble that combined beneath its domes a Koran school, a mosque, a hammam and a soup kitchen. It is thanks to the Greek Anna Missirian that the pink Ottoman-style buildings look as magnificent today as they did when constructed. With a great deal of money and even more diplomatic sensitivity she succeeded, after countless flights between Kavala and Cairo and negotiations with the Egyptian owners that lasted years, in concluding a lease agreement for the monument. Then she converted it into an unusually atmospheric hotel. She attached as much importance to old construction techniques and traditional crafts as to custom-made furniture and the finest materials. The luxurious rooms with vaulted ceilings and floors of waxed chestnut wood are fitted out with velvet and silk, and possess such extras as hand-woven carpets and Egyptian chandeliers, open fireplaces and marble bathtubs in which guests bathe with rose petals, milk and honey. Outdoors, they can stroll through history in colonnades and the orange garden, relax by the patio pool or on the roof with a sea view, and are pampered with fine cuisine: the chef cooks 200 family and monastic recipes from the region. And in the bar after a meal, those who so wish can drink to the health of Muhammad Ali Pasha – and to his rich legacy.

◆ Book to pack: "The Life of Ismail Ferik Pasha" by Rhea Galanaki

DIRECTIONS *Kavala lies on the coast of Eastern Macedonia. Hotel Imaret is in the Old Town, about 1 km/0.5 miles from the harbor and 30 km/ 19 miles from Kavala international airport* · **RATES** *€€€–€€€€* · **ROOMS** *24 rooms and suites* · **FOOD** *The restaurant on the patio has a glass roof that is opened in summer. The menu features Greek and oriental dishes* · **HISTORY** *Renovation of the building, which dates from 1817, was completed in 2004* · **X-FACTOR** *Hand-made soap with olive oil, rose essence and ash is used in the hammam*

EIN REICHES ERBE

Er wurde in Kavala als Sohn eines Tabakhändlers geboren und starb in Alexandria als Gründervater des modernen Ägyptens: Muhammad Ali Pascha (1769–1849) wird in dem Land am Nil noch immer verehrt und bleibt auch in seiner Heimatstadt unvergessen. Ihr stiftete er im frühen 19. Jahrhundert eine der renommiertesten islamischen Bildungsstätten weit und breit – einen Komplex, der unter seinen Kuppeln eine Koranschule, eine Moschee, einen Hammam und eine Suppenküche vereinte. Dass der roséfarbene osmanische Bau heute wieder so prachtvoll dasteht wie zu Zeiten seiner Erbauung, ist der griechischen Mäzenin Anna Missirian zu verdanken. Mit viel Geld und noch mehr diplomatischem Fingerspitzengefühl schaffte sie es, nach ungezählten Flügen zwischen Kavala und Kairo und jahrelangen Verhandlungen mit den ägyptischen Eigentümern einen Pachtvertrag für das Monument zu schließen. Dann ließ sie es zu einem außergewöhnlich stimmungsvollen Hotel umbauen. Auf alte Bautechniken und traditionelles Kunsthandwerk legte sie dabei ebenso viel Wert wie auf maßgefertigte Möbel und feinste Materialien. Die luxuriösen Zimmer mit Gewölbedecken und gewachsten Kastanienholzböden sind in Samt und Seide gekleidet und besitzen Extras wie handgeknüpfte Teppiche und ägyptische Kronleuchter, offene Kamine und Marmorwannen, in denen Bäder mit Rosenblättern, Milch und Honig eingelassen werden. Draußen wandeln die Gäste in Säulengängen und im Orangengarten zwischen Geschichte und Gegenwart, entspannen am Pool im Patio oder auf der Dachterrasse mit Meerblick und lassen sich kulinarisch verwöhnen: Der Küchenchef kocht nach 200 Familien- und Klosterrezepten, die aus der Region stammen. Und wer mag, kann nach dem Essen an der Bar auf das Wohl von Muhammad Ali Pascha anstoßen – und auf dessen reiches Erbe. ◆ Buchtipp: „Das Leben des Ismail Ferik Pascha" von Rhea Galanaki

ANREISE *Kavala liegt an der Küste Ostmakedoniens. Das Hotel Imaret steht in der Altstadt, ca. 1 km vom Hafen und 30 km vom internationalen Flughafen Kavala entfernt* · **PREISE** *€€€–€€€€* · **ZIMMER** *24 Zimmer und Suiten* · **KÜCHE** *Das Restaurant im Patio hat ein Glasdach, das im Sommer geöffnet werden kann. Auf der Karte stehen griechisch-orientalische Gerichte* · **GESCHICHTE** *Die Renovierung des Baus von 1817 wurde 2004 abgeschlossen* · **X-FAKTOR** *Im Hammam wird handgeschöpfte Seife mit Olivenöl, Rosenextrakt und Asche verwendet*

UN RICHE HÉRITAGE

Fils d'un marchand de tabac de Kavala, il est mort à Alexandrie comme père fondateur de l'Égypte moderne : Méhémet Ali (1769–1849) est toujours vénéré sur les rives du Nil et reste inoubliable dans sa ville natale. Au début du XIXe siècle, il a fait édifier ici l'un des établissements d'enseignement islamique les plus réputés au monde – un complexe qui abritait sous ses coupoles une école coranique, une mosquée, un hammam et une soupe populaire. Si le bâtiment de style ottoman de couleur rose a retrouvé sa magnificence d'antan, il le doit à la mécène grecque Anna Missirian. Avec beaucoup d'argent et encore plus de sens de la diplomatie, après d'innombrables allers et retours entre Kavala et Le Caire et des années de négociations avec les propriétaires égyptiens, elle a réussi à conclure un contrat pour la location du monument. Elle l'a ensuite fait transformer en un hôtel à l'atmosphère exceptionnelle, mettant autant l'accent sur les techniques de construction anciennes et l'artisanat traditionnel que sur le mobilier réalisé sur mesure et les matériaux les plus nobles. Les chambres luxueuses aux plafonds voûtés et aux sols en châtaignier ciré sont habillées de velours et de soie et proposent des extras tels que des tapis noués à la main et des lustres égyptiens, des cheminées ouvertes et des baignoires en marbre, dans lesquelles on laisse couler des bains au lait et au miel où flottent des pétales de rose. À l'extérieur, les clients déambulent sous les portiques et dans l'orangeraie entre le passé et le présent, se détendent au bord de la piscine dans le patio ou sur le toit en terrasse qui offre une vue sur la mer, et s'adonnent aux plaisirs culinaires : le chef cuisine selon 200 recettes de famille et de monastères de la région. Et après le repas, au bar, si vous le souhaitez, vous pouvez porter un toast à Méhémet Ali – et à ce qu'il a laissé aux générations futures. ◆ À lire : « La vie d'Ismaïl Férik Pacha » par Rhea Galanaki

ACCÈS *Kavala est située sur la côte de la Macédoine orientale. L'hôtel Imaret se trouve au cœur de la cité historique, à environ 1 km du port et 30 km de l'aéroport international de Kavala* · **PRIX** *€€€–€€€€* · **CHAMBRES** *24 chambres et suites* · **RESTAURATION** *Le toit de verre du patio qui abrite le restaurant peut être ouvert l'été. Au menu, des plats de la cuisine gréco-orientale* · **HISTOIRE** *La restauration de l'édifice datant de 1817 s'est terminée en 2004* · **LES « PLUS »** *Le savon artisanal utilisé dans le hammam est fabriqué avec de l'huile d'olive, de l'extrait de rose et de la cendre*

EAGLES PALACE

OURANOUPOLI, CHALKIDIKI, CENTRAL MACEDONIA

EAGLES PALACE

630 75 Ouranoupoli, Chalkidiki, Central Macedonia
Tel. +30 23774 400 50 and +30 23774 400 60 · info@eaglespalace.gr
www.eaglespalace.gr

A LIVING LEGEND

Its logo is adorned by the double-headed eagle, the symbol of the Byzantine Empire and the Greek Orthodox Church. Its architecture points to Mount Athos, the autonomous holy republic of monasteries that lies close by. Its owners are among the longest-standing hotel families in the country, and the opera star Maria Callas has numbered among its guests: the Eagles Palace is a living legend. Since 1973 this hotel has graced the coast of Chalkidiki, not far from the picturesque village of Ouranoupoli. Its rooms, suites and bungalows – which have always been equipped in a luxurious, airily Mediterranean style – have recently been renovated by the French designer Fabienne Spahn in natural and pastel shades. She has also given the resort's Elemis Spa a facelift, and the restaurants some beauty treatment. In this way the gourmet temple "Kamares by Spondi" got a makeover in white, blue, gold and purple that is every bit as eye-catching as the creative menu composed by Arnaud Bignon, a chef with two Michelin stars to his name. The hotel concierges are also masters of their trade: they organize snorkeling off the sunny little islands of Drenia and Ammouliani, a champagne tour in a sailing boat at sunset, an excursion to Stagira, the birthplace of Aristotle, or a visit to the archaeological sites of Vergina, once the location of Aigai, the capital city of the Macedonian kingdom. Despite its affinity to Greek history, the Eagles Palace also acquaints its guests with contemporary Greece: for some years now, the owners have regularly invited young authors, photographers and painters to be artists-in-residence for a week.
◆ Book to pack: "Mount Athos Diary" in "The Broken Road" by Patrick Leigh Fermor

DIRECTIONS *The Eagles Palace lies on the coast of the Chalkidiki Peninsula in northern Greece. The distance to the international airport of Thessaloniki is 112 km/70 miles* · **RATES** *€€–€€€€* · **ROOMS** *157 rooms, suites and bungalows with a garden or sea view, some of them with a pool* · **FOOD** *"Melathron" has an all-day buffet, "Armyra" serves fish specialties à la carte at midday and in the evening. In "Kamares by Spondi" (only open to adults) modern Greek cuisine is served for dinner. The "Vinum Grill" is open on warm summer evenings between July and September. There are also 4 bars* · **HISTORY** *The hotel belongs to the Tornivoukas family, which has been in this business since 1925, when they founded the first luxury hotel in Thessaloniki* · **X-FACTOR** *The broad stretch of sand at the Eagles Palace is one of the loveliest beaches in Greece*

EINE LEBENDE LEGENDE

Sein Logo ziert der doppelköpfige Adler, Symbol des byzantinischen Reichs und der griechisch-orthodoxen Kirche. Seine Architektur verweist auf den heiligen Berg Athos, die autonome Klosterrepublik, die ganz in der Nähe liegt. Seine Eigentümer gehören zu den ältesten Hoteliersfamilien des Landes, und unter seinen Gästen war schon der Opernstar Maria Callas: Das Eagles Palace ist eine lebende Legende. Seit 1973 steht das Hotel an der Küste der Chalkidiki, nicht weit vom pittoresken Dorf Ouranoupoli entfernt. Seine Zimmer, Suiten und Bungalows – schon immer mediterran-luftig und luxuriös angelegt – wurden zuletzt von der französischen Designerin Fabienne Spahn in Pastell- und Naturtönen renoviert. Sie hat zudem das Elemis-Spa des Resorts aufgefrischt und den Restaurants eine Schönheitskur verpasst. So bekam der Gourmettempel „Kamares by Spondi" ein Make-up in Weiß, Blau, Gold und Violett, das genauso aufsehenerregend ist wie die kreative Karte, die der Zweisternekoch Arnaud Bignon komponiert hat. Zu den Meistern ihres Fachs zählen auch die Concierges des Hotels: Sie organisieren den Schnorchelausflug vor den kleinen Sonneninseln Drenia und Ammouliani ebenso wie den Champagner-Segeltörn in den Sonnenuntergang, die Fahrt nach Stagira, wo Aristoteles geboren wurde, oder den Besuch der Ausgrabungsstätten von Vergina, wo sich einst Aigai, die Hauptstadt des Königreichs Makedonien, befand. Trotz aller Affinität zur griechischen Geschichte bringt das Eagles Palace seinen Gästen aber auch das zeitgenössische Griechenland näher: Seit einigen Jahren laden die Besitzer regelmäßig junge Autoren, Fotografen und Maler zu Artists-in-Residence-Wochen ein.
◆ Buchtipp: „Der Berg" von Gerhard Roth

ANREISE *Das Eagles Palace liegt an der Küste der nordgriechischen Halbinsel Chalkidiki. Der internationale Flughafen Thessaloniki ist 112 km entfernt* · **PREISE** *€€–€€€€* · **ZIMMER** *157 Zimmer, Suiten und Bungalows mit Garten- oder Meerblick und zum Teil mit Pool* · **KÜCHE** *Das „Melathron" bietet ganztags Büfetts, das „Armyra" mittags und abends Fischspezialitäten à la carte. Im „Kamares by Spondi" (nur für Erwachsene geöffnet) wird zum Dinner moderne griechische Küche serviert. Der „Vinum Grill" ist an warmen Sommerabenden zwischen Juli und September offen. Zudem gibt es 4 Bars* · **GESCHICHTE** *Das Haus gehört der Familie Tornivoukas, die seit 1925 in der Branche ist – damals gründete sie das erste Luxushotel in Thessaloniki* · **X-FAKTOR** *Der breite Sandstrand des Eagles Palace ist einer der schönsten Strände in Griechenland*

UNE LÉGENDE VIVANTE

Son logo est orné de l'aigle bicéphale, symbole de l'Empire byzantin et de l'Église orthodoxe grecque. Son architecture fait référence au Mont-Athos, la république monastique autonome, toute proche. Quant à ses propriétaires, ils font partie des plus anciennes familles d'hôteliers du pays, et la diva Maria Callas a séjourné chez eux : le Eagles Palace est une légende vivante. Depuis 1973, l'hôtel se dresse sur la côte de la Chalcidique, près du pittoresque village d'Ouranoupoli. Ses chambres, suites et bungalows, lumineux et aérés, toujours luxueux et orientés vers la Méditerranée, ont été récemment rénovés par la designer française Fabienne Spahn dans des tons pastel et naturels. Elle a également rafraîchi le spa Elemis de l'hôtel et prodigué des soins de beauté aux restaurants. Ainsi, le temple gastronomique « Kamares by Spondi » a été maquillé en blanc, bleu, or et violet, ce qui est tout aussi fascinant que le menu plein d'imagination composé par le chef deux étoiles Arnaud Bignon. Les concierges de l'hôtel sont également passés maîtres dans leur art : ils organisent des excursions de plongée au large des petites îles ensoleillées de Drenia et d'Ammouliani ainsi que des croisières en voilier au champagne vers le soleil couchant, un voyage à Stagira, où est né Aristote, ou encore une visite des sites de fouilles de Vergina, où se trouvait autrefois Aigai, la capitale du royaume de Macédoine. Malgré tous ses liens avec l'histoire grecque, le Eagles Palace fait également mieux connaître la Grèce contemporaine à ses hôtes : depuis quelques années, les propriétaires invitent régulièrement de jeunes auteurs, photographes et peintres à participer à des semaines d'artistes en résidence.
◆ À lire : « Après J.-C. » par Vassilis Alexakis

ACCÈS *Situé sur la côte de la péninsule de Chalcidique, au nord de la Grèce. L'aéroport international de Thessalonique est à 112 km* · **PRIX** *€€–€€€€* · **CHAMBRES** *157 chambres, suites et bungalows avec vue sur le jardin ou sur la mer, en partie avec piscine* · **RESTAURATION** *Le « Melathron » propose des buffets toute la journée, l'« Armyra » des spécialités de poisson à la carte midi et soir. Au « Kamares by Spondi » (pour adultes uniquement), une cuisine grecque moderne est servie pour le dîner. Le « Vinum Grill » est ouvert les chaudes soirées d'été, entre juillet et septembre. Il y a également 4 bars* · **HISTOIRE** *La maison appartient à la famille Tornivoukas, des hôteliers depuis 1925 – à l'époque elle a fondé le premier hôtel de luxe à Thessalonique* · **LES « PLUS »** *La large plage de sable de l'Eagles Palace est l'une des plus belles de Grèce*

ELIVI SKIATHOS

KOUKOUNARIES BEACH, SKIATHOS ISLAND

ELIVI SKIATHOS

Koukounaries Beach, 370 02 Skiathos
Tel. +30 24274 409 00 · info@elivihotels.com
www.elivihotels.com

WHERE THE BLACK SWANS LIVE

The famous black swan of Skiathos is the protagonist of this resort. It turns up as a sculpture indoors, adorns the walls on black-and-white images, and gave its name to the most attractive villa. As majestically and proudly as it glides over the water, thus Elivi lies on the southwest coast of the island – on gently rolling hills, surrounded by dense, dark-green vegetation and with a view of four picture-postcard beaches. Designed by 3SK Stylianidis Architects, a studio in Athens, it comprises three parts. The Xenia Hotel at the highest point of the premises has the most interesting history: it was constructed in 1963 as part of a national building program for the tourism organization, intended to give a boost to the Greek hotel sector. Its modernist façade has been preserved, a whiff of 1960s atmosphere is in the air of the white-and-beige styled rooms with their floor-to-ceiling windows, and the rooms on the ground floor share a pool with direct access from every veranda. Next to it were built the Nest and Grace zones, whose exclusive suites and villas provide even more privacy and are all equipped with a private pool. Elivi also lives up to the highest culinary standards. The cuisine is fresh, creative and delicious – whether on the terrace of the Greek taverna, beneath the olive trees of the Mediterranean restaurant or at the Japanese sushi tables. Romantics are entranced by a candlelight dinner in "Leda & The Swan," right by the sea. This intimate restaurant is, incidentally, the only place far and wide where the black swan changes color: it was named after the mythical Queen Leda, to whom Zeus came as a lover in the shape of a white swan. ◆ Film to watch: "Mamma Mia" (2008) by Phyllida Lloyd with Meryl Streep and Pierce Brosnan was partly filmed on Skiathos

DIRECTIONS *In a nature reserve in the southwest of Skiathos, 14 km/9 miles from the harbor and 15 km/10 miles from the island airport* · **RATES** *€€–€€€€* · **ROOMS** *160 rooms – split between the Xenia Hotel (32), the Nest Villas & Suites (67) and the Grace Rooms & Suites (61)* · **FOOD** *6 restaurants, 3 bars and 4 beach bars* · **HISTORY** *The family-owned resort was opened in June 2018* · **X-FACTOR** *The spa, which uses products from Elemis*

WO DIE SCHWARZEN SCHWÄNE LEBEN

Der berühmte schwarze Schwan von Skiathos ist der Protagonist dieses Resorts. Er taucht als Skulptur im Haus auf, ziert auf Schwarz-Weiß-Bildern die Wände und gab der schönsten Villa ihren Namen. Ebenso majestätisch und stolz wie er übers Wasser gleitet, liegt das Elivi an der Südwestküste der Insel – an leicht geschwungenen Hügeln, umgeben von dichter, dunkelgrüner Vegetation und mit Blick auf vier Bilderbuchstrände. Vom Athener Studio 3SK Stylianidis Architects gestaltet, umfasst es drei Teile: Die interessanteste Geschichte hat das Xenia Hotel auf dem höchsten Punkt des Geländes – es entstand 1963 im Rahmen eines nationalen Bauprogramms der Tourismuszentrale, das die griechische Hotelbranche ankurbeln sollte. Seine modernistische Fassade wurde bewahrt, in den in Weiß und Beige gehaltenen Zimmern mit raumhohen Fensterfronten liegt noch ein Hauch Sixties-Flair in der Luft, und die Räume im Erdgeschoss teilen sich gemeinschaftlich einen Pool mit direktem Zugang von allen Veranden. Daneben entstanden die Bereiche Nest und Grace, deren exklusive Suiten und Villen noch mehr Privatsphäre und je einen Privatpool bieten. Höchsten Ansprüchen genügt das Elivi auch auf kulinarischem Gebiet. Seine Küche ist frisch, kreativ und köstlich – ob auf der Terrasse der griechischen Taverne, unter den Olivenbäumen des mediterranen Restaurants oder an der japanischen Sushi-Tafel. Romantiker macht ein Candle-Light-Dinner im „Leda & The Swan" direkt am Meer glücklich. Dieses intime Restaurant ist übrigens der einzige Ort weit und breit, an dem der schwarze Schwan seine Farbe wechselt: Das Lokal wurde nach der mythischen Königin Leda benannt, der sich Zeus in Gestalt eines weißen Schwans näherte, um ihre Liebe zu gewinnen. ◆ Filmtipp: „Mamma Mia" (2008) von Phyllida Lloyd, mit Meryl Streep und Pierce Brosnan, wurde zum Teil auf Skiathos gedreht

ANREISE *In einem Naturschutzgebiet im Südwesten von Skiathos gelegen, 14 km vom Hafen und 15 km vom Flughafen der Insel entfernt* · **PREISE** *€€–€€€€* · **ZIMMER** *160 Zimmer – verteilt auf das Xenia Hotel (32), die Nest Villas & Suites (67) und die Grace Rooms & Suites (61)* · **KÜCHE** *6 Restaurants, 3 Bars und 4 Beachbars* · **GESCHICHTE** *Das Resort ist in Familienbesitz und wurde im Juni 2018 eröffnet* · **X-FAKTOR** *Das Spa, in dem Pflegeprodukte von Elemis verwendet werden*

CYGNES NOIRS, CYGNE BLANC

Le célèbre cygne noir de Skiathos est l'emblème de cet hôtel. Il apparaît sous forme de sculpture dans la maison, sur des photos en noir et blanc décorant les murs, et il a donné son nom à la plus belle villa. Aussi majestueux et fier que le cygne glissant sur l'eau, l'Elivi se dresse sur la côte sud-ouest de l'île – sur des collines légèrement ondulées, entouré d'une végétation dense et sombre, et avec une vue sur quatre plages sorties tout droit d'un livre d'images. Conçu par le studio 3SK Stylianidis Architects d'Athènes, il est composé de trois parties. L'histoire la plus intéressante est celle de l'hôtel Xenia, situé sur le point le plus élevé du site – il a été construit en 1963 dans le cadre d'un programme national de construction de l'Office du tourisme pour stimuler l'industrie hôtelière grecque. Sa façade moderniste a été préservée, les chambres blanches et beiges avec des fenêtres du sol au plafond ont gardé un peu de l'atmosphère des années soixante, et les chambres du rez-de-chaussée partagent une piscine à laquelle on accède directement de toutes les vérandas. Les zones Nest et Grace ont été créées à côté, leurs suites et villas exclusives offrent encore plus d'intimité et disposent chacune d'une piscine privée. L'Elivi répond également aux normes culinaires les plus exigeantes. Sa cuisine à base de produits frais est créative et délicieuse – que ce soit sur la terrasse de la taverne grecque, sous les oliviers du restaurant méditerranéen ou à la table des sushis japonais. Les romantiques apprécieront un dîner aux chandelles chez « Leda & The Swan », au bord de la mer. On notera que ce restaurant intime est le seul endroit où le cygne n'est pas noir, mais blanc ; il doit en effet son nom à la mythique reine Léda, que Zeus réussit à séduire sous la forme d'un cygne blanc. ◆ À voir : « Mamma Mia ! » (2008) de Phyllida Lloyd, avec Meryl Streep et Pierce Brosnan. Le film a été en partie tourné à Skiathos

ACCÈS *Dans une réserve naturelle au sud-ouest de Skiathos, à 14 km du port et 15 km de l'aéroport de l'île* · **PRIX** *€€–€€€€* · **CHAMBRES** *160 chambres réparties entre le Xenia Hotel (32), les Nest Villas & Suites (67) et les Grace Rooms & Suites (61)* · **RESTAURATION** *6 restaurants, 3 bars et 4 bars de plage* · **HISTOIRE** *L'hôtel, ouvert en juin 2018, est une entreprise familiale* · **LES « PLUS »** *Le spa, avec les produits de soins de la marque Elemis*

EUPHORIA RETREAT

MYSTRAS, SPARTI

EUPHORIA RETREAT

231 00 Mystras, Sparti
Tel. +30 2731 306 111 · reservations@euphoriaretreat.com
www.euphoriaretreat.com

EQUILIBRIUM

After overcoming cancer as a young woman, Marina Efraimoglou conquered the world of investment banking – until, as time passed, the exhaustion outweighed the success, and she realized that she needed to balance her life again. During this period she explored traditional Chinese medicine and the theory of the five elements, which is about the specific energies and healing powers of water, wood, fire, earth and metal. She combined this lore with the ancient Greek attitude to life as a joyful and sensual process of abundant, exciting opportunities – and conceived a holistic wellness resort with the aim of establishing harmony between body, mind and soul for its guests. After a long search that lasted some ten years, she found the perfect place for her Euphoria Retreat in Mystras, a ruined Byzantine city. Inspired by Byzantine forms and colors, and in collaboration with Deca Architecture and with Natalia Efraimoglou & Partners, she furnished beautiful rooms in shades of gold with touches of red and blue (the six rooms of the wonderfully refurbished Leoncini Mansion dating from 1830, which are available for exclusive hire, are especially elegant). The spa, too, takes its cue from historic architecture: built into the hillside on four levels, it is a miracle of geometric shapes, striking effects of light and minimalist design. From the Sphere Pool beneath a dome and the Byzantine hammam to the magnificent tepidarium, it provides all of the amenities of a luxury spa – and, it goes without saying, customized wellness programs that are individually prepared for every guest. This also includes nutrition: on the basis of the Mediterranean diet, the "Gaia" restaurant serves healthy menus and runs courses that enable guests to cook the recipes for themselves at home. ◆ Book to pack: "A Guide to Chinese Medicine" by Harriet Beinfield and Efrem Korngold

DIRECTIONS *Mystras is situated on the Peloponnese, west of Sparta. The nearest international airports are Kalamata (96 km/60 miles) and Athens (247 km/155 miles)* · **RATES** *€€€–€€€€* · **ROOMS** *45 rooms and suites, all individually designed. Children from the age of 14 are welcome* · **FOOD** *Seasonal organic products from local suppliers are used for the Mediterranean dishes; the chefs cooperate with nutritionists and doctors* · **HISTORY** *Opened in July 2018* · **X-FACTOR** *A holistic spa in venerable surroundings: Mystras is a Unesco World Heritage site*

IM GLEICHGEWICHT

Nachdem sie als junge Frau eine Krebserkrankung überstanden hatte, eroberte sie die Welt des Investmentbankings – bis nach einiger Zeit die Erschöpfung größer wurde als der Erfolg und sie merkte, dass sie ihr Leben wieder ins Gleichgewicht bringen musste. Damals lernte Marina Efraimoglou die Traditionelle Chinesische Medizin und die Theorie der fünf Elemente kennen, die sich um die spezifischen Energien und heilenden Kräfte von Wasser, Holz, Feuer, Erde sowie Metall dreht. Beides verband sie mit der antiken griechischen Auffassung vom Leben als freudvollem und sinnlichem Prozess voller spannender Möglichkeiten – und konzipierte ein ganzheitliches Wellnessresort, das Körper, Geist und Seele seiner Gäste in Einklang bringen sollte. In der byzantinischen Ruinenstadt Mystras fand sie nach rund zehn Jahre langer Suche den perfekten Platz für ihr Euphoria Retreat. Inspiriert von byzantinischen Formen und Farben und gemeinsam mit Deca Architecture sowie Natalia Efraimoglou & Partners richtete sie hier wunderschöne Zimmer in Goldtönen und mit Akzenten in Rot und Blau ein (besonders elegant sind die sechs Räume der herausragend renovierten Leoncini Mansion von 1830, die exklusiv gemietet werden kann). Auch das Spa zeigt Anklänge an alte Architektur: In den Berg gebaut und vier Etagen umfassend, ist es ein Wunderwerk aus geometrischen Formen, effektvollen Lichtspielen und minimalistischem Design. Vom Sphären-Pool unter einer Kuppel über den byzantinischen Hammam bis hin zum edlen Tepidarium bietet es sämtliche Annehmlichkeiten eines Luxus-Spas – und natürlich maßgeschneiderte Wohlfühlprogramme, die für jeden Gast individuell zusammengestellt werden. Sie umfassen auch die Ernährung: Basierend auf der Mittelmeer-Diät serviert das Restaurant „Gaia" gesunde Menüs und bietet Kurse an, damit man die Rezepte zu Hause nachkochen kann. ◆ Buchtipp: „Traditionelle Chinesische Medizin" von Harriet Beinfield und Efrem Korngold

ANREISE *Mystras liegt auf dem Peloponnes westlich von Sparta, die nächsten internationalen Flughäfen sind Kalamata (96 km) und Athen (247 km)* · **PREISE** *€€€–€€€€* · **ZIMMER** *45 Zimmer und Suiten, alle individuell gestaltet. Kinder sind ab 14 Jahren willkommen* · **KÜCHE** *Für die mediterrane Kost werden saisonale Bioprodukte aus der Region verwendet; die Köche kooperieren mit Ernährungsberatern und Ärzten* · **GESCHICHTE** *Im Juli 2018 eröffnet* · **X-FAKTOR** *Ein holistisches Spa in altehrwürdiger Umgebung: Mystras gehört zum Unesco-Weltkulturerbe*

EN ÉQUILIBRE

Après avoir survécu à un cancer dans sa jeunesse, elle a conquis le monde de la banque d'investissement – et puis, plus tard, l'épuisement l'a emporté sur la satisfaction et elle s'est rendue compte qu'il lui fallait retrouver son équilibre. Marina Efraimoglou a alors appris la médecine traditionnelle chinoise et la théorie des cinq éléments, qui tourne autour des énergies spécifiques et des pouvoirs de guérison de l'eau, du bois, du feu, de la terre et du métal. Combinant les deux avec l'idée grecque antique de la vie considérée comme un processus joyeux et sensuel plein de possibilités excitantes – elle a conçu un hôtel de bien-être holistique qui mettrait en harmonie le corps, l'esprit et l'âme de ses hôtes. Après une dizaine d'années de recherches, elle a trouvé dans la ville byzantine en ruines de Mystras l'endroit idéal pour créer l'Euphoria Retreat. S'inspirant des formes et des couleurs byzantines et en collaboration avec Deca Architecture et Natalia Efraimoglou & Partners, elle a aménagé de magnifiques chambres dans des tons dorés avec des accents de rouge et de bleu (les six pièces de la Leoncini Mansion de 1830, remarquablement rénovée et qui peut être louée en exclusivité, sont particulièrement élégantes). Le spa montre aussi des réminiscences de l'architecture ancienne : construit dans la montagne et couvrant quatre étages, c'est une merveille de formes géométriques, d'effets de lumière et de design minimaliste. De la piscine sphérique sous un dôme, au noble tépidarium, en passant par le hammam byzantin, il offre toutes les commodités d'un spa de luxe – et, bien sûr, des programmes de bien-être conçus individuellement pour chaque client. La nutrition n'a pas été oubliée : basé sur le régime méditerranéen, le restaurant « Gaia » propose des menus sains et des cours permettant de cuisiner les recettes à la maison. ◆ À lire : « Between Heaven and Earth: A Guide to Chinese Medicine » par Harriet Beinfield et Efrem Korngold

ACCÈS *Mystras est située dans le Péloponnèse, à l'ouest de Sparte, les aéroports internationaux les plus proches sont Kalamata (96 km) et Athènes (247 km)* · **PRIX** *€€€–€€€€* · **CHAMBRES** *45 chambres et suites, toutes meublées et décorées de manière individuelle. Les enfants sont les bienvenus à partir de 14 ans* · **RESTAURATION** *Des produits bio de saison et de la région sont utilisés pour préparer les plats aux saveurs méditerranéennes ; les cuisiniers travaillent avec des diététiciens et des médecins* · **HISTOIRE** *Ouvert en juillet 2018* · **LES « PLUS »** *Un spa holistique dans un environnement vénérable : Mystras est inscrite au patrimoine mondial de l'Unesco*

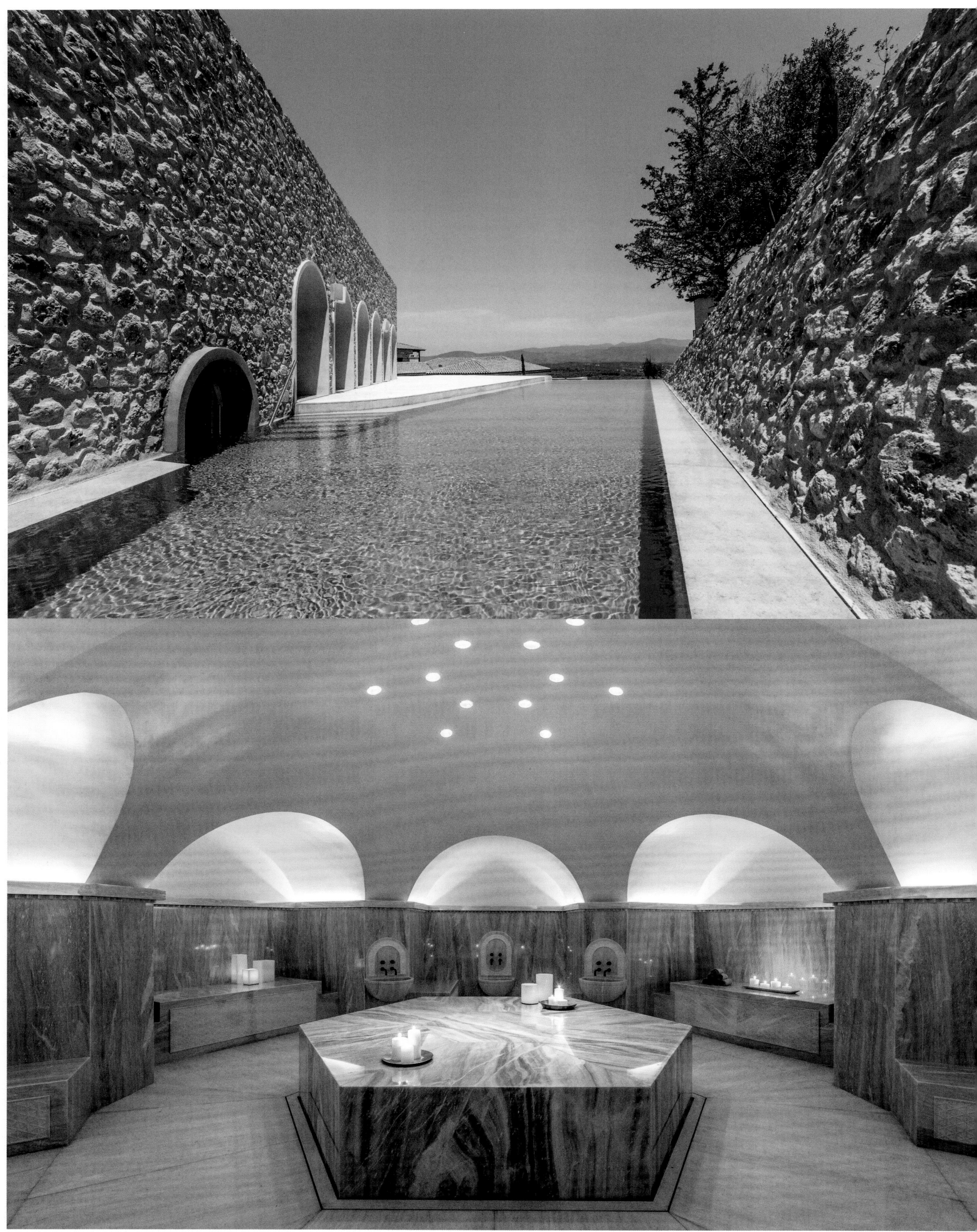

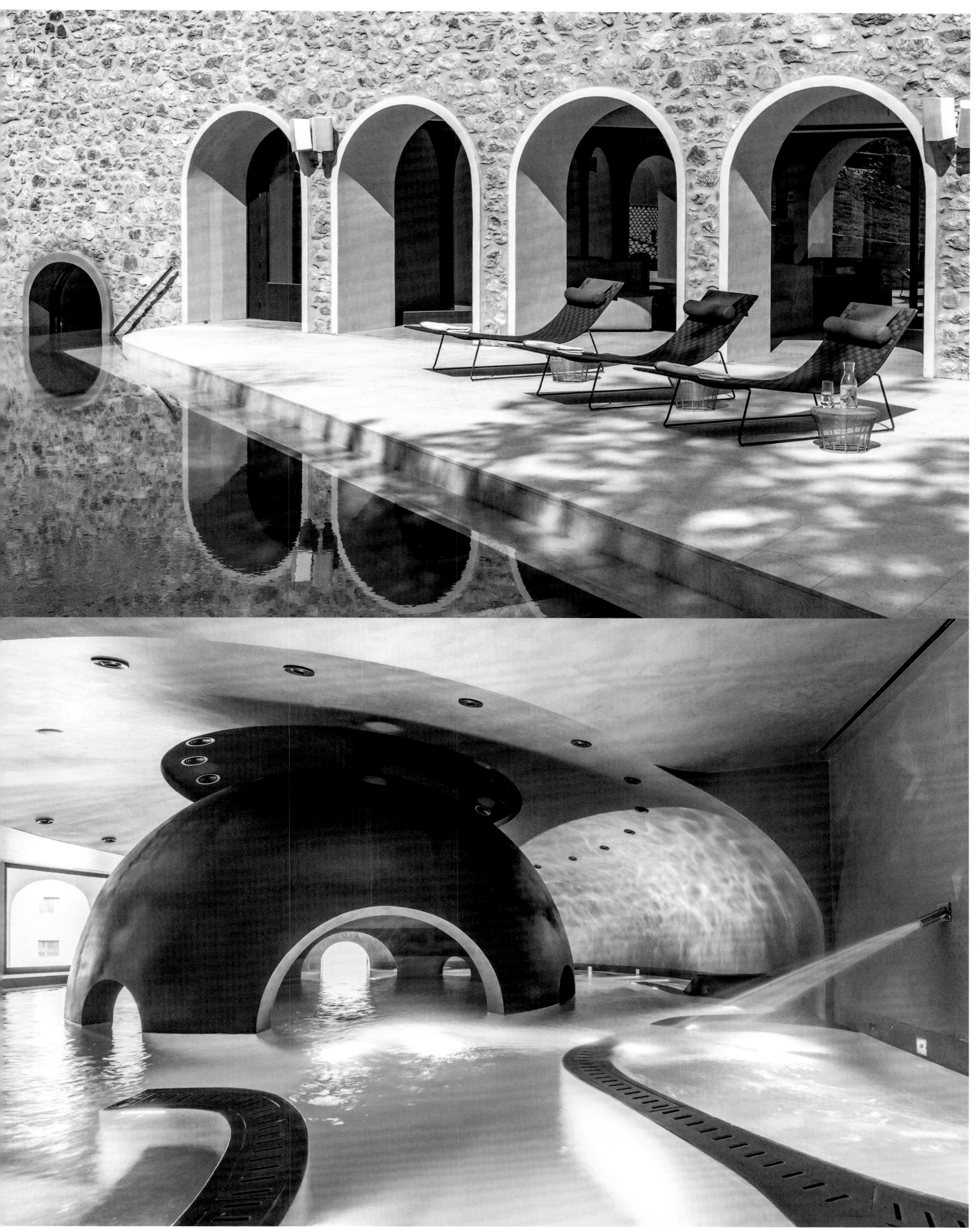

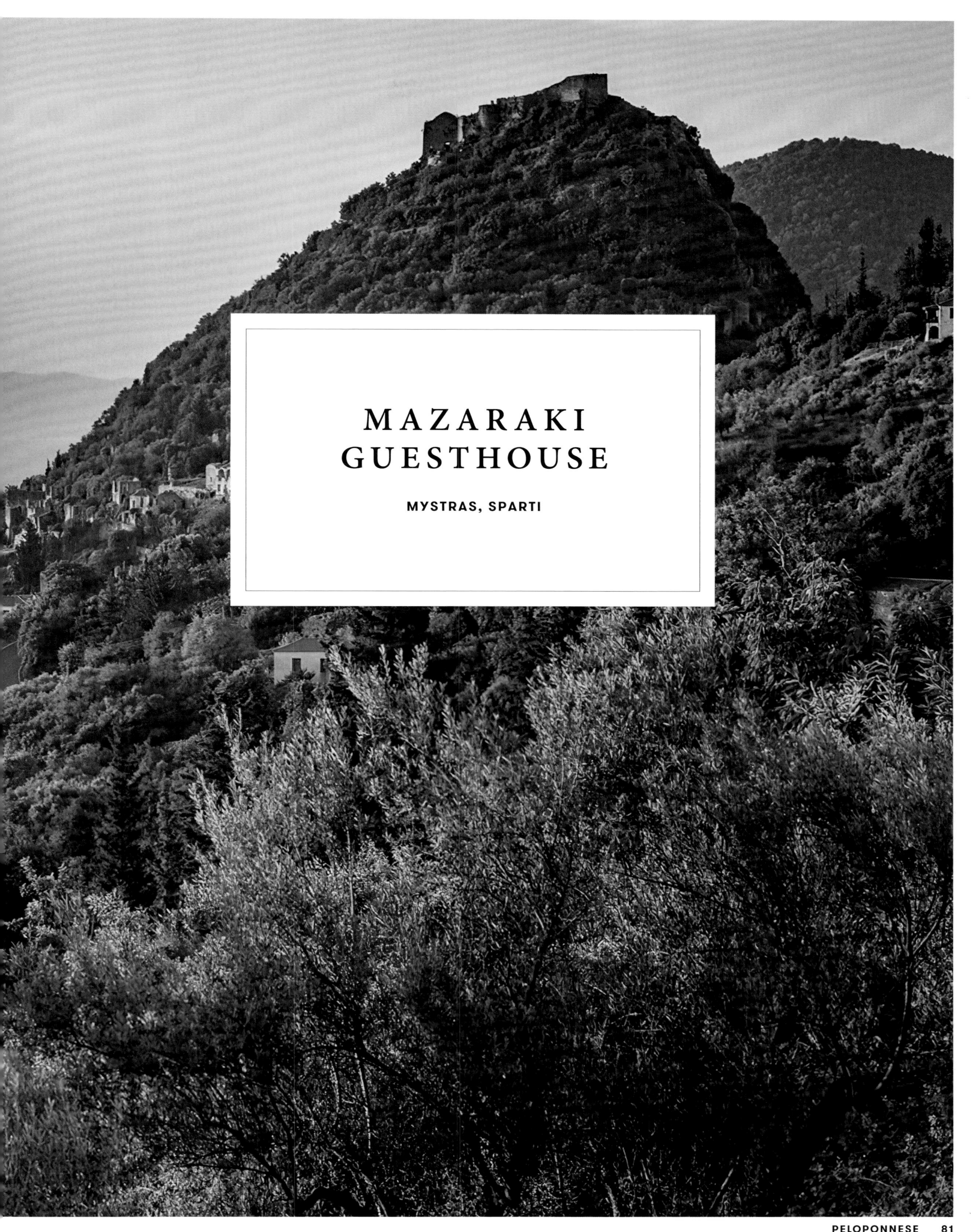

MAZARAKI GUESTHOUSE

MYSTRAS, SPARTI

MAZARAKI GUESTHOUSE

Pikoulianika, 231 00 Mystras, Sparti
Tel. +30 27310 204 14 · info@xenonasmazaraki.gr
www.xenonasmazaraki.gr

THE MAGIC OF MYSTRAS

This fortified town was built on a hill in the thirteenth century and became a center of Byzantine power, art and culture. Mystras has a great history to which the remains of the governor's palace, the mansions of noble families, churches and monasteries testify. For everyone who would like to explore and hike around these world-famous ruins on high ground at the foot of the Taygetos mountain range (Mystras is spread across a site with an altitude range of hundreds of feet – good shoes are a boon here!), the best place to stay is this delightful hotel, which is situated only a few minutes' walk from the entrance to the archaeological site. The architect George Giaxolgou converted several buildings in rustic style into an idyllic ensemble, and Eleni Manolopoulou designed the interiors of the pretty houses in natural shades with the use of natural materials. It is evident that in her main profession she designs theater scenery and costumes, and likes to create playful stage sets: in the Sky suite, the ceiling, fabrics and even the telephone on the bedside table are light blue, while miniature hot-air balloons float in the room called Aerostat, and Bicycle has a real bike built into the surface for its wash basin. A day at the Mazaraki Guesthouse begins with a breakfast basket filled with Greek treats that is placed by the door, and ends by the pool in the garden, in the shared living area with a fireplace and library, or on the private balconies and terraces of the guest rooms – with a stunning view across the plain of Sparta, the mountains and magical Mystras.
◆ Book to pack: "Baudolino" by Umberto Eco

DIRECTIONS *The guesthouse is in the village of Pikoulianika, at a distance of 60 km/40 miles from the international airport in Kalamata and 250 km/155 miles from Athens airport. It is recommended to have a car when staying* · **RATES** *€–€€* · **ROOMS** *11 rooms and suites, 10 of them with a kitchenette* · **FOOD** *The hotel has a coffee and wine bar. For lunch and dinner, guests cook for themselves or eat in one of the small village restaurants* · **HISTORY** *Opened in 2008* · **X-FACTOR** *Thanks to the nearby mountains, a good base for walkers, climbers and mountainbikers*

DIE MAGIE VON MYSTRAS

Die Stadt wurde im 13. Jahrhundert als Bergfestung errichtet und entwickelte sich zum Zentrum byzantinischer Macht, Kunst und Kultur: Mystras hat eine große Geschichte, von der bis heute die Überreste des ehemaligen Statthalterpalasts, der Herrenhäuser, Kirchen und Klöster zeugen. Wer die weltberühmte Ruinenstadt auf einem Hügel vor dem Taygetos-Gebirge entdecken und erwandern möchte (Mystras zieht sich über mehrere Hundert Höhenmeter – gute Schuhe tun gute Dienste!), wohnt am besten in diesem hinreißenden Hotel, das nur ein paar Gehminuten vom Eingang zum archäologischen Gelände entfernt liegt. Der Architekt George Giaxolgou hat aus mehreren Gebäuden im rustikalen Landhausstil eine idyllische Siedlung gemacht, und Eleni Manolopoulou hat das Interieur der hübschen Häuser in Naturtönen und mit Naturmaterialien eingerichtet. Dass sie im Hauptberuf Bühnen- und Kostümbildnerin ist und die Dinge gerne spielerisch in Szene setzt, merkt man: In der Suite Sky sind Decke, Stoffe und selbst das Telefon auf dem Nachttisch in Hellblau gehalten, durch den Raum Aerostat schweben Miniatur-Heißluftballone, und im Zimmer Bicycle wurde ein echtes Zweirad in den Waschtisch im Bad integriert. Der Tag im Mazaraki Guesthouse beginnt mit einem Frühstückskorb voller griechischer Delikatessen, der vor die Tür gestellt wird, und endet am Pool im Garten, im gemeinsamen Wohnbereich mit Kamin und Bibliothek oder auf den privaten Balkonen und Terrassen der Zimmer – mit Bilderbuchblick über die Ebene von Sparta, die Berge und das magische Mystras. ◆ Buchtipp: „Baudolino" von Umberto Eco

ANREISE *Das Gasthaus liegt im Dorf Pikoulianika, die nächsten internationalen Flughäfen sind Kalamata (65 km) und Athen (250 km). Vor Ort ist ein Auto empfehlenswert* · **PREISE** *€–€€* · **ZIMMER** *11 Zimmer und Suiten, 10 davon mit Kitchenette* · **KÜCHE** *Zum Hotel gehört eine Kaffee- und Weinbar. Mittags und abends kocht man selbst oder geht in die kleinen Dorfrestaurants* · **GESCHICHTE** *2008 eröffnet* · **X-FAKTOR** *Dank der nahen Berge eine gute Basis für Wanderer, Kletterer und Mountainbiker*

LA MAGIE DE MYSTRAS

La cité a été construite au XIIIe siècle sous la forme d'une forteresse de montagne et est devenue le centre du pouvoir, de l'art et de la culture byzantins : Mystras (ou Mistra) a une grande histoire, dont témoignent aujourd'hui encore les vestiges de l'ancien palais du gouverneur, les demeures seigneuriales, les églises et les monastères. Si vous voulez découvrir et explorer à pied la ville en ruines mondialement connue, située sur une colline en face des montagnes du Taygète (Mystras s'étend sur plusieurs centaines de mètres d'altitude – de bonnes chaussures seront bienvenues !), le meilleur endroit où séjourner est cet hôtel ravissant, qui n'est qu'à quelques minutes de marche de l'entrée du site archéologique. L'architecte George Giaxolgou a transformé plusieurs bâtiments de style rustique en un lotissement idyllique, et Eleni Manolopoulou a décoré l'intérieur des jolies maisons dans des tons naturels en utilisant des matériaux naturels. Impossible d'ignorer qu'elle est décoratrice de théâtre et créatrice de costumes dans son métier principal et qu'elle aime mettre les choses en scène de façon ludique : dans la suite Sky, le plafond, les tissus et même le téléphone sur la table de chevet sont bleu ciel, des montgolfières miniatures flottent dans la chambre Aerostat, et dans la chambre Bicycle, un vrai vélo a été intégré au lavabo de la salle de bains. La journée à la Mazaraki Guesthouse commence par un panier de petit-déjeuner rempli de gourmandises grecques devant la porte et se termine près de la piscine dans le jardin, dans la salle de séjour commune avec cheminée et bibliothèque ou sur les balcons et terrasses privés des chambres qui offrent une vue sublime sur la plaine de Sparte, les montagnes et Mystras l'envoûtante. ◆ À lire : « Baudolino » par Umberto Eco

ACCÈS *L'hôtel est situé dans le village de Pikoulianika, les aéroports internationaux les plus proches sont Kalamata (65 km) et Athènes (250 km). Une voiture est recommandée sur place* · **PRIX** *€–€€* · **CHAMBRES** *11 chambres et suites, dont 10 avec kitchenette* · **RESTAURATION** *L'hôtel dispose d'un bar-café et d'un bar à vins. Le midi et le soir, on peut préparer ses repas soi-même ou se restaurer dans les petits restaurants du village* · **HISTOIRE** *Ouvert en 2008* · **LES « PLUS »** *Les montagnes sont proches, c'est un bon point de départ pour les randonneurs, les grimpeurs et les amateurs de vélo tout-terrain*

AMANZOE

NEAR PORTO HELI, KRANIDI, ARGOLIDA

AMANZOE

Agios Panteleimonas, near Porto Heli, 213 00 Kranidi, Argolida
Tel. +30 27547 72 888 · amanzoe@aman.com
www.aman.com/resorts/amanzoe

CLASSICAL BEAUTY

The benchmark was challenging, very challenging indeed: the Acropolis, the most famous building of ancient Greece, was chosen as the model for this resort. Yet Edward Tuttle, the principal architect of Aman Hotels, met the challenge with his usual mastery and made the Amanzoe Hotel into a classical beauty. Here everything revolves around clear lines and perfect proportions, with an infallible sense of space, harmony and timelessness. The white pavilions, each a modern temple with a flat roof, columned façade and private pool, lie on a gentle hill with a view of cypresses and olive groves or look out on to the sparkling blue Aegean Sea. The interiors are a play of cold and warm materials beneath high ceilings, with marble, natural stone and oak wood creating elegant contrasts. The cabins down by the water also have large terraces with direct access to the beach, while the villas, the largest of which possesses nine bedrooms on six stories, are distinguished by ultimate, Aman-style luxury. The spa, too, lives up to the highest standards. Run by a team of experts in which no role, from the wellness concierge to the doctor, was overlooked, it combines Asian treatments with a Greek lore of healing that goes back to Hippocrates. Guests can experience for themselves that honey, yogurt and olive oil from Hellas are not merely culinary delights but also genuine beauty elixirs. As for cooking: the chefs at Amanzoe are considered masters of their trade. They serve their creative dishes in very special places – for example, on the candlelit stage of the hotel's own amphitheater, an unforgettable scene. ◆ Book to pack: "Greek Myths" by Olivia E. Coolidge

DIRECTIONS *In the east of the Peloponnese, 2 hrs 30 min from Athens airport; transfer by helicopter on request (25 min)* · **RATES** *€€€€* · **ROOMS** *38 pavilions, 4 cabins on the beach, 8 villas with up to 9 bedrooms, butler and cook* · **FOOD** *Greek and Mediterranean dishes are served in the main restaurant, the pool restaurant and the beach club. The menu in "Nama," open only in the evenings, is Japanese. Not to be missed: the bar, where the cocktails are named after Greek gods* · **HISTORY** *Opened in 2012* · **X-FACTOR** *Yoga courses in the open pavilion*

EINE KLASSISCHE SCHÖNHEIT

Die Messlatte lag hoch, sehr hoch sogar: Die Akropolis, das berühmteste Bauwerk der griechischen Antike, sollte als Vorbild für dieses Resort dienen. Doch Edward Tuttle, Haus- und Hofarchitekt der Aman Hotels, erreichte sie gewohnt souverän und machte aus dem Amanzoe eine klassische Schönheit. Alles dreht sich hier um klare Linien und perfekte Proportionen, um ein untrügliches Gefühl für Raum, Harmonie und Zeitlosigkeit. Die weißen Pavillons, moderne Tempel mit Flachdach, Säulenfassade und Privatpool, liegen an einem sanften Hügel und schauen auf Zypressen und Olivenhaine oder auf die blau schimmernde Ägäis. Innen spielen sie unter hohen Decken mit kalten und warmen Materialien – Marmor, Naturstein und Eichenholz sorgen für elegante Kontraste. Die Cabanas direkt am Wasser bieten zusätzlich große Terrassen mit direktem Zugang zum Strand, während in den Villen, von denen die größte neun Schlafzimmer auf sechs Etagen umfasst, ultimativer Luxus à la Aman herrscht. Auch das Spa genügt höchsten Ansprüchen: Geführt von einem Expertenteam, in dem vom Wellness-Concierge bis zum Arzt kein Posten vergessen wurde, verbindet es asiatische Anwendungen mit griechischer Heilkunde, die bis zu Hippokrates zurückreicht – man erfährt am eigenen Leib, dass Honig, Joghurt und Olivenöl aus Hellas nicht nur kleine Köstlichkeiten sind, sondern auch echte Schönheitselixiere. Apropos Kulinarik: Die Köche des Amanzoe gelten als Meister ihres Fachs und servieren ihre Kreationen sogar an ganz speziellen Orten – zum Beispiel auf der von Kerzen beleuchteten Bühne des hoteleigenen Amphitheaters, eine unvergessliche Szene. ◆ Buchtipp: „Sagen des klassischen Altertums" von Gustav Schwab

ANREISE *Im Osten des Peloponnes gelegen, 2,5 Std. vom Flughafen Athen entfernt; auf Anfrage Helikoptertransfer möglich (25 min)* · **PREISE** *€€€€* · **ZIMMER** *38 Pavillons, 4 Cabanas am Strand, 8 Villen mit bis zu 9 Schlafzimmern, Butler und Koch* · **KÜCHE** *Griechisch-mediterrane Gerichte gibt es im Haupt- und Poolrestaurant sowie im Beachklub. Das nur abends geöffnete „Nama" kocht japanisch. Nicht verpassen: die Bar, deren Cocktails nach griechischen Göttern benannt sind* · **GESCHICHTE** *2012 eröffnet* · **X-FAKTOR** *Die Yogakurse im offenen Pavillon*

UNE BEAUTÉ CLASSIQUE

L'Acropole, le bâtiment le plus célèbre de l'Antiquité grecque, devait servir de modèle, c'est dire que la barre était placée très très haut. Mais Edward Tuttle, architecte attitré des hôtels Aman, a fait montre de sa virtuosité habituelle en dotant l'Amanzoe d'une beauté classique. Ici, tout tourne autour de lignes claires et de proportions parfaites, dénote un sens aigu de l'espace, de l'harmonie et de l'intemporalité. Les pavillons blancs, temples modernes aux toits plats et colonnades et aux piscines privées, se dressent sur une colline aux pentes douces et donnent sur des cyprès et des oliveraies ou sur le bleu chatoyant de la mer Égée. À l'intérieur, ils jouent avec des matériaux froids et chauds sous de hauts plafonds – le marbre, la pierre naturelle et le bois de chêne offrent des contrastes élégants. Les cabanes du front de mer sont dotées de grandes terrasses avec accès direct à la plage, tandis que les villas, dont la plus grande compte neuf chambres sur six étages, offrent le nec plus ultra du luxe à la Aman. Le spa satisfait lui aussi les plus hautes exigences : dirigé par une équipe d'experts dans laquelle aucun poste n'a été oublié, du concierge du bien-être au médecin, il associe les traitements asiatiques à la médecine grecque du temps d'Hippocrate. Vous découvrirez ici que le miel, le yaourt et l'huile d'olive d'Hellas sont aussi de véritables élixirs de beauté. En parlant de délices culinaires, les chefs d'Amanzoe sont considérés comme des maîtres dans leur art et servent même leurs créations dans des endroits très particuliers – par exemple sur la scène éclairée aux bougies de l'amphithéâtre de l'hôtel, une scène inoubliable. ◆ À lire : « Mythes grecs » de Lucilla Burn

ACCÈS *À l'est du Péloponnèse, à 2,5 h de l'aéroport d'Athènes; transfert en hélicoptère sur demande (25 min)* · **PRIX** *€€€€* · **CHAMBRES** *38 pavillons, 4 cabanes de plage, 8 villas abritant jusqu'à 9 chambres à coucher, avec majordome et cuisinier* · **RESTAURATION** *Des plats de la cuisine gréco-méditerranéenne sont servis dans le restaurant principal et le restaurant de la piscine ainsi que dans le club de la plage. Le « Nama » ouvert uniquement le soir propose des plats japonais. À ne pas manquer: le bar, dont les cocktails portent le nom de dieux grecs* · **HISTOIRE** *Ouvert en 2012* · **LES « PLUS »** *Les cours de yoga dans le pavillon ouvert*

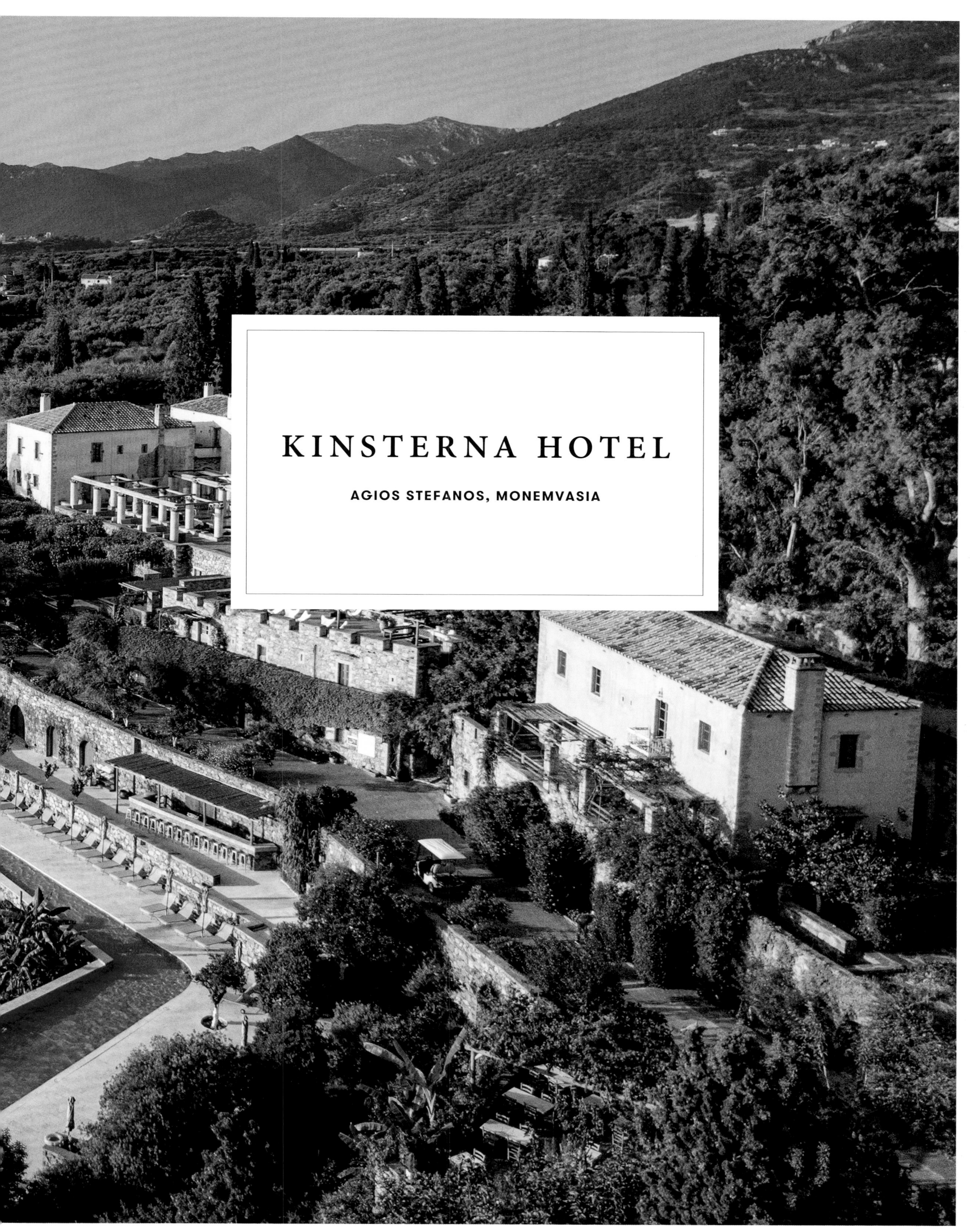

KINSTERNA HOTEL

AGIOS STEFANOS, MONEMVASIA

KINSTERNA HOTEL

Agios Stefanos, 230 70 Monemvasia
Tel. +30 27320 663 00 · info@kinsternahotel.gr
www.kinsternahotel.gr

FAITHFULLY RESTORED

The name means "the only entrance" – and indeed, only a narrow causeway leads to the old fortified town of Monemvasia, which lies on a rock off the coast of the Peloponnese and was considered impregnable for centuries. There is a wonderful view of the small peninsula from the Kinsterna Hotel, which itself resembles a fortress and looks back on a long history. Historians are not entirely in agreement about whether its oldest parts date from the late seventeenth or early eighteenth century – it is undisputed, however, that the building reflects the Byzantine, Venetian and Ottoman heritage of the region. From the impressive cistern in the courtyard, flanked by twenty columns, and the massive stone vaults in many rooms to the slender embrasures in the walls, the whole complex was restored faithfully and with great expert knowledge. The architects, designers, engineers and local artisans worked closely with archaeologists, creating a special atmosphere that blends the past with the present both indoors and outdoors. The twenty-five-acre Mediterranean gardens were newly laid out according to historic models. Kinsterna was once able to supply its own needs – and today, as in the past, wine is pressed on the estate from the grapes that are grown there, the Greek spirit tsipouro is distilled from the must, and olive oil is produced. The kitchen staff of the hotel restaurant harvest fruit, vegetables and herbs on site, private freshwater springs feed the pools, and guests in the spa are treated with natural products such as honey, peppermint and lemon grass. ◆ Book to pack: "Monovassiá" by Yannis Ritsos, the poet's homage to his birthplace Monemvasia

DIRECTIONS *7 km/4 miles southwest of Monemvasia; the nearest international airports are Kalamata (185 km/115 miles) and Athens (334 km/207 miles)* · **RATES** *€€–€€€€* · **ROOMS** *31 rooms and suites, 20 residences and 2 villas with pools* · **FOOD** *Greek gourmet menus are prepared at "Sterna," while "Mouries" serves Mediterranean dishes of the day. There is also an open-air taverna (open in summer only), a bar, and a pool bar* · **HISTORY** *The current owners bought the estate in 2002 and restored it between 2006 and 2010* · **X-FACTOR** *The in-house library with historic books about Kinsterna and Monemvasia*

ORIGINALGETREU RESTAURIERT

Ihr Name bedeutet so viel wie „einziger Zugang" – und in der Tat führt nur ein schmaler Damm zur alten Festungsstadt Monemvasia, die auf einem Felsen vor der Küste des Peloponnes liegt und über Jahrhunderte als uneinnehmbar galt. Einen herrlichen Blick auf die kleine Halbinsel eröffnet das Kinsterna Hotel, das selbst festungsgleich erbaut wurde und eine lange Geschichte erzählt. Ob seine ältesten Teile aus dem späten 17. oder frühen 18. Jahrhundert stammen, darüber sind sich Historiker nicht ganz einig – sicher ist aber, dass der Bau das byzantinische, venezianische und osmanische Erbe der Region widerspiegelt. Von der beeindruckenden, mit 20 Säulen gesäumten Zisterne im Hof über die mächtigen Steingewölbe in manchen Räumen bis hin zu den schmalen Schießscharten in den Mauern: Das gesamte Anwesen wurde originalgetreu und mit viel Fachwissen restauriert – Architekten, Designer, Ingenieure und einheimische Handwerker arbeiteten eng mit Archäologen zusammen und schufen drinnen wie draußen eine ganz besondere Atmosphäre, die Vergangenheit und Gegenwart vereint. Auch die zehn Hektar großen mediterranen Gärten wurden nach altem Vorbild neu angelegt. Einst konnte sich Kinsterna selbst versorgen, und wie damals wird heute auf dem Grundstück wieder Wein aus eigenen Trauben gekeltert, Tsipouro (griechischer Tresterbrand) destilliert und Olivenöl gepresst. Die Küchenbrigaden der hoteleigenen Restaurants ernten Obst, Gemüse und Kräuter direkt vor der Tür, private Süßwasserquellen speisen die Pools, und im Spa pflegen Naturprodukte wie Honig, Pfefferminze und Zitronengras. ◆ Buchtipp: „Monovassiá" von Jannis Ritsos, eine Hommage des Dichters an seinen Geburtsort Monemvasia

ANREISE *7 km südwestlich von Monemvasia gelegen, die nächsten internationalen Flughäfen sind Kalamata (185 km) und Athen (334 km)* · **PREISE** *€€–€€€€* · **ZIMMER** *31 Zimmer und Suiten, 20 Residenzen und 2 Villen mit Pool* · **KÜCHE** *Das „Sterna" serviert griechische Gourmetmenüs, das „Mouries" mediterrane Tagesgerichte. Außerdem gibt es eine Taverne unter freiem Himmel (nur im Sommer geöffnet), eine Bar und eine Poolbar* · **GESCHICHTE** *Der heutige Besitzer kaufte das Anwesen 2002 und sanierte es von 2006 bis 2010* · **X-FAKTOR** *Die hauseigene Bibliothek mit historischen Büchern über Kinsterna und Monemvasia*

UNE RESTAURATION MINUTIEUSE

Son nom signifie « seul accès » – et il est vrai que seule une digue étroite mène à l'ancienne citadelle de Monemvassia, qui est située sur un rocher au large de la côte du Péloponnèse et a été considérée comme imprenable pendant des siècles. L'hôtel Kinsterna, construit lui aussi comme une forteresse et qui a une longue histoire à raconter, offre une vue magnifique sur la petite péninsule. Les historiens ne sont pas d'accord quant à savoir si les parties les plus anciennes remontent à la fin du XVIIe ou au début du XVIIIe siècle, ce qui est certain c'est que le bâtiment est le reflet du patrimoine byzantin, vénitien et ottoman de la région. De l'impressionnante citerne bordée de 20 colonnes dans la cour, aux solides voûtes de pierre dans certaines pièces, en passant par les étroites meurtrières dans les murs, l'ensemble de la propriété a été restauré à l'identique et avec beaucoup de savoir-faire spécialisé – des architectes, des designers, des ingénieurs et des artisans locaux ont travaillé en étroite collaboration avec des archéologues et ont créé, tant à l'intérieur qu'à l'extérieur, une atmosphère très particulière qui unit le passé et le présent. Les jardins méditerranéens de dix hectares ont également été réaménagés selon l'ancien modèle. Kinsterna pouvait autrefois subvenir à ses besoins et, comme par le passé, la propriété a sa vigne pour faire du vin, distiller du tsipouro (alcool de marc grec), et ses oliviers pour l'huile d'olive. Les brigades de cuisine des restaurants de l'hôtel récoltent des fruits, des légumes et des fines herbes au pied de la porte, des sources d'eau douce privées alimentent les piscines, et dans le spa on utilise des produits naturels tels que le miel, la menthe poivrée et la citronnelle pour soigner la peau. ◆ À lire : « Femmes de Monemvassia » par Jannis Ritsos, un hommage du poète à la ville où il est né

ACCÈS *À 7 km au sud-ouest de Monemvassia, les aéroports internationaux les plus proches sont Kalamata (185 km) et Athènes (334 km)* · **PRIX** *€€–€€€€* · **CHAMBRES** *31 chambres et suites, 20 résidences et 2 villas avec piscine* · **RESTAURATION** *Le « Sterna » propose des menus grecs pour gourmets, le « Mouries » des plats du jour de la cuisine méditerranéenne. Il y a également une taverne en plein air (ouverte l'été seulement), un bar et un pool bar* · **HISTOIRE** *Le propriétaire a acheté le domaine en 2002 et l'a restauré de 2006 à 2010* · **LES « PLUS »** *La bibliothèque de la maison abrite des ouvrages historiques sur Kinsterna et Monemvassia*

TAINARON BLUE RETREAT

VATHIA, EAST MANI

TAINARON BLUE RETREAT

230 62 Vathia, East Mani
Tel. +30 2733 300 461 and +30 697 3007 006 · hide@tainaronblue.com
www.tainaron-blue.com

A TOWER ROOM

Mani on the Peloponnese is the most mysterious area in Greece – a remote region of rugged beauty, full of myths (the entrance to Hades, the legendary underworld, is said to have been situated at its southernmost tip) and home to a race of people who for a long time had a reputation for being fearless and unpredictable. To protect themselves from pirates, conquerors or simply from vengeful neighbours, the inhabitants of Mani used to construct strong defensive and residential towers. One of these has now been turned into unconventional accommodation. The owners, both of whom work mainly as architects, have restored the tower on Cape Tenaro with great expertise, with the aim of preserving as much of its original structure as possible. They used local stone and, according to ancient tradition, mortar made from earth, clay, lime and sand that has the same shade of color as the rocks. In this way the building appears to have grown out of the ground. The low doors, small windows and steep wooden steps of the interior were retained and combined with minimalistic modern design. The three rooms are characterized equally by their historical atmosphere and by every amenity of a contemporary hotel, from beds with mattresses of natural fiber to stylish bathrooms and air conditioning. Tainaron Blue also has a restaurant exclusively for guests, where traditional recipes from Mani are prepared. Specialties such as orzo noodles with sun-dried tomatoes, capers and smoked monastery cheese are simply delicious! If the weather is not too hot, guests should definitely eat outside on the terrace to get their fill of the sweeping view of a fascinating landscape. ◆ Book to pack: "Creators, Conquerors and Citizens: A History of Ancient Greece" by Robin Waterfield

DIRECTIONS *On the Mani peninsula, the southernmost point of mainland Greece. The nearest international airports are Kalamata (125 km/ 78 miles) and Athens (340 km/210 miles)* · **RATES** *€€–€€€* · **ROOMS** *Only 3 rooms for a maximum of 9 guests* · **FOOD** *Within the tower is a communal kitchen in vintage design. The restaurant delights its guests with regional dishes for lunch and dinner* · **HISTORY** *The tower was originally built in the early nineteenth century. Kassiani and Kostas Zouvelos discovered it in 1994 and opened the hotel in May 2015* · **X-FACTOR** *Even the pool has a panoramic view*

TURMZIMMER

Die Mani auf dem Peloponnes ist Griechenlands geheimnisvollste Gegend. Eine abgeschiedene Region von schroffer Schönheit, voller Mythen (so soll an ihrer südlichsten Spitze der Eingang zum Hades, der sagenumwobenen Unterwelt, gelegen haben) und mit einem Menschenschlag, der lange als ebenso unerschrocken wie unberechenbar galt. Um sich vor Piraten, Eroberern oder einfach nur rachsüchtigen Nachbarn zu schützen, konstruierten die Bewohner der Mani einst mächtige Wohn- und Wehrtürme – einer davon beherbergt heute diese unkonventionelle Unterkunft. Die Besitzer, beide im Hauptberuf Architekten, haben den Turm am Kap Tenaro mit viel Fachwissen restauriert, um seine originale Struktur so weit wie möglich zu erhalten. Sie verwendeten lokalen Stein und verfugten ihn nach alter Tradition mit einem Mörtel aus Erde, Ton, Kalk und Sand, der dieselbe Farbschattierung wie der Fels hat – so scheint der Bau aus dem Grund herauszuwachsen. Die niedrigen Türen, kleinen Fenster und steilen Holzstufen im Inneren wurden bewahrt und mit minimalistisch-modernem Design verbunden. In den drei Zimmern herrschen sowohl historisches Ambiente als auch aller Hotelkomfort der Gegenwart, vom Bett mit Naturfasermatratze übers schicke Bad bis hin zur Klimaanlage. Exklusiv für Gäste besitzt das Tainaron Blue auch ein Restaurant, in dem nach überlieferten Rezepten der Mani gekocht wird: Die Spezialitäten wie Orzo-Nudeln mit sonnengetrockneten Tomaten, Kapern und geräuchertem Klosterkäse sind einfach nur köstlich! Wenn es nicht zu heiß ist, sollte man unbedingt draußen auf der Terrasse essen und sich am weiten Blick über ein faszinierendes Land sattsehen. ◆ Buchtipp: „Orpheus" von Salih Jamal

ANREISE *Auf der Halbinsel Mani, am südlichsten Punkt des griechischen Festlands gelegen. Die nächsten internationalen Flughäfen sind Kalamata (125 km) und Athen (340 km)* · **PREISE** *€€–€€€* · **ZIMMER** *Nur 3 Zimmer für max. 9 Gäste* · **KÜCHE** *Im Turm gibt es eine Gemeinschaftsküche im Vintage-Design. Mittags und abends verwöhnt das Restaurant mit regionalen Gerichten* · **GESCHICHTE** *Ursprünglich wurde der Turm Anfang des 19. Jahrhunderts erbaut. Das Ehepaar Kassiani und Kostas Zouvelos entdeckten ihn 1994 und eröffneten im Mai 2015 das Hotel* · **X-FAKTOR** *Selbst der Pool bietet einen Panoramablick*

DANS LA TOUR

Le Magne sur le Péloponnèse est la région la plus mystérieuse de Grèce. Dotée d'une beauté sauvage, fourmillant de mythes (la pointe la plus méridionale du Magne aurait été l'entrée de l'Hadès, le légendaire royaume des ombres), elle aurait abrité un peuple longtemps considéré comme intrépide autant qu'imprévisible. Afin de se protéger des pirates, des conquérants ou simplement de voisins avides de vengeance, les habitants du Magne ont jadis construit de solides tours d'habitation et de défense, dont l'une abrite aujourd'hui ce logement non conventionnel. Les propriétaires, tous deux architectes de profession, ont restauré la tour du Cap Tenaro avec un grand savoir-faire afin de préserver autant que possible sa structure d'origine. Ils ont utilisé la pierre locale et l'ont jointoyée selon l'ancienne tradition avec un mortier fait de terre, d'argile, de chaux et de sable, qui a la même nuance de couleur que la roche – ainsi le bâtiment semble pousser hors du sol. Les portes basses, les petites fenêtres et les marches en bois raides à l'intérieur ont été conservées et mariées à un design moderne minimaliste. Les trois chambres partagent à parts égales une ambiance historique et tout le confort d'un hôtel moderne, des lits avec matelas en fibres naturelles à la salle de bains élégante sans oublier la climatisation. Tainaron Blue dispose également d'un restaurant exclusivement réservé à ses hôtes où l'on cuisine selon des recettes traditionnelles du Magne : les spécialités telles que les pâtes orzo aux tomates séchées, câpres et fromage fumé du couvent sont tout simplement délicieuses ! S'il ne fait pas trop chaud, vous devrez absolument manger sur la terrasse et profiter de la vue imprenable sur un pays fascinant. ◆ À lire : « On raconte en Laconie… Contes populaires grecs du Magne » traduits et présentés par Margarita Xanthakou

ACCÈS *Sur la péninsule Magne, au sud du Péloponnèse. Les aéroports internationaux les plus proches sont Kalamata (125 km) et Athènes (340 km)* · **PRIX** *€€–€€€* · **CHAMBRES** *3 chambres seulement pour 9 hôtes maximum* · **RESTAURATION** *Dans la tour une cuisine commune en design vintage. Le restaurant vous gâte midi et soir avec des plats de la cuisine régionale* · **HISTOIRE** *La tour a été construite au début du XIXe siècle. Kassiani et Kostas Zouvelos l'ont découverte en 1994 et ont ouvert l'hôtel en mai 2015* · **LES « PLUS »** *Même la piscine offre une vue panoramique sur les environs*

KYRIMAI HOTEL

GEROLIMENAS, EAST MANI

KYRIMAI HOTEL

230 62 Gerolimenas, East Mani
Tel. +30 27330 542 88 and +30 27330 593 38 · info@kyrimai.gr
www.kyrimai.gr

A HOTEL FULL OF HISTORY

As late as the second half of the nineteenth century, Mani was almost completely unknown. Hardly anyone beyond its borders had ever heard of this remote region in the south of the Peloponnese. Then two merchants put it on the map: in Gerolimenas, a town on the coast, Michael Katsimantis and Theodore Kyrimis founded a trading company which, in the years when it flourished, shipped local products to major European ports – 70,000 live quail per year were exported to Marseille, for example. It is still possible to visit and even stay in the company headquarters, built in the 1870s, as the descendants of Theodore Kyrimis have transformed it into a hotel. The former wine store has become the reception area, in the tower that once symbolized the owner's power there is now a guest bedroom with a 360-degree view, and a private museum full of historic books, pictures and letters from the past now occupies the place where wood was once stacked. Wherever possible, the original building fabric was preserved or replaced faithful to the original details. All rooms and suites have walls of local stone, wooden ceilings and typical small windows (so it is recommended to book a sea view and a room with a balcony or terrace), and are designed in country-house style. That Mani nowadays can also hold its head up high in culinary matters is shown by the excellent house restaurant, which takes its inspiration from traditional recipes. Diners who want to enjoy these time-hallowed specialties should sit at one of the round tables: they pay homage to the traditional "sofra," a low round table at which families used to eat. ◆ Book to pack: "Mani" by Patrick Leigh Fermor

DIRECTIONS *On the coast of Mani, in the south of the Peloponnese. The nearest international airports are Kalamata (115 km/70 miles) and Athens (326 km/202 miles)* · **RATES** *€–€€€€* · **ROOMS** *24 rooms and suites* · **FOOD** *From the organic breakfast to the fine dinner, the restaurant delights diners with Greek and Maniot dishes, as well as a wonderful terrace* · **HISTORY** *The historic home with storehouse has been a hotel since 2003. It was last renovated in 2019* · **X-FACTOR** *The quiet location right by the sea*

EIN GESCHICHTSTRÄCHTIGES HOTEL

Noch in der zweiten Hälfte des 19. Jahrhunderts war die Mani fast völlig unbekannt – kaum jemand außerhalb ihrer Grenzen hatte jemals von dieser abgelegenen Region im Süden des Peloponnes gehört. Doch dann brachten sie zwei Kaufleute auf die Landkarte: Michael Katsimantis und Theodore Kyrimis gründeten im Küstenort Gerolimenas ein Handelsunternehmen, das zu seiner Blütezeit einheimische Produkte in die größten europäischen Häfen verschiffte – so wurden zum Beispiel jährlich 70.000 lebende Wachteln nach Marseille exportiert. Den in den 1870ern erbauten Firmensitz kann man noch heute besuchen und sogar bewohnen, denn die Nachfahren von Theodore Kyrimis haben ihn in ein Hotel verwandelt: Aus dem ehemaligen Weinlager wurde die Rezeption, im Turm, der einst die Macht der Besitzer symbolisierte, entstand ein Gästezimmer mit 360-Grad-Ausblick, und wo früher Holz gestapelt wurde, erzählt inzwischen ein privates Museum voller historischer Bücher, Bilder und Briefe von der Geschichte der Region. Wo immer möglich, wurde die alte Bausubstanz erhalten oder detailgetreu ersetzt. Alle Zimmer und Suiten haben Wände aus einheimischem Stein, Holzdecken sowie die typisch kleinen Fenster (daher am besten Meerblick und einen Raum mit Balkon oder Außenbereich buchen) und sind im Landhausstil gehalten. Dass sich die Mani auch in puncto Kulinarik nicht länger versteckt hält, beweist das ausgezeichnete Restaurant des Hauses, das von traditionellen Rezepten inspiriert ist. Wer die Spezialitäten nach überlieferter Art genießen will, wählt einen runden Tisch: Er ist eine Hommage an die traditionelle „sofra", eine niedrige runde Tafel, an der die Familie früher gemeinsam aß. ◆ Buchtipp: „Athos der Förster" von Maria Stefanopoulou

ANREISE *An der Küste der Mani, im Süden des Peloponnes gelegen. Die nächsten internationalen Flughäfen sind Kalamata (115 km) und Athen (326 km)* · **PREISE** *€–€€€€* · **ZIMMER** *24 Zimmer und Suiten* · **KÜCHE** *Vom organischen Frühstück bis zum feinen Abendessen: Das Restaurant begeistert mit griechischen und maniotischen Gerichten sowie einer Traumterrasse* · **GESCHICHTE** *Das historische Wohnhaus mit Warenlager ist seit 2003 ein Hotel. Zuletzt wurde es 2019 renoviert* · **X-FAKTOR** *Die ruhige Lage direkt am Meer*

UN HÔTEL CHARGÉ D'HISTOIRE

Dans la seconde moitié du XIXe siècle, le Magne était encore pratiquement inconnu – au-delà de ses frontières personne ou presque n'avait entendu parler de cette région reculée du sud du Péloponnèse. Et puis deux marchands, Michael Katsimantis et Theodore Kyrimis, l'ont sortie de l'anonymat en créant une société de commerce dans la ville côtière de Gerolimenas, qui, à son apogée, expédiait des produits locaux vers les plus grands ports européens – exportant par exemple chaque année 70 000 cailles vivantes vers Marseille. Le siège de la société, construit dans les années 1870, peut encore être visité aujourd'hui et même habité, car les descendants de Theodore Kyrimis l'ont transformé en hôtel, métamorphosant l'ancien entrepôt de vin en réception, aménageant une chambre d'hôtes avec une vue à 360 degrés dans la tour qui symbolisait autrefois le pouvoir des propriétaires – et là où le bois était empilé, un musée privé plein de livres, de photos et de lettres historiques évoque maintenant les temps passés. L'ancienne structure du bâtiment a été préservée autant que possible ou remplacée avec un grand respect des détails. Toutes les chambres et suites ont des murs en pierre locale, des plafonds en bois ainsi que les petites fenêtres typiques de la région (il est donc préférable de réserver une chambre dotée d'un balcon ou d'un espace extérieur) et sont décorées dans le style d'une maison de campagne. Le Magne ne cache plus sa cuisine non plus, ce dont témoigne l'excellent restaurant de la maison, avec ses plats inspirés de recettes traditionnelles. Ceux qui veulent déguster les spécialités comme on le faisait autrefois choisissent une table ronde, rendant ainsi hommage à la « sofra », une table ronde basse où la famille avait l'habitude de manger. ◆ À lire : « Athos le forestier » par Maria Stefanopoulou

ACCÈS *Sur la côte du Magne, au sud du Péloponnèse. Les aéroports internationaux les plus proches sont Kalamata (115 km) et Athènes (326 km)* · **PRIX** *€–€€€€* · **CHAMBRES** *24 chambres et suites* · **RESTAURATION** *Du petit-déjeuner bio au dîner raffiné, le restaurant propose des mets grecs et maniotes savoureux ainsi qu'une terrasse de rêve* · **HISTOIRE** *L'habitation historique dotée d'un entrepôt est un hôtel depuis 2003. La dernière rénovation date de 2019* · **LES « PLUS »** *Le calme des lieux, tout près de la mer*

PIRGOS MAVROMICHALI

LIMENI, EAST MANI

PIRGOS MAVROMICHALI

230 62 Limeni, East Mani
Tel. +30 27330 510 42 and +30 697 375 74 99 · info@pirgosmavromichali.gr
www.pirgosmavromichali.gr

MICHALIS' LEGACY

The history of the Mavromichalis family began in the fourteenth century with a little Greek boy named Michalis. He fled from the Turks, losing his parents on the dangerous journey from Thrace to Mani. As the Maniots of those days believed that an orphan had a "black" ("mavro") destiny, they named him Mavromichalis. However, in spite of this superstition, the boy became a successful and honored man who married the daughter of a landowner and founded with her a family whose members were without exception strong, brave, and beautiful too. In the course of generations they settled at the harbor of Limeni, among other places, and built a tower house ("pirgos") there that much later became this unique hotel. Michalis' descendants have restored their inheritance from top to bottom, combining the historic buildings to form a harmonious ensemble with a simple yet simultaneously elegant appearance. The rooms and suites, some of which are on two stories, are plain and unadorned, but equipped with every amenity. They look out onto the sea, which is crystal clear on this part of the coast. The sunny terraces lead straight down to the water, and their upper area accommodates a renowned Greek restaurant. Visitors should also take time to enjoy a stroll through the old village of Limeni, which is unusually well preserved. For those who want to be more active, the rough beauty of Mani can be explored on walks or bike tours to ruined castles, monasteries and gorges. ◆ Book to pack: "The Hill of Kronos" by Peter Levi

DIRECTIONS *In a stunningly beautiful bay near Limeni. The nearest international airports are Kalamata (87 km/54 miles) and Athens (303 km/188 miles)* · **RATES** *€–€€€* · **ROOMS** *13 rooms and suites* · **FOOD** *A fine breakfast and fresh regional dishes. The restaurant opens exclusively for hotel guests* · **HISTORY** *The tower house opened as a hotel in 2010* · **X-FACTOR** *Open-air dinner – in the evening, the terraces and buildings are romantically illuminated*

MICHALIS' VERMÄCHTNIS

Die Geschichte der Familie Mavromichalis begann im 14. Jahrhundert mit einem kleinen griechischen Jungen namens Michalis. Er flüchtete vor den Türken aus Thrakien in die Mani und verlor auf der gefährlichen Reise seine Eltern. Da die Manioten damals dachten, ein Waisenkind habe ein „schwarzes" („mavro") Schicksal, nannten sie ihn Mavromichalis. Doch allem Aberglauben zum Trotz wurde aus dem Jungen ein erfolgreicher und ehrbarer Mann, der die Tochter eines Landbesitzers heiratete und mit ihr eine Familie gründete, deren Mitglieder allesamt außergewöhnlich stark, tapfer und noch dazu schön waren. Sie ließen sich im Laufe von Generationen auch am Hafen von Limeni nieder und errichteten dort ein Turmhaus („pirgos"), aus dem dann viel später dieses einzigartige Hotel wurde. Michalis' Nachfahren haben ihr Erbe von Grund auf saniert und die historischen Gemäuer zu einem harmonischen Ensemble verbunden, das einfach und elegant zugleich erscheint. Die Zimmer und die zum Teil zweistöckigen Suiten sind schlicht und schnörkellos, aber mit allen Annehmlichkeiten ausgestattet und schauen aufs Meer, das an dieser Stelle der Küste kristallklar ist. Die Sonnenterrassen führen direkt hinunter zum Wasser und bieten im oberen Bereich Platz für ein renommiertes griechisches Restaurant. Genießer sollten auch einmal durch das alte Dorf Limeni bummeln, das außergewöhnlich gut erhalten ist – und wer aktiver sein möchte, kann die raue Schönheit der Mani während einer Wanderung oder Radtour zu Burgruinen, Klöstern und Schluchten entdecken.
◆ Buchtipp: „Prinzessin Isabeau" von Angelos Terzakis

ANREISE *In einer Traumbucht beim Dorf Limeni gelegen. Die nächsten internationalen Flughäfen sind Kalamata (87 km) und Athen (303 km)* · **PREISE** *€–€€€* · **ZIMMER** *13 Zimmer und Suiten* · **KÜCHE** *Feines Frühstück und frische regionale Gerichte. Das Restaurant ist exklusiv für Hotelgäste geöffnet* · **GESCHICHTE** *Das Turmhaus wurde 2010 als Hotel eröffnet* · **X-FAKTOR** *Ein Dinner unter freiem Himmel – abends sind Terrassen und Gebäude stimmungsvoll beleuchtet*

L'HÉRITAGE DE MICHALIS

L'histoire de la famille Mavromichalis commence au XIVe siècle avec Michalis, un petit garçon grec. Fuyant les Turcs, il a quitté la Thrace pour rejoindre le Magne et a perdu ses parents au cours de ce dangereux voyage. Comme les Maniotes de l'époque pensaient que le destin d'un orphelin serait « noir » (« mavro »), ils l'ont appelé Mavromichalis. Mais, triomphant de toutes les superstitions, le garçon est devenu un homme honorable et prospère qui a épousé la fille d'un propriétaire terrien et fondé avec elle une famille dont les membres étaient tous exceptionnellement forts, courageux et beaux. Au fil des générations, ils se sont également installés dans le port de Limeni et y ont construit une tour d'habitation (« pirgos »), qui deviendra bien plus tard cet hôtel unique en son genre. Les descendants de Michalis ont restauré leur héritage de fond en comble, transformant les murs historiques en un ensemble harmonieux qui semble à la fois simple et élégant. Les chambres et les suites, dont certaines ont deux étages, sont simples et sans fioritures, mais équipées de tout le confort et donnent sur la mer, limpide à cet endroit de la côte. Les terrasses ensoleillées mènent directement à la plage et la partie supérieure accueille un restaurant grec renommé. Les bons vivants devraient également se promener dans le village historique de Limeni, qui est exceptionnellement bien préservé, quant à ceux qui veulent être plus actifs, ils peuvent découvrir la beauté sauvage du Magne au cours d'une randonnée à pied ou en bicyclette vers les châteaux forts en ruine, les monastères et les gorges.
◆ À lire : « La princesse Isabeau » par Angelos Terzakis

ACCÈS *Dans une baie idyllique près du village de Limeni. Les aéroports internationaux les plus proches sont Kalamata (87 km) et Athènes (303 km)* · **PRIX** *€–€€€* · **CHAMBRES** *13 chambres et suites* · **RESTAURATION** *Petit-déjeuner raffiné et cuisine régionale à base de produits frais. Le restaurant est réservé aux clients de l'hôtel* · **HISTOIRE** *La tour d'habitation est devenue un hôtel en 2010* · **LES « PLUS »** *Le dîner à l'extérieur – la terrasse et les bâtiments illuminés offrent une ambiance unique*

THE PATRICK & JOAN LEIGH FERMOR HOUSE

KARDAMYLI, WEST MANI

THE PATRICK & JOAN LEIGH FERMOR HOUSE

240 22 Kardamyli, West Mani
Tel. +30 210 367 10 90 · leighfermorhouse@benaki.gr
www.benaki.org

AN ENGLISHMAN IN GREECE

Sir Patrick Michael Leigh Fermor (1915–2011), simply known as Paddy, was one of the most charismatic and charming personalities of the twentieth century. He was a passionate traveler and adventurer, an author and a scholar, a soldier and a war hero. As a child, he was a rebel who was expelled from several schools in England. As a young man he walked from Hoek van Holland to Istanbul. As an agent of the British Special Operations Executive during the Second World War, he organized resistance to the German occupation of Crete and kidnapped the German commander of Crete, Heinrich Kreipe. As a travel writer, he finally found a home for his soul on the coast of Mani. Leigh Fermor, who loved Greece and whose life seems to have come straight out of a novel, spent many years in Kardamyli – in a house that he built with architect Nikos Hatzimichalis, located above a bay on a plot of land that he and his wife Joan, a photographer, bought in the 1960s. In 1996 the Leigh Fermors bequeathed it to the Benaki Museum, expressing the wish that it be used as a retreat for scholars, intellectuals and honorary guests. According to the donation agreement, the house can also be rented for the summer months in order to cover the running costs. In his nonchalant British manner, Leigh Fermor attached little importance either to heating and air conditioning or to a modern water and power supply. Comprehensive refurbishment was therefore carried out by the Benaki Museum, funded by the Stavros Niarchos Foundation. The most elegant of the buildings is the Main House with its wonderful living-room-cum-library, while the pretty Guest House is the most romantic and the Traditional House, where the author had his study, is the most authentic. The estate next to the sea can be reserved for exclusive use. Residents can enjoy the pool, the nearby private pebble beach and the picture-perfect Mediterranean garden with its cypresses, olive trees and oleanders. ◆ Book to pack: "Patrick Leigh Fermor. An Adventure" by Artemis Cooper; film to watch: "Before Midnight" (2013) by Richard Linklater, with Ethan Hawke and Julie Delpy, was filmed in the area around Kardamyli, partly in Leigh Fermor's garden

DIRECTIONS *The nearest international airports are Kalamata (49 km/ 30 miles) and Athens (300 km/185 miles)* · **RATES** *€€€€ (3 nights minimum stays for some dates)* · **ROOMS** *3 rooms in the Main House, 1 room in the Guest House, 1 room in the Traditional House (all for 2 persons with a living area and a private bathroom)* · **FOOD** *In addition to breakfast, lunch and dinner can be served on request. For self-caterers, the Main House has a kitchen, and the two smaller buildings each have a kitchenette* · **HISTORY** *Available to rent since summer 2020* · **X-FACTOR** *An inspiring place, not only for fans of Patrick Leigh Fermor*

EIN ENGLÄNDER IN GRIECHENLAND

Sir Patrick Michael Leigh Fermor (1915–2011), auch einfach als „Paddy" bekannt, war eine der charismatischsten und charmantesten Persönlichkeiten des 20. Jahrhunderts. Er war ein leidenschaftlicher Reisender und Abenteurer, ein Schriftsteller und Gelehrter, ein Soldat und Kriegsheld. Als Kind war er ein Rebell und wurde in England mehrerer Schulen verwiesen. Als junger Mann wanderte er zu Fuß von Hoek van Holland bis nach Istanbul. Als Agent des britischen Geheimdienstes organisierte er im Zweiten Weltkrieg auf Kreta den Widerstand gegen die deutsche Besatzung und entführte Heinrich Kreipe, den deutschen Kommandanten der Insel. Und als Reiseschriftsteller fand er schließlich an der Küste der Mani seine Seelenheimat: Leigh Fermor liebte Griechenland und verbrachte lange Jahre seines romanhaften Lebens in Kardamyli – in diesem über einer Bucht gelegenen Haus, das er mit dem Architekten Nikos Hatzimichalis baute, auf einem Grundstück, das er Mitte der 1960er-Jahre mit seiner Frau Joan, einer Fotografin, erworben hatte. 1996 vermachte das Ehepaar ihr Anwesen dem Benaki-Museum – verbunden mit dem Wunsch, es als Retreat für Gelehrte, Intellektuelle und Ehrengäste zu nutzen. Die Schenkungsvereinbarung erlaubt zudem, dass das Haus im Sommer vermietet werden kann, um die Unterhaltskosten zu decken. Da Leigh Fermor nach britisch-nonchalanter Art weder auf Heizung und Klimaanlage noch auf moderne Wasser- und Stromleitungen viel Wert gelegt hatte, wurden die Gebäude unter Leitung des Benaki-Museums und finanziert von der Stiftung Stavros Niarchos saniert. Am elegantesten präsentiert sich das Haupthaus mit seiner Wohnbibliothek, am romantischsten das hübsche Gästehaus und am authentischsten das Traditionshaus, in dem sich das Studio des Schriftstellers befand. Man kann das direkt am Meer gelegene Anwesen exklusiv oder zimmerweise buchen – dann teilen sich die Bewohner den Pool, den nahen Privatstrand sowie den mediterranen Bilderbuchgarten voller Zypressen, Olivenbäume und Oleander. ◆ Buchtipp: „Mani. Reisen auf der südlichen Peloponnes" von Patrick Leigh Fermor; Filmtipp: „Before Midnight" (2013) von Richard Linklater, mit Ethan Hawke und Julie Delpy, wurde rund um Kardamyli gedreht, unter anderem in Leigh Fermors Garten

ANREISE *Die nächsten internationalen Flughäfen sind Kalamata (49 km) und Athen (300 km)* · **PREISE** *€€€€ (an einigen Daten 3 Nächte Mindestaufenthalt)* · **ZIMMER** *3 Zimmer im Haupthaus, 1 Zimmer im Gästehaus, 1 Zimmer im Traditionshaus (alle für 2 Personen, mit Wohnbereich und eigenem Bad)* · **KÜCHE** *Neben Frühstück wird auf Wunsch auch Mittag- und Abendessen serviert. Für Selbstversorger besitzt das Haupthaus eine Küche, die beiden kleineren Häuser haben je eine Kitchenette* · **GESCHICHTE** *Seit 2020 kann das Anwesen im Sommer gemietet werden* · **X-FAKTOR** *Ein inspirierender Ort, nicht nur für Anhänger von Patrick Leigh Fermor*

UN ANGLAIS EN GRÈCE

Sir Patrick Michael « Paddy » Leigh Fermor (1915–2011) a été l'une des personnalités les plus charismatiques et charmantes du XXᵉ siècle. Il était un voyageur et un aventurier passionné, un écrivain et un érudit, un soldat et un héros de guerre. Enfant, il est expulsé de plusieurs écoles en Angleterre à cause de son caractère rebelle. Jeune homme, il voyage à pied de Hoek van Holland à Istanbul. Plus tard agent des services secrets britanniques, il organisera la résistance contre l'occupation allemande en Crète pendant la Seconde Guerre mondiale et enlèvera Heinrich Kreipe, le commandant allemand de l'île. Et en tant qu'écrivain voyageur, il a finalement trouvé sa patrie intérieure sur la côte du Magne : cet amoureux de la Grèce a passé de nombreuses années de sa vie captivante à Kardamýli, dans cette maison située au-dessus d'une baie et qu'il a construite avec l'architecte Nikos Hatzimichalis sur un terrain acquis au milieu des années 1960 avec sa femme Joan, photographe. En 1996, il l'a léguée au Musée Benaki en demandant de l'utiliser comme « retraite » pour les savants, les intellectuels et les invités d'honneur. L'accord de donation permet également de louer la maison en été pour couvrir les frais d'entretien. Comme Leigh Fermor avait, avec une nonchalance toute britannique, accordé peu d'importance au chauffage et à la climatisation ou aux conduites d'eau et lignes électriques modernes, les bâtiments ont été entièrement rénovés sous la direction du musée Benaki et les travaux financés par la fondation Stavros Niarchos. La Maison principale est la plus élégante avec sa magnifique bibliothèque, la plus romantique est la jolie Maison d'hôtes et la plus authentique est la Maison traditionnelle qui abritait le studio de l'écrivain. Vous pouvez réserver la propriété située en bord de mer en exclusivité ou chambre par chambre – les résidents se partagent alors la piscine, la plage privée toute proche et le jardin méditerranéen où s'épanouissent cyprès, oliviers et lauriers-roses. ◆ À lire : « Mani – Voyages dans le sud du Péloponnèse » par Patrick Leigh Fermor ; à voir : « Before Midnight » (2013) de Richard Linklater, avec Ethan Hawke et Julie Delpy. Le film a été tourné autour de Kardamýli, entre autres dans le jardin de Leigh Fermor

ACCÈS *Les aéroports internationaux les plus proches sont Kalamata (49 km) et Athènes (300 km)* · **PRIX** *€€€€ (séjour de 3 nuits minimum à certaines dates)* · **CHAMBRES** *3 chambres dans la Maison principale, 1 chambre dans la Maison d'hôtes, 1 chambre dans la Maison traditionnelle (toutes doubles, avec espace séjour et salle de bains)* · **RESTAURATION** *En plus du petit-déjeuner, le déjeuner et le dîner sont servis sur demande. La Maison principale dispose d'une cuisine, les deux autres, plus petites, ont une kitchenette* · **HISTOIRE** *Depuis 2020, la propriété peut être louée l'été* · **LES « PLUS »** *Un lieu qui donne envie de créer, et pas seulement à ceux qui vénèrent Patrick Leigh Fermor*

DEXAMENES

KOUROUTA BEACH, AMALIADA, ELIS

DEXAMENES

Kourouta Beach, 272 00 Amaliada, Elis
Tel. +30 697 252 18 06 and +30 26220 25 999 · info@dexamenes.com
www.dexamenes.com

CHEERS!

Thanks to the black corinth, a sweet red grape, the Peloponnese has been one of the most important Greek wine areas for centuries. Some of the most famous vineyards and the best grape varieties in Greece are still found here. When production was industrialized in the 1920s, this winery was built near Amaliada – right by the water, so that bottles could be shipped overseas directly. After the plant for pressing grapes was decommissioned, businessman Nikos Karaflos converted it into a hotel, which now attracts lovers of both wine and architecture. In collaboration with K-Studio from Athens, he turned the wine tanks into rooms for guests, retaining the raw, functional atmosphere of this former industrial facility. The walls of naked concrete, on which the passage of time has left its mark, frame a minimalistic interior with polished terrazzo floors, black steel frames, structured glass and high-quality wood. In addition to beds by the Greek ecological brand Coco-Mat and aesthetic bathrooms, each room has a terrace overlooking the quiet courtyard and back yards or with a view of the sea. For families and groups of friends the hotel also has a neoclassical beach villa, which once served as a laboratory, office and company director's residence, and has been given a modern makeover. The former engine room has been converted into a tavern with subdued industrial design. So raise a glass of red wine to a special destination! ◆ Book to pack: "Little Infamies" by Panos Karnezis

DIRECTIONS *On the northwest coast of the Peloponnese. The nearest airports are Patras Araxos (45 min), Kalamata (1 hr 40 min) and Athens (3 hrs)* · **RATES** *€–€€€* · **ROOMS** *34 suites and 1 villa with 2 suites, 1 room with 3 bunk beds and kitchen* · **FOOD** *The tavern and bar serve classic Greek dishes. Cookery courses and wine tastings are also organized* · **HISTORY** *Opened in spring 2019* · **X-FACTOR** *The summer art program, in which artists-in-residence exhibit their work in the hotel*

ZUM WOHL!

Dank der Schwarzen Korinthe, einer süßen roten Traube, ist der Peloponnes seit Jahrhunderten eine der wichtigsten Weinregionen Griechenlands – bis heute findet man hier einige der renommiertesten Weingüter und besten Rebsorten des Landes. Als die Produktion in den 1920ern industrialisiert wurde, entstand diese Kelterei bei Amaliada – direkt am Wasser erbaut, sodass die Flaschen ohne Umwege nach Übersee verschifft werden konnten. Aus der später stillgelegten Anlage machte der Unternehmer Nikos Karaflos ein Hotel, das Wein- ebenso wie Architekturliebhaber anzieht: Gemeinsam mit dem Athener K-Studio verwandelte er die Weintanks in Gästezimmer und erhielt dabei die raue, funktionale Atmosphäre des einstigen Betriebs. Die nackten Betonwände, auf denen die Zeit ihre Spuren hinterlassen hat, rahmen ein minimalistisches Interieur mit polierten Terrazzoböden, schwarzen Stahlrahmen, strukturiertem Glas und hochwertigem Holz ein. Neben Betten der griechischen Ökomarke Coco-Mat und ästhetischen Bädern besitzt jeder Raum eine Terrasse mit Blick auf die ruhigen Innen- und Hinterhöfe oder aufs Meer. Für Familien oder Freunde bietet das Hotel zudem eine neoklassizistische Strandvilla, die früher als Labor, Büro und Direktorenresidenz diente und modern renoviert wurde. Und im ehemaligen Maschinenraum entstand eine Taverne im reduzierten Industriedesign – ein Glas Rotwein auf ein ganz besonderes Reiseziel! ◆ Buchtipp: „Und beim Licht des Wolfes kehren sie wieder“ von Siranna Sateli

ANREISE *An der Nordwestküste des Peloponnes gelegen. Nächste Flughäfen sind Patras Araxos (45 min), Kalamata (1 Std. 40 min) und Athen (3 Std.)* · **PREISE** *€–€€€* · **ZIMMER** *34 Suiten und 1 Villa mit 2 Suiten, 1 Zimmer mit 3 Stockbetten sowie Küche* · **KÜCHE** *Taverne und Bar bieten griechische Klassiker an. Zudem werden Kochkurse und Weinverkostungen organisiert* · **GESCHICHTE** *Im Frühjahr 2019 eröffnet* · **X-FAKTOR** *Das sommerliche Kunstprogramm, bei dem Artists in Residence im Hotel ausstellen*

À VOTRE SANTÉ !

Depuis des siècles, grâce au Corinthe noir, un raisin doux et juteux, le Péloponnèse est l'une des plus importantes régions viticoles de Grèce. Aujourd'hui encore, on peut y trouver certains des vignobles les plus réputés et des meilleurs cépages du pays. Lorsque la production a été industrialisée dans les années 1920, ces celliers ont été construits près d'Amaliada, au bord de l'eau, pour faciliter le transport des bouteilles à l'étranger. Après la fermeture, l'entrepreneur Nikos Karaflos a transformé les lieux en un hôtel qui attire à la fois les amateurs de vin et d'architecture : avec le K-Studio d'Athènes, il a transformé les cuves à vin en chambres d'hôtes tout en préservant le caractère rude et fonctionnel de l'ancienne installation. Les murs en béton nu, sur lesquels le temps a laissé des traces, encadrent un intérieur minimaliste avec des sols en terrazzo poli, des cadres en acier noir, du verre structuré et du bois de qualité. En plus des lits de la marque écologique grecque Coco-Mat et des salles de bains esthétiques, chaque chambre dispose d'une terrasse avec vue sur les cours intérieures et les arrière-cours tranquilles ou sur la mer. Pour les familles ou les groupes d'amis, l'hôtel propose également une villa de plage néoclassique, qui servait autrefois de laboratoire, de bureau et de résidence aux directeurs et qui a été rénovée dans un style moderne. Et une taverne au design industriel réduit a vu le jour dans l'ancienne salle des machines – on lève son verre à une destination très particulière ! ◆ À lire : « Le crépuscule des loups » de Zyránna Zatéli

ACCÈS *Sur la côte nord-ouest du Péloponnèse. Les aéroports les plus proches sont Patras Araxos (45 min de route), Kalamata (1 h 40) et Athènes (3 h)* · **PRIX** *€–€€€* · **CHAMBRES** *34 suites et 1 villa avec 2 suites, 1 chambre avec 3 lits superposés et une cuisine* · **RESTAURATION** *La taverne et le bar proposent des classiques de la cuisine grecque. Des cours de cuisine et des dégustations de vins sont également organisés* · **HISTOIRE** *Ouvert au printemps 2019* · **LES « PLUS »** *Le programme artistique estival, durant lequel des artistes en résidence exposent leurs œuvres*

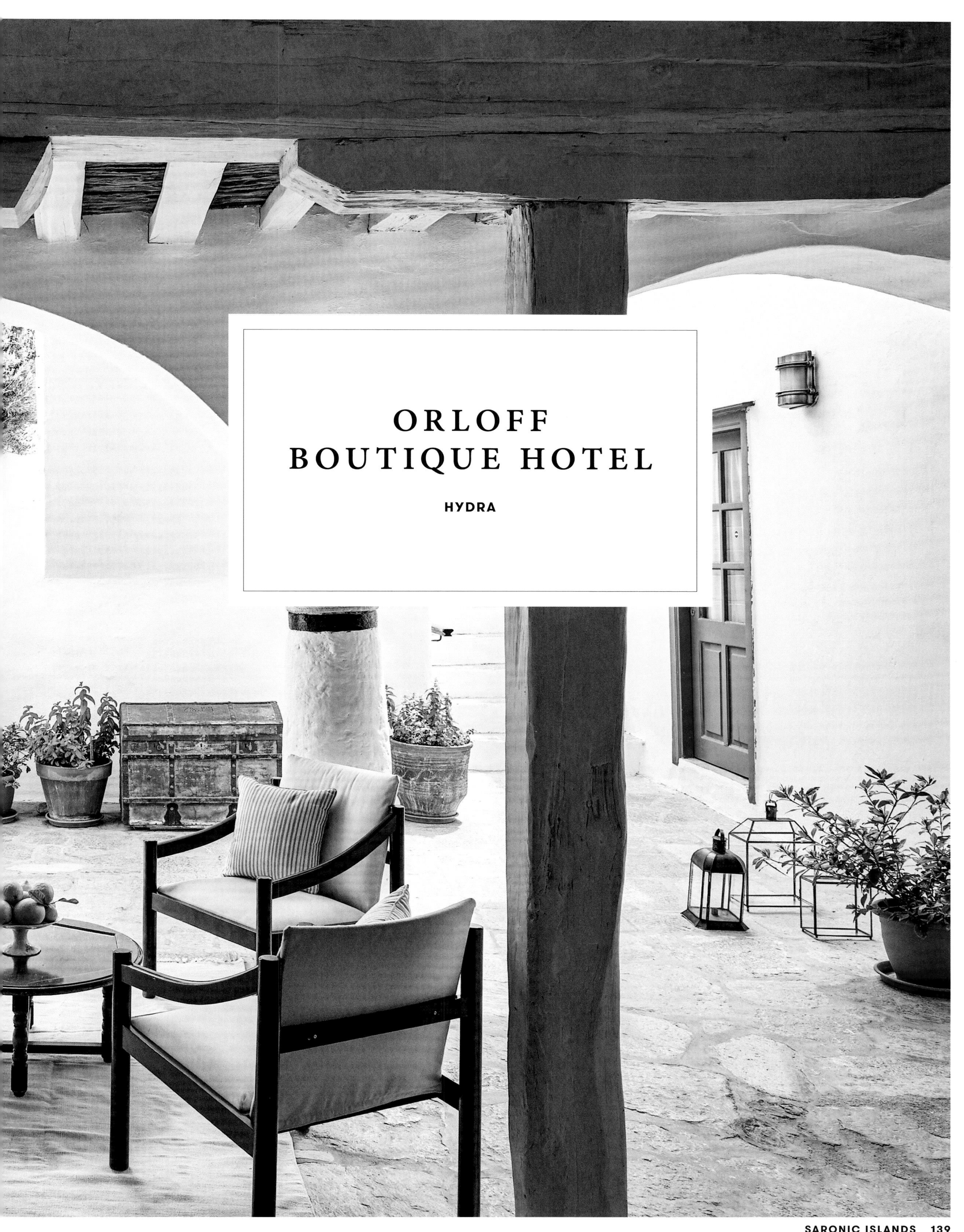

ORLOFF BOUTIQUE HOTEL

HYDRA

ORLOFF BOUTIQUE HOTEL

Rafalia Street 9, 180 40 Hydra
Tel. +30 22980 525 64 and +30 22980 524 95 · hotel@orloff.gr
www.orloff.gr

RUSSIAN ROOTS

A long time ago, a small monastery stood here. In about 1790 this building arose over its ruins – as the holiday home of a Russian count from the family of Alexei Orloff, whom Catherine the Great sent to the Mediterranean to support the Greeks in their struggle against the Turks. Today's owners still keep alive the memory of the nobleman who built the house: they have turned what used to be his private office, with a view from tall windows over the town and the surrounding hills, into one of the loveliest guest rooms. A total of eight rooms have been furnished with antiques from the time when the house was built, including the attractive corner library. The well-tended historic atmosphere blends with the Greek and Mediterranean feeling of the house, where the design plays skillfully on the typical blue-and-white color scheme, originals by modern Greek painters such as Panayiotis Tetsis and Dimitris Mytaras are on display, and the garden resembles an oasis. It was the inspiration for the composition of the in-house perfume, named "George Orloff of Hydra," a delicate scent of hesperidia, geranium, jasmine and lavender. Every morning the garden is the guests' favorite spot for enjoying an outstanding Greek breakfast to the strains of quiet classical music. The service is as refined as the ambience: the hosts are extremely obliging and have an unerring sense for which excursion, which taverna or which beach should be on their guests' must-see lists. It would be hard to find better travel advisers on Hydra. ◆ Film to watch: "Phaedra" (1962) by Jules Dassin, with Melina Mercouri and Anthony Perkins

DIRECTIONS *5 minutes' walk west of the harbor at Hydra; porters are available for heavy suitcases* · **RATES** *€–€€€* · **ROOMS** *7 rooms and 1 suite on two floors* · **FOOD** *Breakfast is served in the hotel (definitely try the homemade lemon marmalade). The owners are pleased to recommend restaurants for lunch and dinner* · **HISTORY** *Opened as a hotel in 1986 and last renovated in 2020* · **X-FACTOR** *Timeless beauty*

RUSSISCHE WURZELN

Vor langer Zeit stand hier ein kleines Kloster, auf dessen Ruinen um 1790 dieses Haus entstand – als Feriendomizil eines russischen Grafen aus der Familie von Alexej Orlow, den Katharina die Große in den Mittelmeerraum entsandt hatte, um die Griechen bei ihrem Kampf gegen die Türken zu unterstützen. Die Erinnerung an den adligen Bauherrn halten die heutigen Besitzer noch immer lebendig: Sie haben sein ehemaliges Privatbüro, das aus hohen Fenstern über die Stadt und die umliegenden Hügel blickt, in eines der schönsten Gästezimmer umgewandelt. Die insgesamt acht Räume wurden mit Antiquitäten aus der Bauzeit des Hauses ausgestattet, darunter eine formschöne Eckbibliothek. Das gepflegte historische Flair mischt sich mit der griechisch-mediterranen Atmosphäre des Hauses, das geschickt mit dem typisch blau-weißen Farbschema spielt, Originale moderner griechischer Maler wie Panayiotis Tetsis oder Dimitris Mytaras zeigt und einen oasengleichen Garten besitzt. Dieser war schon Quell für die Komposition des hauseigenen Parfüms „George Orloff of Hydra", das zart nach Hesperidium, Geranie, Jasmin und Lavendel duftet, und ist jeden Morgen Lieblingsplatz aller Gäste, die bei leiser klassischer Musik ein ausgezeichnetes griechisches Frühstück genießen. So feinsinnig wie das Ambiente ist auch der Service: Die Gastgeber sind sehr zuvorkommend und besitzen ein untrügliches Gespür dafür, welches Ausflugsziel, welche Taverne oder welcher Strand auf der persönlichen Urlaubswunschliste noch gefehlt haben – bessere Reiseberater findet man auf Hydra schwerlich. ◆ Filmtipp: „Phaedra" (1962) von Jules Dassin, mit Melina Mercouri und Anthony Perkins

ANREISE *5 Gehminuten westlich des Hafens von Hydra gelegen, Gepäckträger helfen mit schweren Koffern* · **PREISE** *€–€€€* · **ZIMMER** *7 Zimmer und 1 Suite mit zwei Etagen* · **KÜCHE** *Im Hotel wird Frühstück serviert (nicht verpassen: die hausgemachte Zitronenmarmelade). Die Besitzer empfehlen gerne Restaurants für Mittag- und Abendessen* · **GESCHICHTE** *1986 als Hotel eröffnet und 2020 zuletzt renoviert* · **X-FAKTOR** *Zeitlos schön*

RACINES RUSSES

Il y avait autrefois ici un petit monastère sur les ruines duquel cette maison a été construite vers 1790, pour devenir la résidence de vacances d'un comte russe de la famille d'Alexeï Orlov, que la Grande Catherine avait envoyé en Méditerranée pour soutenir les Grecs dans leur lutte contre les Turcs. La mémoire du noble bâtisseur est toujours vivante chez les propriétaires actuels : ils ont transformé son ancien bureau privé, dont les hautes fenêtres donnent sur la ville et les collines environnantes, en l'une des plus belles chambres d'hôtes. Les huit pièces ont été meublées avec des antiquités datant de l'époque de construction de la maison, y compris une élégante bibliothèque d'angle. L'ambiance historique soigneusement entretenue se marie à l'atmosphère gréco-méditerranéenne de la maison, qui joue habilement avec les couleurs bleu et blanc typiques, abrite des œuvres originales de peintres grecs modernes tels que Panayiotis Tetsis ou Dimitris Mytaras et possède un jardin aux airs d'oasis. C'est dans ce jardin qu'a été composé le parfum « George Orloff of Hydra » aux délicates senteurs d'agrumes, de géranium, de jasmin et de lavande. Chaque matin, c'est le lieu préféré de tous les hôtes, qui y dégustent un excellent petit-déjeuner grec en écoutant de la musique classique douce. Le service est aussi subtil que l'ambiance : les hôtes sont très serviables et savent parfaitement quelle excursion, taverne ou plage manque à votre liste personnelle de souhaits de vacances – il est difficile de trouver de meilleurs conseillers de voyages sur Hydra. ◆ À voir : « Phèdre » (1962) de Jules Dassin, avec Melina Mercouri et Anthony Perkins

ACCÈS *À 5 minutes à pied à l'ouest du port d'Hydra, des porteurs de bagage aident à transporter les valises lourdes* · **PRIX** *€–€€€* · **CHAMBRES** *7 chambres et 1 suite de deux étages* · **RESTAURATION** *Le petit-déjeuner est servi à l'hôtel (il faut goûter la confiture de citron maison). Les propriétaires recommandent volontiers des adresses de restaurants où l'on peut déjeuner et dîner* · **HISTOIRE** *Ouvert en tant qu'hôtel en 1986, rénové en 2020* · **LES « PLUS »** *D'une beauté intemporelle*

FOUR SEASONS HYDRA

VLYCHOS BEACH, HYDRA

FOUR SEASONS HYDRA

Vlychos Beach, 180 40 Hydra
Tel. +30 22980 536 98 and +30 698 424 82 08 · info@fourseasonshydra.gr
www.fourseasonshydra.gr

FIT FOR THE SILVER SCREEN

An Italian actress and a Canadian songwriter-poet made the Greek island of Hydra famous as an international destination: this is where Sophia Loren starred in the film "Boy on a Dolphin" (1957), in which she played the role of a sponge diver with impressive backdrops on land and underwater, and where Leonard Cohen found in 1960 a house, inspiring surroundings and love. This made Hydra an artists' colony and a must-see for half of Hollywood – with the jet set arriving from Athens and the whole world, as well as tourists who were simply eager to see this unique island. To this day, Hydra seems to perform an effortless balancing act between exclusivity and simplicity. The property prices are exorbitantly high, and in the high season one chic yacht is moored next to another in the harbor. At the same time, the island insists on remaining car-free and taking visitors to their accommodation by boat, donkey or horse. Possibly the prettiest place to stay is the Four Seasons Hydra, which shares only its name and its outstanding reputation with the famous hotel chain. Ideally located on Vlychos Beach, the house dating from the late nineteenth century once belonged to a sea captain. Today it has eight suites, named after the seasons and the elements of nature, individually fitted out in bright colors with hand-made country-house furniture and a touch of bohemian atmosphere. The competition for the best room could easily be decided in favor of any of them – but the Autumn Suite, in pale yellow with a balcony looking to the sea and a view of the sunset, is a real gem. Every evening, sundown is a masterpiece in blood-orange, fiery red and blue-black; no artist on Hydra could render it more beautifully.
◆ Book to pack: "Flowers for Hitler" by Leonard Cohen; film to watch: "Boy on a Dolphin" (1957) von Jean Negulesco

DIRECTIONS *The ferry from Piraeus to Hydra takes 1 hr 30 min. The hotel is 5 minutes by boat, 35 minutes' walk south of the harbor (the hotel's own boat takes guests for free)* · **RATES** *€€–€€€€* · **ROOMS** *8 suites, 1 of them in a separate villa* · **FOOD** *"Tassia's Tavern" serves fresh fish and Greek specialties beneath a pergola* · **HISTORY** *The house was built between 1870 and 1890. It has been a hotel since 2005* · **X-FACTOR** *A trip in the hotel's own sailboat*

KINOTAUGLICH

Eine italienische Schauspielerin sowie ein kanadischer Dichter und Liedermacher machten die griechische Insel Hydra als internationales Reiseziel berühmt: Sophia Loren drehte hier den Film „Der Knabe auf dem Delphin“ (1957), in dem sie eine Schwammtaucherin darstellte und vor beeindruckenden Kulissen an Land sowie unter Wasser in Szene gesetzt wurde, und Leonard Cohen fand hier 1960 ein Haus, eine inspirierende Umgebung und eine große Liebe. So wurde Hydra erst zum Must-see für halb Hollywood und zur Künstlerkolonie – anschließend kamen der Jetset aus Athen und aller Welt sowie Touristen, die ganz einfach auf dieses einzigartige Eiland neugierig geworden waren. Bis heute balanciert Hydra scheinbar mühelos zwischen Exklusivität und Einfachheit: So sind die Grundstückspreise astronomisch hoch, und im Hafen liegen zur Hochsaison schicke Jachten Seite an Seite. Zugleich besteht die Insel darauf, autofrei zu bleiben und ihre Besucher per Boot, Esel oder Pferd zu ihren Unterkünften zu bringen. Die vielleicht hübscheste Adresse ist das Four Seasons Hydra, das mit der berühmten Hotelkette nur den Namen und ausgezeichneten Ruf gemeinsam hat. Ideal am Vlychos Beach gelegen, gehörte das Ende des 19. Jahrhunderts erbaute Haus einst einem Kapitän. Heute beherbergt es acht Suiten, die nach Jahreszeiten und Naturelementen benannt und individuell in hellen Tönen, mit handgefertigten Landhausmöbeln und einem Hauch Boheme eingerichtet sind. Die Wahl zum Lieblingszimmer könnte jeder Raum mit Leichtigkeit gewinnen – ein echtes Schmuckstück aber ist die Autumn Suite in blassem Gelb, mit Balkon zum Meer und Blick auf den Sonnenuntergang. Dieser ist jeden Abend ein Meisterwerk in Blutorange, Feuerrot und Blauschwarz; kein Künstler auf Hydra könnte ihn schöner malen. ◆ Buchtipp: „Blumen für Hitler“ von Leonard Cohen; Filmtipp: „Der Knabe auf dem Delphin“ (1957) von Jean Negulesco

ANREISE *Von Piräus aus erreicht man Hydra mit der Fähre in 1,5 Std. Das Hotel liegt 5 Boots- oder 35 Gehminuten südlich des Hafens (ein hoteleigenes Boot transportiert die Gäste kostenfrei)* · **PREISE** *€€–€€€€* · **ZIMMER** *8 Suiten, 1 davon in einer separaten Villa* · **KÜCHE** *„Tassia's Tavern“ serviert unter einer Pergola am Strand frischen Fisch und griechische Spezialitäten* · **GESCHICHTE** *Das Haus wurde zwischen 1870 und 1890 erbaut. Seit 2005 ist es ein Hotel* · **X-FAKTOR** *Ein Törn mit dem hoteleigenen Segelboot*

COMME AU CINÉMA

Une actrice italienne et un poète et chanteur-compositeur canadien ont rendu célèbre l'île grecque d'Hydra qui est devenue une destination internationale : Sophia Loren y a tourné en 1957 le film « Ombres sous la mer », dans lequel elle interprétait une pêcheuse d'éponges dans des décors impressionnants sur terre comme sous l'eau, et Leonard Cohen y a trouvé une maison, un environnement éveillant l'inspiration et un grand amour en 1960. En un premier temps, Hydra est devenue un lieu incontournable pour la moitié d'Hollywood et une colonie d'artistes – puis la jet-set est venue d'Athènes et du monde entier, ainsi que des touristes simplement curieux de voir cette île unique. Jusqu'à ce jour, Hydra semble aisément trouver un équilibre entre exclusivité et simplicité : les prix des terrains sont astronomiques et les yachts chics se côtoient dans le port en haute saison. Dans le même temps, les habitants de l'île insistent pour que la voiture soit interdite et que les visiteurs soient amenés à leur logement par bateau, à dos d'âne ou de cheval. La plus belle adresse est peut-être celle du Four Seasons Hydra, qui n'a de commun avec la célèbre chaîne hôtelière que le nom et l'excellente réputation. Idéalement située sur la plage de Vlychos, la maison, construite à la fin du XIXe siècle, a appartenu à un capitaine. Aujourd'hui, elle abrite huit suites, qui portent le nom des saisons et des éléments naturels et sont meublées et décorées individuellement dans des tons clairs, avec des meubles rustiques faits à la main et une touche de bohème. N'importe quelle chambre pourrait facilement devenir votre chambre préférée – mais la suite Automne est un véritable joyau, de couleur jaune pâle, avec un balcon donnant sur la mer et une vue sur le coucher du soleil. Chaque soir, celui-ci est un chef-d'œuvre d'orange brûlée, de rouge flamboyant et de noir bleuté ; aucun artiste sur Hydra ne pourrait le peindre plus magnifiquement. ◆ À lire : « Des fleurs pour Hitler » par Leonard Cohen ; à voir : « Ombres sous la mer » (1957) de Jean Negulesco

ACCÈS *Hydra se trouve à 1,5 h du Pirée en ferry. L'hôtel est situé à 5 min de bateau ou 35 min à pied au sud du port (transport gratuit des clients avec le bateau de l'hôtel)* · **PRIX** *€€–€€€€* · **CHAMBRES** *8 suites, dont l'une dans une villa à part* · **RESTAURATION** *Sur la plage, « Tassia's Tavern » sert des plats de poisson et des spécialités grecques sous une pergola* · **HISTOIRE** *La maison a été construite entre 1870 et 1890. L'hôtel a été ouvert en 2005* · **LES « PLUS »** *Une croisière à bord du voilier de l'hôtel*

POSEIDONION GRAND HOTEL

DAPIA, SPETSES

POSEIDONION GRAND HOTEL

Dapia, 180 50 Spetses
Tel. +30 22980 745 53 · res@poseidonion.com
www.poseidonion.com

THE TOP ADDRESS IN TOWN

Sotirios Anargyros was a merchant from Spetses who emigrated to America and made a fortune there as a tobacco dealer. Returning to his homeland a wealthy man, he built the island's first luxury hotel – in American dimensions and French style. With its cream façade, its wrought-iron balconies and elegant roof structure, the Poseidonion Grand Hotel resembles the palaces of the Côte d'Azur and even possesses a lavender garden. Since it opened in 1914 it has been a favorite destination for the rich and beautiful from Athens, international stars and the European aristocracy – Prince Nikolaos of Greece married Tatiana Blatnik here in 2010, celebrating with more than 350 blue-blooded guests. The hotel had just reopened that year following a thorough renovation, a joint project by the Greek architectural practices Vois and 3SK Stylianidis Architects. Since then it has displayed an impressive blend of public areas marked by the glitter and glamour of bygone days, and exquisite rooms in modern design. Highly recommended are the Pool Suite with its garden and swimming pool, as well as the two-level Cupola Suite, whose curving wooden roof is reminiscent of a traditional kaiki boat. The Poseidonion was the first hotel in Greece to offer spa treatments. This heritage sets a high standard, of course, so the hotel has an excellent wellness zone using Mediterranean care products, for example for peeling treatment with olive stones, grape seeds and orange water. Rested and relaxed, guests can give personal thanks to the hotel's founder at the end of their vacation: close to the Poseidonion, a bronze statue of Sotirios Anargyros greets passers-by. ◆ Book to pack: "The Magus" by John Fowles

DIRECTIONS *The hotel stands majestically by the harbor of Dapia. Ferries to Spetses leave from Piraeus (2 hrs 30 min to 3 hrs, depending on the route), and helicopter transfer from Athens (20 min) can be organized on request* · **RATES** *€€–€€€€* · **ROOMS** *52 rooms and suites* · **FOOD** *In the "Library Brasserie," Mediterranean dishes are on the menu, while "Palms" on the veranda serves snacks and cocktails. The organic farm Bostani in the hills of Spetses with its rustic restaurant also belongs to the hotel* · **HISTORY** *Reopened in summer 2009 after a five-year refurbishment* · **X-FACTOR** *From June to October the Poseidonion runs the Ciné Titania open-air cinema*

DAS ERSTE HAUS AM PLATZ

Sotirios Anargyros war ein Kaufmann aus Spetses, der nach Amerika auswanderte und dort ein Vermögen als Tabakhändler machte. Nachdem er wohlhabend in seine Heimat zurückgekehrt war, ließ er das erste Luxushotel der Insel bauen – in amerikanischen Dimensionen und im französischen Stil: Mit seiner cremefarbenen Fassade, seinen schmiedeeisernen Balkonen und der eleganten Dachkonstruktion erinnert das Poseidonion Grand Hotel an die Paläste der Côte d'Azur und besitzt sogar einen Lavendelgarten. Seit seiner Eröffnung im Jahr 1914 ist es ein Lieblingsziel der Schönen und Reichen aus Athen, internationaler Stars und des europäischen Adels – Prinz Nikolaos von Griechenland heiratete hier 2010 Tatiana Blatnik und feierte mit mehr als 350 blaublütigen Gästen. Damals war das Hotel gerade nach einer Rundumrenovierung, einem Co-Projekt der griechischen Architekturbüros Vois und 3SK Stylianidis Architects, wiedereröffnet worden. Seither verbindet es effektvoll öffentliche Bereiche, in denen noch der Glanz und Glamour vergangener Zeiten herrschen, und edle Zimmer im modernen Design. Besonders empfehlenswert sind die Pool Suite mit Garten und Schwimmbecken sowie die Cupola Suite auf zwei Ebenen, deren gewölbte Holzdecke an das traditionelle Boot „kaiki" erinnert. Das Poseidonion war das erste Hotel Griechenlands, in dem Spa-Behandlungen angeboten wurden. Ein solches Erbe verpflichtet natürlich, und so besitzt das Haus einen exzellenten Wellnessbereich, in dem mediterrane Produkte pflegen, zum Beispiel ein Peeling mit Olivensteinen und Traubenkernen sowie Orangenwasser. Rundum erholt kann man sich am Ende des Urlaubs sogar persönlich beim Gründer des Hotels bedanken: Ganz in der Nähe des Poseidonion wartet eine Bronzestatue von Sotirios Anargyros auf Passanten. ◆ Buchtipp: „Land" von Perikles Monioudis

ANREISE *Das Hotel thront am Hafen von Dapia. Fährverbindungen nach Spetses bestehen ab Piräus (je nach Route 2,5–3 Std.), auf Wunsch werden auch Helikoptertransfers ab Athen organisiert (20 min)* · **PREISE** *€€–€€€€* · **ZIMMER** *52 Zimmer und Suiten* · **KÜCHE** *In der „Library Brasserie" stehen mediterrane Menüs auf der Karte, im „Palms" auf der Veranda Snacks und Cocktails. Zudem gehört die Biofarm Bostani in den Hügeln von Spetses zum Hotel, dort gibt es ein rustikales Restaurant* · **GESCHICHTE** *Nach fünfjähriger Renovierung im Sommer 2009 neu eröffnet* · **X-FAKTOR** *Von Juni bis Oktober betreibt das Poseidonion das Freiluftkino Ciné Titania*

UN EMPLACEMENT DE PREMIER CHOIX

Sotirios Anargyros, natif de Spetses émigré en Amérique, y a fait fortune comme marchand de tabac. De retour dans son pays, il a fait construire le premier hôtel de luxe de l'île – dimensions américaines et style français. Avec sa façade couleur crème, ses balcons en fer forgé et sa toiture élégante, le Poseidonion Grand Hotel évoque les palaces de la Côte d'Azur et possède même un jardin de lavande. Depuis son ouverture en 1914, il est la destination favorite de l'élite belle et fortunée d'Athènes, des stars internationales et de l'aristocratie européenne. Le prince Nikolaos de Grèce y a épousé Tatiana Blatnik en 2010 et a fêté l'événement avec plus de 350 invités au sang bleu. À l'époque, l'hôtel venait de rouvrir après une rénovation complète, un projet commun des cabinets d'architectes grecs Vois et 3SK Stylianidis Architects. Depuis lors, il combine efficacement les espaces publics, où règnent encore le glamour et le charme d'autrefois, avec des pièces nobles au design moderne. La Pool Suite avec jardin et piscine et la Cupola Suite sur deux niveaux, dont le plafond voûté en bois rappelle le bateau traditionnel « kaiki », sont particulièrement recommandées. Le Poseidonion a été le premier hôtel en Grèce à proposer des soins thermaux. Un tel héritage oblige, et l'hôtel dispose donc d'un excellent espace de spa où l'on utilise des produits méditerranéens, par exemple des massages exfoliants aux noyaux d'olive et pépins de raisin et à l'eau de fleurs d'oranger. À la fin de vos vacances, parfaitement dispos, vous pouvez même remercier le fondateur de l'hôtel en personne : tout près du Poseidonion, une statue en bronze de Sotirios Anargyros attend les passants. ◆ À lire : « La langue maternelle » par Vassilis Alexakis

ACCÈS *L'hôtel se dresse majestueusement dans le port de Dapia. On peut rejoindre Spetses en ferry à partir du Pirée (2,5 à 3 h selon la route empruntée), des transferts en hélicoptère peuvent également être organisés sur demande à partir d'Athènes (20 min)* · **PRIX** *€€–€€€€* · **CHAMBRES** *52 chambres et suites* · **RESTAURATION** *Cuisine méditerranéenne au menu de la « Library Brasserie », des snacks et cocktails servis dans la véranda du « Palms Bar ». De plus, la ferme bio Bostani, dans les collines de Spetses, appartient à l'hôtel, on y trouve un restaurant rustique* · **HISTOIRE** *Rouvert durant l'été 2009 après cinq ans de travaux* · **LES « PLUS »** *Le Poseidonion gère le cinéma en plein air Ciné Titania de juin à octobre*

ARTION
KAFES

ONAR

AHLA BEACH, ANDROS

ONAR

Ahla Beach, 845 00 Andros
Tel. +30 210 807 43 24 and +30 695 629 29 15 · info@onar-andros.gr
www.onar-andros.gr

BACK TO NATURE

To think of the Cyclades usually means to conjure up images in blue and white, a picture-postcard Greece. Andros, however, has a different color: the northernmost and second-largest island in the Cyclades is green. It owes these natural surroundings, unusually luxuriant for the region, to its four rivers, countless streams, lakes and waterfalls that irrigate the land. There is even a source of mineral water that bubbles up from the depths of the earth – so it is no wonder that Andros was once known under the name Hydroussa, "rich in water." On the east side of the island at the beach of Ahla lie wetlands with extremely rare flora and fauna. This area is part of the European Natura 2000 network and is home to the Onar eco-hotel. Its owner, Mateo (Teo) Pantzopoulos, wanted to fulfill a long-standing wish here (the name Onar is derived from the Greek word for "dream") by creating a place that is in harmony with nature. He built the sixteen cottages as sustainably as possible, using local stone, wood and reeds. They are decorated in calming, earthy colors and fitted with large windows and open-air seating so that the inside and outside flow into one another. Renewable energy is generated, and an organic garden has been planted – alongside the products of local farmers and fishermen, it is the main supplier to the hotel restaurant. Those who take a break with Teo should first and foremost switch off (WiFi is available only on request), raise their awareness of the beauty of nature, and rediscover it respectfully – on a walk along the beach, a boat trip or a hike in the mountains. Thanks to the size of the houses, the easygoing atmosphere and the variety of excursions on offer, children too love Onar and an "unplugged" holiday. ◆ Book to pack: "The Women of Andros" by Ioanna Karystiani

DIRECTIONS *To reach Andros, take a ferry from Rafina near Athens or from Mykonos (2 hrs to 2 hrs 30 min, several times daily). Transfer to the remote hotel (50 min) can be arranged, but it is better to hire a four-wheel-drive car so as to be flexible while staying there* · **RATES** *€€–€€€€* · **ROOMS** *16 cottages and villas* · **FOOD** *Breakfast, lunch and dinner are served at communal tables. The food is mostly organic and good rustic Greek cooking. There is also a kitchenette in every house* · **HISTORY** *Designed by the Greek architectural practice Zege, and opened in 2008* · **X-FACTOR** *At the beginning and end of the season, the hotel runs yoga retreats and meditation courses*

ZURÜCK ZUR NATUR

Wer an die Kykladen denkt, hat normalerweise Weiß und Blau sowie ein Griechenland wie aus dem Fotoalbum vor Augen. Auf Andros dominiert aber eine andere Farbe: Die nördlichste und zweitgrößte Kykladeninsel ist grün. Ihre für die Region ungewöhnlich üppige Natur verdankt sie vier Flüssen, ungezählten Bächen, Seen und Wasserfällen, die das Land speisen. Sogar eine Mineralwasserquelle sprudelt aus den Tiefen der Erde – kein Wunder, dass Andros früher auch unter dem Namen Hydroussa, die Wasserreiche, bekannt war. Im Osten der Insel erstreckt sich am Strand von Ahla ein Feuchtgebiet mit besonders seltener Flora und Fauna, das zum europäischen Netzwerk Natura 2000 gehört und Heimat des Ökohotels Onar ist. Der Besitzer Mateo (Teo) Pantzopoulos wollte sich hier einen lang gehegten Wunsch erfüllen (der Name Onar leitet sich vom griechischen Wort für „Traum" ab) und einen Ort in Einklang und Harmonie mit der Natur schaffen. So ließ er die 16 Cottages möglichst nachhaltig aus lokalem Stein, Holz und Schilf konstruieren. Sie sind in ruhigen Erdtönen gehalten und mit großen Fenstern sowie Freisitzen versehen, damit Innen- und Außenwelt ineinander übergehen. Auch an alternativen Energien wurde getüftelt und ein Biogarten angelegt, der neben einheimischen Bauern und Fischern wichtigster Lieferant des hoteleigenen Restaurants ist. Wer bei Teo Urlaub macht, soll in erster Linie abschalten (WiFi gibt es nur auf Anfrage), sich die Schönheit der Natur wieder bewusst machen und diese mit Respekt neu entdecken – ob beim Strandspaziergang, bei einer Bootsfahrt oder einer Bergwanderung. Dank der Größe der Häuser, der lockeren Atmosphäre und der abwechslungsreichen Ausflugsmöglichkeiten lieben auch Kinder das Onar und ihren Urlaub „unplugged". ◆ Buchtipp: „Die Frauen von Andros" von Ioanna Karystiani

ANREISE *Andros ist mit der Fähre ab Rafina bei Athen und ab Mykonos erreichbar (mehrmals täglich, 2–2,5 Std.). Der Transfer zum einsam gelegenen Hotel (50 min) kann arrangiert werden – besser ist aber ein Mietwagen mit Allradantrieb, damit man während des Aufenthalts flexibel ist* · **PREISE** *€€–€€€€* · **ZIMMER** *16 Häuser und Villen* · **KÜCHE** *Frühstück, Mittag- und Abendessen wird an Gemeinschaftstafeln serviert, die Mahlzeiten sind überwiegend biologisch und gute griechische Landküche. In jedem Haus steht zudem eine Kitchenette zur Verfügung* · **GESCHICHTE** *Vom griechischen Architekturbüro Zege entworfen und 2008 eröffnet* · **X-FAKTOR** *Zu Beginn und zum Ende der Saison bietet das Hotel Yoga-Retreats und Meditationskurse an*

RETOUR À LA NATURE

Penser aux Cyclades, c'est le plus souvent penser en blanc et en bleu et à une Grèce sortie tout droit d'un album photo. Mais Andros n'est ni blanche ni bleue, la deuxième plus grande île des Cyclades, la plus septentrionale, est verte. Sa végétation, exceptionnellement luxuriante, est due à quatre rivières, d'innombrables ruisseaux, lacs et cascades qui alimentent le pays. Même une source d'eau minérale jaillit des profondeurs de la terre – rien d'étonnant donc si Andros a été autrefois connue sous le nom d'Hydroussa, la riche en eau. Dans l'est de l'île, sur la plage d'Ahla, s'étend une zone humide abritant une flore et une faune particulièrement rares, qui fait partie du réseau européen Natura 2000 et qui abrite l'éco-hôtel Onar. Le propriétaire, Mateo (Teo) Pantzopoulos, caressait depuis longtemps le rêve (le nom Onar vient du mot grec signifiant « rêve ») de créer un lieu en harmonie avec la nature. Il a donc fait construire les 16 cottages de manière aussi durable que possible en pierre de la région, en bois et en roseau. Ils offrent des tons de terre et disposent de grandes fenêtres et de sièges extérieurs pour que les espaces intérieurs et extérieurs se fondent l'un dans l'autre. Les sources d'énergie alternatives n'ont pas été oubliées et un jardin biologique a vu le jour – il est le principal fournisseur du restaurant de l'hôtel à côté des agriculteurs et des pêcheurs locaux. Celui qui passe ses vacances chez Teo devrait avant tout se déconnecter (la WiFi n'est disponible que sur demande), reprendre conscience de la beauté de la nature et la redécouvrir avec respect – que ce soit en se promenant sur la plage, en faisant une excursion en bateau ou une randonnée en montagne. La taille des maisons, l'atmosphère détendue et les possibilités d'excursions variées, font que même les enfants aiment l'Onar et leurs vacances « débranchées ». ◆ À lire : « La petite Angleterre » par Ioanna Karystiani

ACCÈS *Andros est accessible par ferry depuis Rafina près d'Athènes et depuis Mykonos (plusieurs fois par jour, 2 à 2,5 h). Le transfert vers l'hôtel isolé (50 min) peut être organisé, mais il vaut mieux louer un quatre-quatre qui assurera la mobilité durant le séjour* · **PRIX** *€€–€€€€* · **CHAMBRES** *16 maisons et villas* · **RESTAURATION** *Petit-déjeuner, déjeuner et dîner sont servis à des tables communes, la plupart des plats proposés – une bonne cuisine de campagne grecque – sont réalisés avec des produits bio. Chaque maison est dotée d'une kitchenette* · **HISTOIRE** *Conçu par le cabinet d'architectes Zege et ouvert en 2008* · **LES « PLUS »** *L'hôtel propose des retraites de yoga et des cours de méditation au début et en fin de saison*

MÈLISSES

PALEOPOLI, ANDROS

MÈLISSES

Paleopoli, 845 00 Andros
info@melissesandros.com
www.melissesandros.com

A STAY WITH ALLEGRA

She works as a cook, photographer and author; she loves travel, antiques and design; she is Italian and has found a second home in Greece. On Andros she combines all of her passions at Mèlisses, which takes its name from the industrious bees of the island (and perhaps a little bit from herself). Allegra Pomilio runs, to put it in cosmopolitan terms, a bijou bed & breakfast, and receives guests in six delightful rooms, which she has furnished with a great aesthetic and stylistic sense, using original prints by photographers such as Mimmo Jodice and Armin Linke, vintage furniture and finds from flea markets in Italy, Greece, France and Belgium. The Coral Apartment and Sea Urchin Suite each have their own kitchen or outdoor kitchen – which is not really necessary, as Allegra's cooking is Hellas heaven. She has taken master classes from starred chefs such as Alain Ducasse and Heinz Beck, assisted food blogger Mimi Thorisson, and acquired all the tricks, but fortunately not the celebrity attitudes, of her teachers. Her dishes are wonderful, down-to-earth cooking – made without much fuss from fresh ingredients and presented so temptingly that practically every one of them ends up on Instagram. Those who would like to follow her lead can take part in the workshops and retreats that Allegra organizes in cooperation with guest chefs, photographers, stylists and trainers – in addition to cookery courses, the program includes floral design, yoga and meditation. Many guests, both families and groups of friends, book individually tailored courses, making their vacation here a special experience. ◆ Book to pack: "The Colossus of Maroussi" by Henry Miller

DIRECTIONS *To reach Andros take a ferry from Rafina near Athens or from Mykonos (2 hrs to 2 hrs 30 min, several times daily). Mèlisses lies in the Bay of Paleopoli on the west coast of the island, 7 minutes' drive from the village of Batsi. Those who rent a car are advised to take a four-wheel-drive, as the road to the house is unpaved* · **RATES** *€€–€€€* · **ROOMS** *1 guesthouse with 2 bedrooms, kitchen and private pool, 2 suites with an outdoor kitchen and barbecue, 2 rooms (with a shared bathroom)* · **FOOD** *Allegra's Greek breakfast is pure poetry. On request she also cooks for guests in the evening* · **HISTORY** *Allegra fitted out the house in collaboration with her parents and architect Vangelis Stamatelatos. It opened in July 2018* · **X-FACTOR** *The infinity pool and private access to the beach*

ZU GAST BEI ALLEGRA

Sie arbeitet als Köchin, Fotografin und Autorin; sie liebt Reisen, Antiquitäten und Design; sie ist Italienerin und hat in Griechenland eine zweite Heimat gefunden. Auf Andros vereint sie all ihre Leidenschaften im Mèlisses, das nach den emsigen Bienen der Insel benannt ist (und vielleicht auch ein bisschen nach ihr selbst). Allegra Pomilio besitzt, kosmopolitisch gesprochen, ein „Bijou Bed & Breakfast" und empfängt ihre Gäste in sechs zauberhaften Zimmern, die sie mit viel Gespür für Ästhetik und Stil und mit Originalen von Fotografen wie Mimmo Jodice oder Armin Linke, Vintagemöbeln und Flohmarktfunden aus Italien, Griechenland, Frankreich sowie Belgien eingerichtet hat. Das Coral Apartment und die Sea Urchin Suite haben zudem eine eigene Küche beziehungsweise Außenküche – was allerdings nicht wirklich nötig wäre, denn Allegra kocht wie im Himmel über Hellas. Sie hat bei Sterneköchen wie Alain Ducasse und Heinz Beck Meisterkurse belegt, der Foodbloggerin Mimi Thorisson assistiert und sich von ihren Lehrern alle Tricks, aber glücklicherweise keine Starallüren abgeschaut. Ihre Gerichte sind herrliche Hausmannskost – aus frischen Zutaten ohne viel Aufhebens zubereitet und so verlockend präsentiert, dass so gut wie jede ihrer Kreationen auf Instagram landet. Wer es ihr nachtun möchte, kann an Workshops und Retreats teilnehmen, die Allegra gemeinsam mit Gastköchen, Fotografen, Stylisten und Trainern organisiert – neben Kochkursen stehen unter anderem Floraldesign, Yoga und Meditation auf dem Programm. Viele Gäste, sowohl Familien als auch Freundesgruppen, lassen sich ihre Kurse auch individuell zusammenstellen und machen so aus ihrem Urlaub ein ganz besonderes Erlebnis. ◆ Buchtipp: „Der Koloß von Maroussi. Eine Reise nach Griechenland" von Henry Miller

ANREISE *Andros ist mit der Fähre ab Rafina bei Athen und ab Mykonos erreichbar (mehrmals täglich, 2–2,5 Std.). Mèlisses liegt in der Bucht von Paleopoli an der Westküste der Insel, 7 Fahrtminuten südlich des Dorfs Batsi. Wer mit dem Mietwagen anreist, sollte auf Allradantrieb achten, da die Straße zum Haus unbefestigt ist* · **PREISE** *€€–€€€* · **ZIMMER** *1 Gästehaus mit 2 Schlafzimmern, Küche und Privatpool, 2 Suiten mit Außenküche bzw. Grill, 2 Zimmer (mit Gemeinschaftsbad)* · **KÜCHE** *Allegras griechisches Frühstück ist ein Gedicht. Auf Wunsch bekocht sie ihre Gäste auch abends* · **GESCHICHTE** *Allegra stattete das Haus gemeinsam mit ihren Eltern und dem Architekten Vangelis Stamatelatos aus. Eröffnung war im Juli 2018* · **X-FAKTOR** *Der Infinitypool und der Privatzugang zum Strand*

LES HÔTES D'ALLEGRA

Elle est cuisinière, photographe et auteur ; elle aime les voyages, les antiquités et le design ; elle est italienne et a trouvé une seconde patrie en Grèce. Sur l'île d'Andros, elle peut s'adonner à ses passions au Mèlisses, du nom des abeilles très actives sur l'île (elle leur ressemble un peu). Allegra Pomilio est propriétaire d'un « Bijou Bed & Breakfast » et accueille ses hôtes dans six chambres charmantes, qu'elle a meublées et décorées avec un grand sens de l'esthétique et du style, choisissant des œuvres de photographes tels que Mimmo Jodice ou Armin Linke, des meubles vintage et des trouvailles chinées en Italie, en Grèce, en France et en Belgique. L'appartement Coral a sa propre cuisine et la suite Sea Urchin une cuisine extérieure – mais ce ne serait pas vraiment nécessaire, car Allegra est une cuisinière hors-pair. Elle a suivi des master-classes avec des chefs étoilés comme Alain Ducasse et Heinz Beck, a assisté la blogueuse culinaire Mimi Thorisson, apprenant toutes les astuces de ses professeurs, sans rien perdre, heureusement, de sa simplicité et de son naturel. Ses plats sont délicieux – préparés à partir de produits frais et sans chichis, ils sont présentés de manière si séduisante que presque toutes ses créations se retrouvent sur Instagram. Ceux qui souhaitent l'imiter peuvent participer aux ateliers et aux retraites qu'Allegra organise avec des cuisiniers invités, des photographes, des stylistes et des formateurs. Outre les cours de cuisine, le programme comprend des cours de design floral, de yoga et de méditation. De nombreux hôtes, qu'il s'agisse de familles ou de groupes d'amis, font également organiser leurs cours de manière individuelle, ce qui transforme leurs vacances en une expérience bien particulière. ◆ À lire : « Le colosse de Maroussi » par Henry Miller

ACCÈS *Andros est accessible par ferry depuis Rafina près d'Athènes et depuis Mykonos (plusieurs fois par jour, 2–2,5 h). Mèlisses est située dans la baie de Paleopoli sur la côte occidentale de l'île, à 7 min en voiture au sud du village de Batsi. Si vous envisagez de louer une voiture, choisissez plutôt un quatre-quatre, vu que la route menant à la maison n'est pas goudronnée* · **PRIX** *€€–€€€* · **CHAMBRES** *1 maison d'hôtes avec 2 chambres à coucher, cuisine et piscine privée, 2 suites avec cuisine extérieure ou barbecue, 2 chambres (avec salle de bains commune)* · **RESTAURATION** *Le petit-déjeuner grec d'Allegra est fabuleux. Sur demande, elle cuisine aussi le soir* · **HISTOIRE** *Allegra a meublé et décoré la maison avec ses parents et l'architecte Vangelis Stamatelatos. L'ouverture a eu lieu en juillet 2018* · **LES « PLUS »** *La piscine à débordement et l'accès privé à la plage*

ΡΟΔΟΖΑΧΑΡΗ
παραδοσιακα προϊοντα
ΠΑΣΤΕΛΙ ΑΝΔΡΟΥ
ΑΥΓΑ ΝΤΟΠΙΑ
ΜΕΛΙ ΑΝΔΡΟΥ
ΡΑΚΙ - ΚΡΑΣΙ
ΕΛΙΕΣ ΑΝΔΡΟΥ
ΛΟΥΚΑΝΙΚΑ ΝΤΟΠΙΑ
ΓΛΥΚΑ ΚΟΥΤΑΛΙΟΥ
ΧΥΛΟΠΙΤΕΣ - ΤΡΑΧΑΝΑ
ΜΕ ΑΓΟΡΕΣ
ΑΝΩ ΤΩΝ
25€
ΣΑΣ ΚΑΝΟΥΜΕ
ΔΩΡΟ
ΜΙΑ ΟΙΚΟΛΟΓΙΚΗ
ΤΣΑΝΤΑ
ΡΟΔΟΖΑΧΑΡΗ

ΥΔΡΟΥΣΑ II N.A. 158

HOT

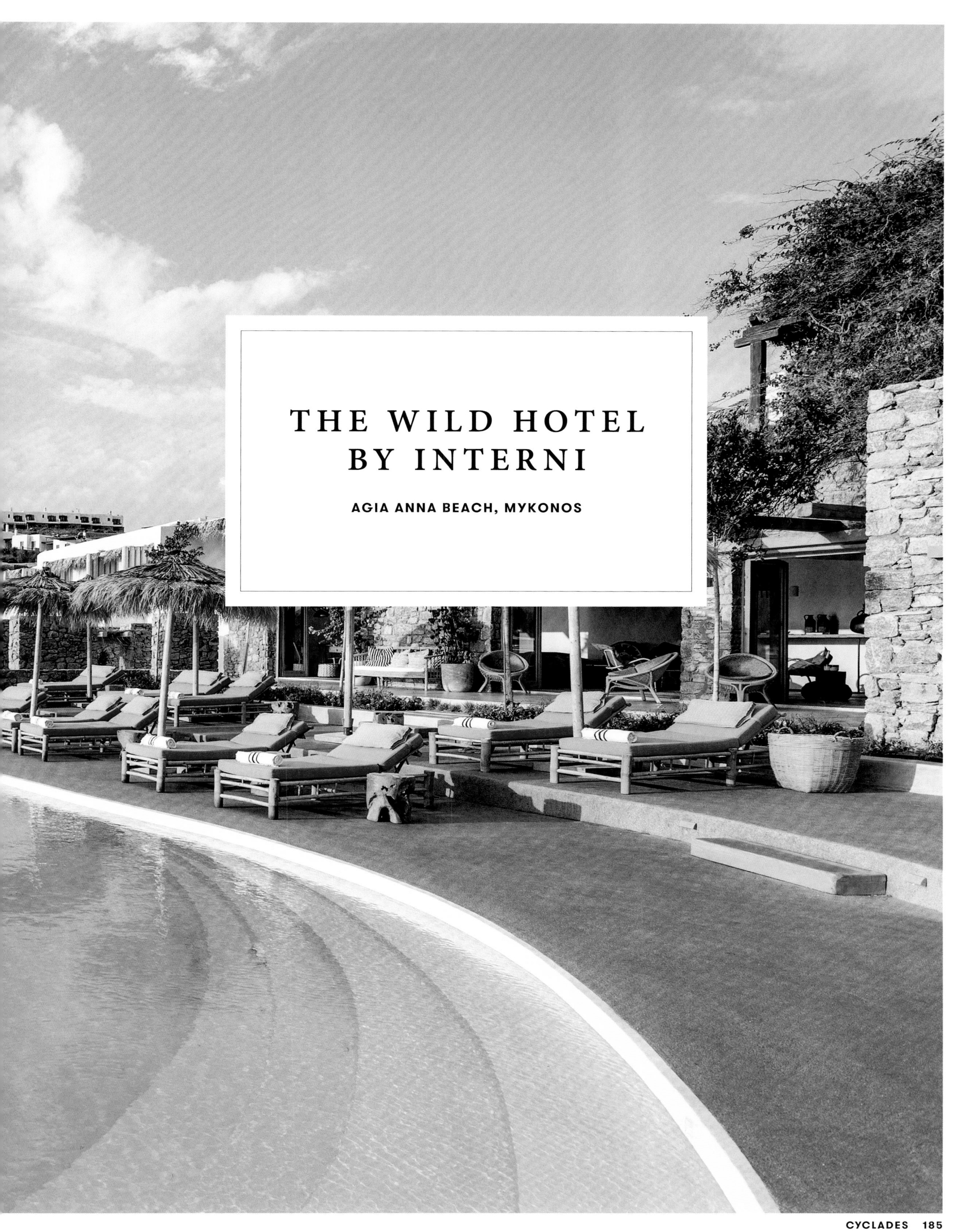

THE WILD HOTEL BY INTERNI

AGIA ANNA BEACH, MYKONOS

THE WILD HOTEL BY INTERNI

846 00 Agia Anna, Mykonos
Tel. +30 22890 725 00 and +30 697 001 71 49 · info@thewildhotel.com
www.thewildhotel.com

ON A WILD COAST

Don't be misled by the name of this hotel. It does not indicate a location for unrestrained parties, but rather is a reference to "the wild ones," meaning the boldest and proudest fishermen of Mykonos, who inhabited the neighboring village many years ago – and to the wild beauty of its surroundings. Here, on the cliffs of the southeast coast of the island, owner Alexandros Varveris aims to breathe new life into a genuine Mykonos and restore to the island the splendor and glamour that the Onassis and Krupp families once brought when they moored in the harbor. Varveris, who already operated the eclectic restaurant "Interni" and luxurious beach clubs on Mykonos, collaborated with the designers at Airtec to create The Wild Hotel. The suites and villas built on several terraces of a natural amphitheater express a blend of cultures. With lots of white, stone and wood, they look to the regional architecture of the Cyclades. To this are added decorative objects with an Asian or African touch, and the aura of Zen surrounds the whole establishment. The pool, which winds along the edge of the cliffs with views of the coast, sea and beach, is regarded as a masterpiece. From here, narrow stone steps lead down to the beach, which lies in a picturesque cove. Just a short time after it opened, the house tavern numbered among the best Greek restaurants far and wide. The menu includes such classics as moussaka and stuffed vine leaves – and fresh fish, of course, caught by the descendants of the wild ones. ◆ Book to pack: "Travels in Greece" by Nikos Kazantzakis

DIRECTIONS *12 km/7 miles from Mykonos airport* · **RATES** *€€–€€€€* · **ROOMS** *37 suites and villas* · **FOOD** *The Greek specialties in the taverna are made using local organic products. There is also a bar* · **HISTORY** *Opened in May 2019* · **X-FACTOR** *The spa with a rock grotto and an outdoor gym area*

AN DER WILDEN KÜSTE

Man darf sich vom Namen dieses Hotels nicht in die Irre führen lassen. Er bezeichnet kein ausschweifendes Partymotto, sondern erinnert an „die Wilden“ – die kühnsten und stolzesten Fischer von Mykonos, die vor vielen Jahren im benachbarten Dorf lebten – sowie an die wilde Schönheit der Umgebung. Hier, an einer Steilküste im Südosten der Insel, möchte Besitzer Alexandros Varveris das authentische Mykonos neu beleben und ihm zugleich den Glanz und Glamour zurückgeben, den die Onassis und Krupps einst mitbrachten, wenn sie im Hafen vor Anker gingen. Varveris, der bereits Betreiber des eklektischen Restaurants „Interni“ und eines luxuriösen Beachklubs auf der Insel war, entwarf The Wild Hotel gemeinsam mit den Designern von Airtec. Die auf mehreren Terrassen eines natürlichen Amphitheaters erbauten Suiten und Villen sind ein Mix der Kulturen: Viel Weiß, Stein und Holz verweisen auf die regionale Architektur der Kykladen – dazu kommen asiatisch oder afrikanisch anmutende Deko-Objekte, und über allem schwebt ein Hauch Zen. Als Meisterwerk gilt der Pool, der sich am Rand der Klippen entlangschlängelt und über die Küste, das Meer und den Strand blickt. Schmale Steintreppen führen von hier zum Strand hinunter, der in einer malerischen Bucht liegt. Die Taverne des Hauses rangierte schon kurz nach ihrer Eröffnung unter den besten griechischen Restaurants weit und breit. Auf der Karte stehen Klassiker wie Moussaka oder gefüllte Weinblätter – und natürlich frischer Fisch, gefangen von den Nachfahren der Wilden. ◆ Buchtipp: „Im Zauber der griechischen Landschaft“ von Nikos Kazantzakis

ANREISE *12 km vom Flughafen Mykonos entfernt* · **PREISE** *€€–€€€€* · **ZIMMER** *37 Suiten und Villen* · **KÜCHE** *Die griechischen Spezialitäten in der Taverne basieren auf lokalen Bioprodukten, zudem gibt es eine Bar* · **GESCHICHTE** *Im Mai 2019 eröffnet* · **X-FAKTOR** *Das Spa mit Felsengrotte und Outdoor-Fitnessbereich*

SUR LA CÔTE SAUVAGE

Que l'on ne se méprenne pas, le nom de cet hôtel ne veut en rien suggérer l'idée de fêtes déchaînées, il évoque le souvenir des « sauvages », les pêcheurs les plus audacieux et les plus fiers de Mycènes, qui ont vécu dans le village voisin il y a de nombreuses années – et vante la beauté farouche des environs. Ici, sur une côte escarpée au sud-est de l'île, le propriétaire Alexandros Varveris veut revitaliser l'authentique Mycènes tout en lui redonnant le faste et le glamour que les Onassis et les Krupp apportaient autrefois avec eux lorsqu'ils mouillaient au port. Varveris, qui dirigeait déjà le restaurant éclectique « Interni » et un luxueux club de plage sur l'île, a conçu le Wild Hotel en collaboration avec les designers d'Airtec. Les suites et villas, construites sur plusieurs terrasses d'un amphithéâtre naturel, sont inspirées de diverses cultures : beaucoup de blanc, de pierre et de bois font référence à l'architecture régionale des Cyclades – on y trouve aussi des objets décoratifs d'aspect asiatique ou africain, et surtout une pincée de zen. La piscine qui serpente le long des falaises et offre une vue sur la côte, la mer et la plage est un chef-d'œuvre. D'étroits escaliers de pierre mènent d'ici à la plage qui s'étend dans une baie pittoresque. Peu après son ouverture, la taverne de la maison a été classée parmi les meilleurs restaurants grecs des alentours. Au menu, des classiques tels que la moussaka ou les feuilles de vigne farcies – et bien sûr du poisson frais, pêché par les descendants des sauvages. ◆ À lire : « Îles grecques, mon amour » de Philippe Lutz

ACCÈS *À 12 km de l'aéroport de Mycènes* · **PRIX** *€€–€€€€* · **CHAMBRES** *37 suites et villas* · **RESTAURATION** *Les spécialités grecques proposées dans la taverne sont à base de produits biologiques de la région, il y a aussi un bar* · **HISTOIRE** *Ouvert en mai 2019* · **LES « PLUS »** *Le spa avec sa grotte et la zone extérieure de remise en forme*

SOHO ROC HOUSE

PARAGA BEACH, MYKONOS

SOHO ROC HOUSE

Paraga Beach, Platis Gialos, 846 00 Mykonos
Tel. +30 22890 274 74 · info.sohorochouse@sohohouse.com
www.sohohouse.com

WELCOME TO THE CLUB

The first Soho House was more or less the result of a coincidence – and a narrow doorway. In 1995 Nick Jones, who ran "Café Bohème" in London's Greek Street, was offered the chance to use a space above his café. However, it could only be accessed through a narrow entrance, which gave Jones the idea of founding behind this modest doorway a club for artists whom he supplied with food and drink in the café downstairs. The idea was a success: today there are Soho Houses in the shape of clubs, restaurants, hotels, spas and offices not only in London and Britain but all over the world – for members who are mainly young (or who feel young, at least), creative and networked, and want to have fun in a stylish way.
The Soho Roc House in Mykonos is the chain's first hotel in Greece, and a perfect fit for the portfolio. Its cuboid white buildings stand Instagram-ready above a rocky bay, and the rooms were furnished by the in-house design team in casual shades of cream, beige and brown, using wood, linen, rattan, wool and ceramics. The intention was to achieve a relaxed, pure and natural look, as if in a summer house belonging to good friends (guests who want to treat themselves to something special should ask for a room looking out onto the sea with a balcony, terrace or garden). For seeing and being seen, the pool bar in lounge style is the best spot – or equally the nearby "Scorpios" beach club, which is also run by Soho House and breathes new life into the ancient Greek concept of the agora ("marketplace," "meeting place") on the beach at Paraga. This is a place to chill out on loungers, chat in the restaurant to chefs and waiters who look like glam rockers, and enjoy some of the best experimental music events on Mykonos in the evenings. ◆ Book to pack: "Island of Secrets" by Jeffrey Siger; film to watch: "The Bourne Identity" (2002) by Doug Liman, with Matt Damon and Franka Potente – Mykonos was the setting for the final scenes

DIRECTIONS *On the south coast of Mykonos, 4 km/2.5 miles from the island airport and 8 km/5 miles from the harbor. The walk from the hotel to the beach club takes about 10 min* · **RATES** *€€–€€€€* · **ROOMS** *45 rooms, which non-members too can book* · **FOOD** *The hotel restaurant serves organic Mediterranean dishes* · **HISTORY** *What used to be the Hotel San Giorgio became Soho Roc House in summer 2020* · **X-FACTOR** *An excellent blend of paradise and party*

WILLKOMMEN IM KLUB

Das erste Soho House ist mehr oder minder dem Zufall zu verdanken – und einer schmalen Tür: 1995 bekam Nick Jones, der in der Londoner Greek Street das „Café Bohème" führte, das Angebot, auch die über dem Lokal liegende Fläche zu nutzen. Diese war jedoch nur durch einen engen Eingang erreichbar, was Jones auf die Idee brachte, hinter der unscheinbaren Pforte einen Klub für Künstler zu gründen, die er unten im Café verköstigte. Das Konzept ging auf: Heute gibt es Soho Houses in Form von Klubs, Restaurants, Hotels, Spas und Büros nicht nur in London und Großbritannien, sondern in aller Welt – für Mitglieder, die mehrheitlich jung (oder sich zumindest so fühlen), kreativ sowie vernetzt sind und stilvoll Spaß haben möchten. Das Soho Roc House Mykonos ist die Hotelpremiere der Kette in Griechenland und passt perfekt ins Portfolio. Seine weißen, würfelartigen Gebäude stehen Instagram-tauglich über einer Felsenbucht, und die Zimmer wurden vom firmeneigenen Designteam lässig in Creme-, Beige- und Brauntönen und mit Holz, Leinen, Rattan, Wolle und Keramik eingerichtet. Entspannt, pur und natürlich sollte es aussehen und wie im Sommerhaus guter Freunde (wer sich etwas Besonderes gönnen möchte, sollte nach einem Zimmer zum Meer und mit Balkon, Terrasse oder Garten fragen). Zum Sehen und Gesehenwerden ist die Poolbar im Loungestil der beste Platz – ebenso wie der nahe Beachklub „Scorpios", der ebenfalls von Soho House betrieben wird und am Strand von Paraga den antiken griechischen Gedanken der Agora („Marktplatz", „Treffpunkt") neu belebt. Hier chillt man auf Sonnenliegen, chattet im Restaurant mit Köchen und Kellnern, die wie Edelrocker aussehen, und bekommt abends einige der besten experimentellen Musikevents auf Mykonos zu hören. ◆ Buchtipp: „So ist das Leben" von Amanda Michalopoulou; Filmtipp: „Die Bourne Identität" (2002) von Doug Liman, mit Matt Damon und Franka Potente, deren Schlussszenen auf Mykonos gedreht wurden

ANREISE *An der Südküste von Mykonos gelegen, 4 km vom Flughafen der Insel und 8 km vom Hafen entfernt. Vom Hotel zum Beachklub läuft man ca. 10 min* · **PREISE** *€€–€€€€* · **ZIMMER** *45 Zimmer, auch ohne Mitgliedschaft buchbar* · **KÜCHE** *Im Hotelrestaurant stehen biologische mediterrane Gerichte auf der Karte* · **GESCHICHTE** *Aus dem ehemaligen Hotel San Giorgio wurde im Sommer 2020 das Soho Roc House* · **X-FAKTOR** *Eine gelungene Mischung aus Paradies und Party*

BIENVENUE AU CLUB

La première Soho House est plus ou moins le fruit du hasard – en fait elle doit sa création à une porte étroite : en 1995, Nick Jones, le patron du « Café Bohème » dans la Greek Street de Londres, s'est vu offrir la possibilité d'utiliser l'espace situé au-dessus du restaurant. Le problème, c'est qu'on ne pouvait y accéder que par une entrée étroite ; Jones eut alors l'idée de fonder, derrière la porte qui passait presque inaperçue, un club réservé aux artistes qu'il restaurait en bas, dans le café. Pari gagné : aujourd'hui, les Soho Houses sous forme de clubs, restaurants, hôtels, spas et bureaux existent non seulement à Londres et en Grande-Bretagne, mais aussi dans le monde entier – et ses membres sont pour la plupart jeunes (ou se sentent jeunes), créatifs, en réseau et veulent s'amuser avec style. La Soho Roc House Mykonos est le premier hôtel de la chaîne en Grèce et s'intègre parfaitement dans son programme. Ses cubiques bâtiments blancs se dressent, dignes d'Instagram, au-dessus d'une crique rocheuse, et les pièces ont été aménagées de manière décontractée par l'équipe de design de la société dans des tons de crème, beige et brun, en utilisant du bois, du lin, du rotin, de la laine et de la céramique. L'ensemble devait être serein, limpide et naturel, ressembler à la maison d'été de bons amis (si vous voulez vous offrir quelque chose de spécial, demandez une chambre face à la mer et dotée d'un balcon, d'une terrasse ou d'un jardin). Le meilleur endroit pour voir et être vu est le bar de la piscine en style lounge – ainsi que le club de plage voisin « Scorpios », également géré par Soho House et qui, sur la plage de Paraga, fait revivre l'idée d'agora de la Grèce antique. Ici, on peut se détendre sur une chaise longue, discuter au restaurant avec des chefs et des serveurs qui ressemblent à de fiers rockeurs et, le soir, écouter certains des meilleurs événements musicaux expérimentaux sur Mykonos. ◆ À lire : « Splendide journée » par Amanda Michalopoulou ; à voir : « La mémoire dans la peau » (2002) de Doug Liman, avec Matt Damon et Franka Potente, dont les dernières scènes ont été tournées à Mykonos

ACCÈS *Sur la côte méridionale de Mykonos, à 4 km de l'aéroport de l'île et à 8 km du port. Une dizaine de minutes de marche de l'hôtel au club de la plage* · **PRIX** *€€–€€€€* · **CHAMBRES** *45 chambres que l'on peut réserver sans être membre* · **RESTAURATION** *Le restaurant de l'hôtel propose une cuisine méditerranéenne à base de produits bio* · **HISTOIRE** *L'ancien Hotel San Giorgio est devenu Soho Roc House durant l'été 2020* · **LES « PLUS »** *Faire la fête au paradis, un mélange réussi*

STENDHAL
DE L'AMOUR
GILBERT CESBRON
JOURNAL SANS DATE
ROBERT LAFFONT

BOUTIQUE HOTEL PLOES

HERMOUPOLIS, SYROS

BOUTIQUE HOTEL PLOES

Apollonos Street 2, 841 00 Hermoupolis, Syros
Tel. +30 22810 793 60 · info@hotelploes.com
www.hotelploes.com

A FINE TOWNHOUSE

In the nineteenth century Syros was one of the leading places of trade in Greece: its port was more important than Piraeus, its shipyards had a global reputation, and its capital Hermoupolis was entirely worthy of its divine patron, the god Hermes. In the town center, with houses in pastel shades and numerous churches, the magnificent buildings dating from those days can still be seen: Miaouli Square, for example, paved in marble, the palatial town hall and the Apollo Theater, a miniature version of La Scala in Milan. Hotel Ploes can hold its head up high alongside these photogenic neighbors: this elegant classical building with two wings is around 150 years old and has been greatly acclaimed for its textbook restoration. The location, too, is first-class: the historic Old Town is only a few steps away, and it is only a stone's throw to the sea, as the hotel even possesses a small rocky beach. Established families once resided here. They included the Lorentzos, who are still the owners of this mansion with its eclectic atmosphere and are pleased to share their passion for history, art and literature with their guests. The latter appreciate the hand-painted coffered ceilings and Venetian chandeliers, recline in antique armchairs or on modern Barcelona chairs, browse through works from the house library, and discover on the walls original works by Greek painters of the late twentieth century, including Michalis Manousakis and Pavlos Samios. All seven bedrooms are individually furnished with every luxury amenity, including marble bathrooms. The hotel's only suite is a highlight: it has a private spa with a steam bath and a massage pool over which a replica of the famous Kouros statue of Naxos stands guard. There is no more stylish way to immerse yourself in Greece! ◆ Book to pack: "The God of Impertinence" by Sten Nadolny

DIRECTIONS *Regional airlines fly to Syros from Athens and Thessaloniki, and the island is also linked to Piraeus by ferry (2 to 4 hrs, depending on the route and type of ferry). The hotel is 4 km/2.5 miles from Syros airport and 1 km/0.5 miles from the harbor* · **RATES** *€€–€€€€* · **ROOMS** *7 rooms and 1 suite* · **FOOD** *"Cafeplous" is a café-bar serving an excellent breakfast, small Greek dishes and drinks* · **HISTORY** *The mansion was built in the nineteenth century and has been a hotel since 2008* · **X-FACTOR** *The terrace with a stunning view of the bay and the Aegean Sea*

EIN STADTPALAIS

Im 19. Jahrhundert war Syros eines der größten Handelszentren Griechenlands: Sein Hafen war bedeutender als Piräus, seine Werften besaßen Weltruf, und seine Hauptstadt Hermoupolis machte ihrem Paten, dem Gott Hermes, alle Ehre. Im Zentrum mit seinen pastellfarbenen Häusern und zahlreichen Kirchen kann man noch die Prachtbauten sehen, die damals entstanden – den mit Marmor gepflasterten Miaouli-Platz etwa, das palastartige Rathaus oder das Apollon-Theater, eine Miniaturausgabe der Mailänder Scala. Das Hotel Ploes muss sich vor solch fotogenen Nachbarn nicht verstecken: Das elegante klassizistische Gebäude mit zwei Flügeln ist rund 150 Jahre alt und erhielt für seine mustergültige Renovierung jede Menge Lob. Auch seine Lage ist erstklassig: Die historische Altstadt ist nur wenige Schritte entfernt, das Meer nur einen Katzen- beziehungsweise Hechtsprung, denn das Hotel besitzt sogar einen kleinen Felsenstrand. Einst residierten hier alteingesessene Familien, dazu gehörten auch die Lorentzos, in deren Besitz das Stadtpalais mit seiner eklektischen Atmosphäre nach wie vor ist und die gern ihre Leidenschaft für Geschichte, Kunst und Literatur mit den Gästen teilen. Man freut sich über handbemalte Kassettendecken und venezianische Lüster, sitzt in antiken Sesseln oder auf modernen Barcelona-Sesseln, schmökert in Werken aus der hauseigenen Bibliothek und entdeckt an den Wänden Originale griechischer Maler aus dem späten 20. Jahrhundert, darunter Werke von Michalis Manousakis und Pavlos Samios. Alle sieben Gästezimmer sind individuell und mit allem Luxus bis hin zu Marmorbädern ausgestattet. Ein Höhepunkt ist die einzige Suite des Hauses – sie hat ein privates Spa mit Dampfbad und Massagepool, der von einer Replik der berühmten Kouros-Statue von Naxos bewacht wird. Stilvoller kann man in Griechenland kaum abtauchen! ◆ Buchtipp: „Ein Gott der Frechheit" von Sten Nadolny

ANREISE *Nach Syros fliegen regionale Fluglinien ab Athen und Thessaloniki, zudem ist die Insel per Fähre ab Piräus erreichbar (2–4 Std., je nach Fährtyp und Route). Das Hotel ist 4 km vom Flughafen Syros und 1 km vom Hafen entfernt* · **PREISE** *€€–€€€€* · **ZIMMER** *7 Zimmer und 1 Suite* · **KÜCHE** *Die Café-Bar „Cafeplous" serviert ein feines Frühstück, kleine griechische Mahlzeiten und Drinks* · **GESCHICHTE** *Der Palazzo stammt aus dem 19. Jahrhundert und ist seit 2008 ein Hotel* · **X-FAKTOR** *Die Terrasse mit sensationellem Blick über die Bucht und die Ägäis*

UN PALAIS URBAIN

Syros a été au XIXe siècle l'un des plus grands centres commerciaux de Grèce : son port était plus important que le Pirée, ses chantiers navals renommés dans le monde entier et sa capitale, Ermoúpoli, la « ville d'Hermès », faisait honneur au dieu qui lui a donné son nom. Au centre, avec ses maisons aux couleurs pastel et ses nombreuses églises, on peut encore voir les magnifiques bâtiments construits à cette époque – la place Miaouli pavée de marbre, par exemple, l'hôtel de ville aux airs de palais ou le théâtre Apollo, une Scala de Milan en miniature. L'hôtel Ploes n'a rien à envier à ces voisins photogéniques : édifié il y a environ un siècle et demi, l'élégant bâtiment néo-classique doté de deux ailes a reçu de nombreux éloges pour sa rénovation exemplaire. Son emplacement est également privilégié : la cité historique n'est qu'à quelques pas, et il n'y a qu'un saut à faire pour être à la mer, car l'hôtel dispose même d'une petite plage rocheuse. De vieilles familles résidaient ici autrefois, c'est le cas des Lorentzo qui possèdent toujours le palais urbain à l'atmosphère éclectique et qui aiment partager leur passion pour l'histoire, l'art et la littérature avec leurs hôtes. Vous pourrez admirer les plafonds à caissons peints à la main et les lustres vénitiens, vous asseoir dans des fauteuils anciens ou dans des fauteuils Barcelona modernes, parcourir les ouvrages de la bibliothèque et découvrir sur les murs des œuvres de peintres grecs de la fin du XXe siècle, Michalis Manousakis et Pavlos Samios par exemple. Les sept chambres sont meublées de manière individuelle et dotées de tout le luxe possible, jusqu'aux salles de bains en marbre. L'un des points forts est la seule suite de la maison qui dispose d'un spa privé avec bain de vapeur et d'une piscine de massage sur laquelle veille une réplique de la célèbre statue du Kouros de Naxos. On peut difficilement s'immerger plus élégamment en Grèce ! ◆ À lire : « Hermès l'insolent » par Sten Nadolny

ACCÈS *Des compagnies aériennes régionales desservent Syros depuis Athènes et Thessalonique, et l'île est également accessible en ferry depuis le Pirée (2 à 4 h, selon le type de ferry et la route). L'hôtel est situé à 4 km de l'aéroport de Syros et à 1 km du port* · **PRIX** *€€–€€€€* · **CHAMBRES** *7 chambres et 1 suite* · **RESTAURATION** *Le café-bar « Cafeplous » propose un petit-déjeuner raffiné, de petits repas de la cuisine grecque et des boissons* · **HISTOIRE** *Le palais date du XIXe siècle, il est devenu un hôtel en 2008* · **LES « PLUS »** *La terrasse qui offre une vue sensationnelle sur la baie et la mer Égée*

2

COCO-MAT ECO RESIDENCES

VAGIA BEACH, SERIFOS

COCO-MAT ECO RESIDENCES

Vagia Beach, 840 05 Serifos
Tel. +30 210 801 06 88 and +30 694 830 31 64 · info@coco-matserifos.com
www.coco-matserifos.com

ISLAND LIFE

Like every Greek island, Serifos has its tales and legends. Perseus is said to have lived here and beheaded the sea monster Medusa. Here, too, Odysseus was kept prisoner in a cave by the treacherous Cyclops. However, the true fame of the island at the western edge of the Cyclades derives from its mineral resources: it is known as the "iron island." Iron ore was extracted in its mountains from the earliest times, on a large scale in the late nineteenth and early twentieth centuries. The buildings that accommodate the Coco-Mat Eco Residences date from this period. Greek architect George Zafiriou, who knows Serifos well, restored them on ecological lines with a fine sense of history. The interiors were designed by Ioanna Founti and Zili Karahaliou, who worked with earthy, blue and gray shades and used natural products such as chestnut wood, cotton and linen – not to mention the coconut fiber thanks to which Coco-Mat was transformed from an unknown Greek manufacturer of beds to an international success story. Even before arriving, guests can choose their favorite mattress, duvet and pillows, specify the right size of slippers, and order fresh organic ingredients if they want to cook for themselves in the little kitchen in their apartment. Then all they need to do after arriving is to enjoy the laid-back atmosphere, the idyllic beach of Vagia and the warm hospitality of the islanders. ◆ Book to pack and film to watch: "Z" by Vassilis Vassilikos; the book was made into a film by Constantin Costa-Gavras in 1969

DIRECTIONS *Serifos has no airport; fast ferries take 2 hrs 30 min to reach the island from Piraeus. The hotel provides transfer from the harbor (10 min)* · **RATES** *€€–€€€€* · **ROOMS** *13 two-story apartments with 1 or 2 bedrooms (for up to 3 or 5 guests)* · **FOOD** *All apartments have a small kitchen for self-caterers, and the lounge bar "The Space" provides Greek and Mediterranean breakfast, lunch and dinner* · **HISTORY** *The houses were built for miners in 1910; the hotel was opened in 2013* · **X-FACTOR** *The island history is preserved here*

INSELLEBEN

Wie jede griechische Insel besitzt auch Serifos seine Sagen und Legenden. So soll Perseus einst hier gelebt und das Seeungeheuer Medusa enthauptet haben und Odysseus in der Höhle eines hinterhältigen Zyklopen gefangen gehalten worden sein. Doch die wirkliche Berühmtheit der Insel am westlichen Rand der Kykladen basiert auf ihren Bodenschätzen: Als „eisernes Eiland" ist sie auch bekannt – in ihren Bergen wurde seit jeher Eisenerz abgebaut, im großen Stil Ende des 19. und Anfang des 20. Jahrhunderts. Aus dieser Epoche stammen die Häuser, die heute die Coco-Mat Eco Residences beherbergen. Der griechische Architekt und Serifos-Kenner George Zafiriou hat sie mit viel Gespür für ihre Historie ökologisch saniert. Das Interieur haben Ioanna Founti und Zili Karahaliou gestaltet, die mit Erd-, Blau- und Grautönen arbeiteten sowie mit Naturprodukten wie Kastanienholz, Baumwolle oder Leinen. Nicht zu vergessen die Kokosnussfaser, dank der Coco-Mat von einer unbekannten griechischen Bettenmanufaktur zu einer internationalen Erfolgsgeschichte wurde. Schon vor der Anreise können Gäste ihre Lieblingsmatratze, -decke und -kissen auswählen, Slipper in ihrer Größe bestellen sowie frische Bioprodukte ordern, wenn sie in der kleinen Küche ihres Apartments selbst am Herd stehen wollen. Dann bleibt vor Ort nur noch, die unkomplizierte Atmosphäre zu genießen, den idyllischen Strand von Vagia und die herzliche Gastfreundschaft der Insulaner. ◆ Buch- und Filmtipp: „Z" von Vassilis Vassilikos; das Buch wurde 1969 von Constantin Costa-Gavras verfilmt

ANREISE *Serifos hat keinen Flughafen; man erreicht die Insel in 2,5 Std. per Schnellboot ab Piräus. Vom Hafen bietet das Hotel einen Transfer an (10 min)* · **PREISE** *€€–€€€€* · **ZIMMER** *13 zweistöckige Apartments mit 1 oder 2 Schlafzimmern (für bis zu 3 oder 5 Gäste)* · **KÜCHE** *Alle Häuser besitzen eine kleine Küche für Selbstversorger. Zudem kümmert sich die Lounge-Bar „The Space" um Frühstück, Mittag- und Abendessen (griechisch-mediterran)* · **GESCHICHTE** *Die ehemaligen Bergarbeiterhäuser wurden 1910 erbaut; das Hotel eröffnete 2013* · **X-FAKTOR** *Hier wird Inselgeschichte nachhaltig bewahrt*

LA VIE INSULAIRE

Comme toutes les îles grecques, Sérifos a ses légendes et ses mythes. Selon eux, c'est ici que Persée aurait vécu et décapité la gorgone Méduse, quant à Ulysse, de retour vers sa patrie, il y aurait été emprisonné dans la grotte du cyclope Polyphème. Mais l'île située à l'extrémité occidentale des Cyclades doit surtout sa célébrité aux richesses naturelles de son sous-sol : elle est également connue sous le nom d'« île de fer » – le minerai de fer a toujours été exploité dans ses montagnes, à grande échelle à la fin du XIXe et au début du XXe siècle. Les maisons qui abritent aujourd'hui les éco-résidences Coco-Mat datent de cette époque. L'architecte grec et spécialiste de Sérifos, George Zafiriou, les a rénovées de manière écologique en faisant preuve d'un sens aigu de leur histoire. L'intérieur a été conçu par Ioanna Founti et Zili Karahaliou, qui ont privilégié les tons de terre, de bleu et de gris ainsi que des produits naturels tels que le bois de châtaignier, le coton ou le lin. Sans oublier la fibre de noix de coco, grâce à laquelle Coco-Mat, un fabricant de lits grec inconnu jusque-là, connaît aujourd'hui un succès international. Avant même leur arrivée, les clients peuvent choisir leur matelas, leur couverture et leur oreiller préférés, commander des pantoufles à leur taille et des produits biologiques frais s'ils veulent préparer eux-mêmes leurs repas dans la petite cuisine de leur appartement. Il ne reste plus qu'à profiter de l'atmosphère décontractée, de la plage idyllique de Vagia et de la chaleureuse hospitalité des habitants. ◆ À lire et à voir : « Z » par Vassilis Vassilikos ; le roman a été porté à l'écran par Constantin Costa-Gavras en 1969

ACCÈS *Sérifos n'a pas d'aéroport ; à 2,5 h en vedette à partir du Pirée. L'hôtel propose un transfert du port à l'hôtel (10 min)* · **PRIX** *€€–€€€€* · **CHAMBRES** *13 appartements de deux étages avec 1 ou 2 chambres (jusqu'à 3 ou 5 personnes)* · **RESTAURATION** *Toutes les maisons disposent d'une petite cuisine. La Lounge Bar « The Space » propose en outre petit-déjeuner, déjeuner et dîner (cuisine gréco-méditerranéenne)* · **HISTOIRE** *À l'origine destinées aux mineurs, les maisons ont été construites en 1910 ; l'hôtel a ouvert ses portes en 2013* · **LES « PLUS »** *L'histoire de l'île est durablement préservée ici*

BEACHHOUSE ANTIPAROS

APANTIMA BEACH, ANTIPAROS

BEACHHOUSE ANTIPAROS

Apantima Beach, 840 07 Antiparos
Tel. +30 22840 640 00 · info@beachhouseantiparos.com
www.beachhouseantiparos.com

RELAX!

Island-hoppers love Antiparos: the boat takes no more than seven minutes to come over from Paros. From the harbor they take a taxi to the interior of the island and explore the Spilion Agiou Ioannou dripstone cave, in which a stalagmite has been growing from the ground for 45 million years – it is said to be the oldest in Europe. After the tour, there is time for a Greek lunch in a taverna down in the town, perhaps a brisk walk to the fifteenth-century Venetian castle, and then it's time to board the ferry again. One day, one island. That's great – and it is also a pity, because Antiparos is worth a longer stay. Paros' little sister, as the island is also called, lets you take a slightly calmer approach to life. Here you have time for a gentle walk, a longer bike tour or a proper hike. Here the waters are excellent for sailing, diving, and kite-surfing, and here you can also spend an entire day on the beach, watching the waves. The Beachhouse, situated in one of the most beautiful bays on Antiparos and wonderfully sheltered from the wind, is an ideal base for a slow-motion vacation. All eight suites in the small house, which was designed by the Athenian architectural studio ARP, have a sea view, chocolate-brown concrete floors and furniture in the style of the Cyclades. Kitchenettes including a refrigerator and coffee machine are handy extras. On the beach, four large pergolas and gnarled juniper trees provide some shade, and it's only a few paces to the bar and restaurant, where traditional Greek dishes get a modern twist and hearty steaks sizzle on the barbecue. If you are still not relaxed enough after sunbathing and dining, go for yoga or a massage – and at last you will have arrived on Antiparos.
◆ Book to pack: "The Discovery of Slowness" by Sten Nadolny

DIRECTIONS *Ferries cross between Paros and Antiparos every 30 minutes, all day. The hotel is in Apantima Bay, 8 km/5 miles south of the harbor (transfer to and from the ferry is organized by the Beachhouse)* · **RATES** *€–€€€* · **ROOMS** *5 suites and 3 family suites, all with a balcony or terrace* · **FOOD** *Breakfast, lunch and dinner are served in the beach restaurant, and excellent cocktails are mixed at the 25-foot-long beach bar* · **HISTORY** *The first part of the hotel was opened in 2013, the second part and the restaurant in 2014* · **X-FACTOR** *The straightforward service*

ENTSPANNEN SIE SICH!

Inselhüpfer lieben Antiparos: Gerade einmal sieben Minuten dauert die Überfahrt von Paros. Vom Hafen aus nehmen sie sich ein Taxi ins Inselinnere und erkunden die Tropfsteinhöhle Spilion Agiou Ioannou, in der ein 45 Millionen Jahre alter Stalagmit aus dem Boden ragt – er soll der älteste in Europa sein. Nach der Tour ein griechisches Mittagessen in einer Taverne unten im Ort, vielleicht noch ein Sprung zur venezianischen Burg aus dem 15. Jahrhundert, dann geht es mit der Fähre wieder zurück. Ein Tag, eine Insel. Das ist schön – und das ist schade, denn Antiparos lohnt einen längeren Besuch. Die kleine Schwester von Paros, wie die Insel auch genannt wird, lässt das Leben ein bisschen geruhsamer angehen. Hier ist Zeit für einen gemütlichen Spaziergang, eine ausgedehnte Radtour oder Wanderung, hier gibt es herausragende Reviere für Segler, Taucher oder Kitesurfer, hier kann man auch nur einen ganzen Tag am Strand liegen und den Wellen zuschauen. Eine ideale Basis für Ferien in Zeitlupe ist dieses Beachhouse, das in einer der schönsten Buchten von Antiparos liegt, die noch dazu wunderbar windgeschützt ist. Alle acht Suiten der kleinen Anlage, die das Athener Architekturstudio ARP entworfen hat, bieten Meerblick, schokobraune Betonböden und Möbel im Stil der Kykladen – praktische Extras sind die Kitchenettes samt Kühlschrank und Kaffeemaschine. Am Strand spenden vier große Pergolas und knorrige Wacholderbäume Schatten, und es sind nur ein paar Schritte zur Bar und zum Restaurant, in dem traditionellen griechischen Gerichten ein moderner Twist verliehen wird und deftige Steaks auf dem Grill brutzeln. Wer nach dem Sonnenbaden und Essen immer noch nicht entspannt genug ist, geht zum Yoga oder zur Massage – und kommt endlich ganz auf Antiparos an. ◆ Buchtipp: „Die Entdeckung der Langsamkeit" von Sten Nadolny

ANREISE *Zwischen Paros und Antiparos pendeln die Fähren ganztags im 30-min-Takt. Das Hotel liegt in der Bucht von Apantima, 8 km südlich des Hafens (der Transfer zum/vom Haus wird organisiert)* · **PREISE** *€–€€€* · **ZIMMER** *5 Suiten und 3 Familiensuiten, alle mit Balkon oder Terrasse* · **KÜCHE** *Frühstück, Mittag- und Abendessen gibt es im Strandrestaurant. An der 8 m langen Strandbar werden gute Cocktails gemixt* · **GESCHICHTE** *2013 wurde der erste Teil des Hotels eröffnet, 2014 folgten der zweite Teil sowie das Restaurant* · **X-FAKTOR** *Der unkomplizierte Service*

DÉTENDEZ-VOUS !

Ceux qui ont l'habitude de se déplacer d'une île à l'autre apprécient Antiparos : la traversée depuis Paros ne dure que sept minutes. Arrivés dans le port, ils prennent un taxi pour se rendre à l'intérieur de l'île et explorent la grotte Spilion Agiou Ioannou qui abrite une forêt de stalactites et où s'élève ce qui est peut-être la plus ancienne stalagmite d'Europe – elle aurait 45 millions d'années. Après la visite, ils prennent un déjeuner grec dans une taverne du village, font peut-être un saut au château vénitien du XVe siècle, puis le ferry repart. Un jour, une île. C'est bien, mais c'est dommage, car Antiparos mériterait une visite plus longue. La petite sœur de Paros, comme on appelle aussi l'île, est propice à la détente. Il est temps de se promener, de faire une longue balade à vélo ou une randonnée, d'excellents endroits attendent les navigateurs, les plongeurs ou les amateurs de kite-surf, ici vous pouvez aussi simplement vous allonger sur la plage et regarder les vagues toute la journée. Située dans l'une des plus belles baies d'Antiparos, qui est également merveilleusement abritée du vent, cette maison de plage est l'endroit idéal pour passer des vacances au ralenti. Les huit suites de ce petit complexe, conçues par le studio d'architecture ARP d'Athènes, offrent toutes une vue sur la mer, un sol en béton brun chocolat et un mobilier de style cycladique. Les kitchenettes, avec réfrigérateur et cafetière électrique à café, sont très pratiques. Sur la plage, quatre grandes pergolas et des genévriers noueux fournissent de l'ombre et ne sont qu'à quelques pas du bar et du restaurant, où les plats traditionnels grecs sont revisités au goût du jour et où de copieux steaks grillent sur le barbecue. Si vous n'êtes toujours pas assez détendu après avoir pris un bain de soleil et un bon repas, allez faire du yoga ou un massage – et arrivez enfin à Antiparos. ◆ À lire : « La découverte de la lenteur » par Sten Nadolny

ACCÈS *Les ferries passent toutes les 30 min entre Paros et Antiparos pendant la journée. L'hôtel est situé dans la baie d'Apantima, à 8 km au sud du port (la maison organise le transfert aller/retour)* · **PRIX** *€–€€€* · **CHAMBRES** *5 suites et 3 suites familiales, toutes dotées d'un balcon ou d'une terrasse* · **RESTAURATION** *Le restaurant de la plage propose petit-déjeuner, déjeuner et dîner. D'excellents cocktails sont servis au bar de la plage, long de 8 m* · **HISTOIRE** *La première partie de l'hôtel a été ouverte en 2013, la seconde partie et le restaurant ont suivi en 2014* · **LES « PLUS »** *Le service, simple et efficace*

Beach House
Antiparos
Enjoy!!

VERINA ASTRA

POULATI, SIFNOS

VERINA ASTRA

Poulati, 840 03 Sifnos
Tel. +30 22840 314 40 · astra@verina.gr
www.verinahotelsifnos.com

STARRY-EYED

You could spend twenty-four hours here simply looking into the blue distance: by day the Aegean Sea shimmers azure, cobalt or turquoise, and by night the sky takes on a deep, inky color as the backdrop for twinkling and glittering – and it was the stunning view of the stars ("astra" in Greek) that gave this boutique hotel its name. Accordingly, each room has the name of a constellation, so guests sleep under the aegis of Cassiopeia, Orion or the Great Bear. What all rooms have in common is their harmonious design in subdued colors with natural materials, and that each has a veranda with an unobstructed view. But from time to time it is worth tearing yourself away from the Instagrammable panoramas to explore the picturesque island of Sifnos, where life is lived at a gentle and easy pace. Like the founder of the Verina Hotel, who was born into a local family of sailors, the members of his enthusiastic team know the island like the backs of their hands. Whether you prefer a stroll through the winding alleys in the old quarter of Apollonia, a hike to historic churches and monasteries or a boat trip to hidden coves, everything is tailored to guests' personal preferences. Those who want to get creative can take part in cookery or photography courses, or learn under the guidance of an island potter the art of ceramics, for which Sifnos has been known for thousands of years. And it goes without saying that the best pots can be decorated with starry patterns before they are fired in the kiln. ◆ Book to pack: "The Greek House: The Story of a Painter's Love Affair with the Island of Sifnos" by Christian Brechneff

DIRECTIONS *On the east coast of Sifnos, near Poulati. The island has no airport and is best reached by ferry from Piraeus (about 3 hrs) or Milos (about 1 hr)* · **RATES** *€€–€€€* · **ROOMS** *14 rooms and suites* · **FOOD** *Mediterranean fusion menus with an emphasis on Greek cooking. Many ingredients are grown in the hotel's own garden* · **HISTORY** *The Athens office of aka lab architects converted 7 existing buildings into this hotel, which opened in 2008* · **X-FACTOR** *The service is so warm-hearted that it is like spending a holiday with friends*

STERNSTUNDEN

Hier könnte man 24 Stunden am Stück einfach ins Blaue schauen: Tagsüber leuchtet die Ägäis in Azur, Kobalt oder Türkis, und nachts bekommt der Himmel einen tiefen Tintenton, vor dem es glitzert und funkelt – die sagenhafte Sicht in die Sterne (griechisch „astra") gab diesem Boutiquehotel seinen Namen. Passend dazu ist jedes Zimmer nach einem Sternbild benannt und steht beispielsweise im Zeichen der Kassiopeia, des Orion oder des Großen Bären. Allen Räumen gemeinsam ist das harmonische Design in dezenten Farben und mit natürlichen Materialien, alle verfügen auch über eine Veranda mit unverbautem Blick. Bisweilen sollte man sich aber von all den Instagram-würdigen Panoramen losreißen und die pittoreske Insel Sifnos erkunden, auf der das Leben so gemächlich wie gemütlich verläuft. Wie der Gründer der Verina-Hotels, der aus einer hiesigen Seefahrerfamilie stammt, so kennt auch sein engagiertes Team das Eiland in- und auswendig. Ob es sich um einen Bummel durch die verwinkelte Altstadt von Apollonia, eine Wanderung zu historischen Kirchen und Klöstern oder eine Bootsfahrt zu versteckten Buchten handelt: Alles wird maßgeschneidert und nach persönlichen Vorlieben zusammengestellt. Wer kreativ sein möchte, kann auch an Koch- und Fotokursen teilnehmen oder bei einem einheimischen Töpfer das Keramikkunstwerk erlernen, für das Sifnos seit Jahrtausenden bekannt ist. Dass die schönsten Stücke vor dem Brennen mit Sternenmustern verziert werden können, steht dabei natürlich außer Frage. ◆ Buchtipp: „The Greek House: The Story of a Painter's Love Affair with the Island of Sifnos" von Christian Brechneff

ANREISE *An der Ostküste von Sifnos bei Poulati gelegen. Die Insel besitzt keinen Flughafen und ist am besten per Fähre von Piräus (ca. 3 Std.) oder Milos (ca. 1 Std.) erreichbar* · **PREISE** *€€–€€€* · **ZIMMER** *14 Zimmer und Suiten* · **KÜCHE** *Mediterrane Fusion-Gerichte mit Schwerpunkt auf griechischer Küche. Zahlreiche Zutaten werden im eigenen Garten angebaut* · **GESCHICHTE** *Das Athener Büro aka lab architects wandelte sieben bestehende Gebäude zu diesem Hotel um; Eröffnung war 2008* · **X-FAKTOR** *Der herzliche Service, fast so, als würde man Ferien bei Freunden verbringen*

NUITS ÉTOILÉES

Ici, on pourrait plonger jour et nuit le regard dans le bleu : le jour, la mer Égée brille dans des tons d'azur, de cobalt ou de turquoise, et la nuit, le ciel prend l'aspect d'une encre d'un bleu profond devant laquelle brillent et scintillent les étoiles (du grec « astra ») qui ont donné leur nom à cet hôtel-boutique. Comme il se doit, chaque chambre porte le nom d'une constellation et est placée par exemple sous le signe de Cassiopée, d'Orion ou de la Grande Ourse. Toutes les chambres ont en commun un design harmonieux, des couleurs subtiles et des matériaux naturels, et toutes disposent d'une véranda avec une vue imprenable sur les environs. Mais il faut parfois s'éloigner de tous les panoramas dignes d'Instagram et explorer la pittoresque île de Sifnos, où la vie est aussi paisible que douillette. Tout comme le fondateur des hôtels Verina, issu d'une famille de marins de la région, son équipe dévouée connaît l'île sur le bout des doigts. Que ce soit une promenade dans les ruelles labyrinthiques de la cité historique d'Apollonia, une randonnée vers des églises et des monastères mémorables ou une excursion en bateau vers des baies cachées : tout est fait sur mesure et organisé selon les préférences personnelles. Ceux qui veulent être créatifs peuvent également participer à des cours de cuisine et de photographie ou apprendre chez un potier local l'art de la céramique pour lequel Sifnos est célèbre depuis des milliers d'années. Il va de soi que les plus belles pièces peuvent être décorées de motifs étoilés avant la cuisson. ◆ À lire : « L'inconnu de Sifnos » de Jean-François Dominiak

ACCÈS *Sur la côte orientale de Sifnos près de Poulati. L'île ne possède pas d'aéroport et le plus simple est de prendre le ferry au Pirée (env. 3 h) ou Milos (env. 1 h)* · **PRIX** *€€–€€€* · **CHAMBRES** *14 chambres et suites* · **RESTAURATION** *Cuisine méditerranéenne revisitée, l'accent étant porté sur la cuisine grecque. De nombreux produits frais sont cultivés dans le jardin* · **HISTOIRE** *Le cabinet athénien aka lab architects a transformé sept bâtiments existants en cet hôtel ouvert en 2008* · **LES « PLUS »** *Le service chaleureux, l'impression de passer les vacances chez des amis*

THE WINDMILL KIMOLOS

KIMOLOS

THE WINDMILL KIMOLOS

840 04 Kimolos
Tel. +30 22870 516 76 and +30 22870 516 77 · kimolos@ariahotels.gr
www.ariahotels.gr

THE SIGNS OF THE WIND

Today they are the emblems of the Cyclades and the most popular motif for tourists' photos, whereas in past times they were the engines of the economy and the communication systems of the islands: windmills, which ground grain for local farmers and at the same time served as weather stations and places to exchange news. Many of them are now empty and abandoned, but some have been turned into museums, restaurants or hotels – as in the case of this mill on Kimolos. Built about 170 years ago, painted radiant white and restored in the traditional manner, it holds five guest rooms. They are bathed in bright light, skillfully and simply furnished in shades of gray and white, and adorned with nautical accessories. Every room has its individual floor plan, often following the rounded shape of the mill, and its own terrace or balcony. The best views of the coast and sea are to be had from the Strogilo duplex suite with its stunning terrace on the first floor and from the Agnantio double room, one story higher with a miniature balcony (guests up there should be prepared for a breeze, however, as windmills usually aren't constructed in sheltered bays). The main occupations during a day here are to let your gaze sweep across the glittering blue Aegean Sea and your thoughts journey to distant horizons: Kimolos is a sleepy island, and therefore a perfect spot to switch off and put some distance between yourself and everyday life. The options for short trips include nearby beaches, the harbor at Psathi and the picturesque village of Chorio, which grew up around a fort and is worth visiting for its churches and archaeological museum. ◆ Book to pack: "Offshore" by Petros Markaris

DIRECTIONS *The volcanic island of Kimolos has no airport. It can be reached by ferry from Piraeus (4 hrs 30 min to 7 hrs 30 min, depending on the route and type of ferry) or from the neighboring island of Milos (10–25 min). The windmill stands on a hill, 600 m/2,000 feet from the harbor* · **RATES** *€–€€ (3 nights minimum stay in the main season)* · **ROOMS** *5 rooms, including 1 suite for up to 4 guests* · **FOOD** *The "Windmill Café & Bar" serves breakfast, afternoon tea and snacks. There are several restaurants at the harbor and in the village* · **HISTORY** *The windmill dates from 1852* · **X-FACTOR** *The last glass of wine in the evening beneath a starry sky*

IM ZEICHEN DES WINDES

Heute sind sie die Wahrzeichen der Kykladen und die beliebtesten Fotomotive der Touristen, früher trieben sie die Wirtschaft und Kommunikation auf den Inseln an: Die Windmühlen mahlten einst das Getreide der einheimischen Bauern und dienten zugleich als Nachrichtenzentrale und Wetterstation. Viele von ihnen stehen inzwischen leer, doch einige wurden in Museen, Restaurants oder Hotels umgewandelt – so wie diese Mühle auf Kimolos. Vor rund 170 Jahren erbaut, in strahlendes Weiß getaucht und im traditionellen Stil restauriert, bietet sie fünf Gästezimmer. Diese sind hell und lichtdurchflutet, geschickt und schnörkellos in weißen sowie grauen Tönen eingerichtet und mit maritimen Accessoires verziert. Jeder Raum hat einen individuellen Grundriss, der den zum Teil runden Formen der Mühle folgt, und eine eigene Terrasse oder einen Balkon. Die beste Sicht auf Küste und Meer eröffnen die Duplex-Suite Strogilo mit ihrer Traumterrasse im ersten Stock sowie das noch eine Etage höher gelegene Doppelzimmer Agnantio mit Miniaturbalkon (auf eine Brise muss man dort oben allerdings gefasst sein, denn Windmühlen stehen nun mal nicht in geschützten Buchten). Den Blick über die blau glitzernde Ägäis und die Gedanken in weite Ferne schweifen zu lassen, ist die Hauptbeschäftigung des Tages – Kimolos ist eine beschauliche Insel und damit ein perfekter Platz, um Abstand vom Alltag zu bekommen und abzuschalten. Kürzere Ausflüge führen zu nahen Stränden, an den Hafen von Psathi und ins pittoreske Dorf Chorio, das rund um eine Festung errichtet wurde, sehenswerte Kirchen und ein archäologisches Museum besitzt. ◆ Buchtipp: „Offshore" von Petros Markaris

ANREISE *Kimolos hat keinen Flughafen. Die Vulkaninsel ist per Fähre ab Piräus (4,5–7,5 Std., je nach Route und Fährtyp) oder von der Nachbarinsel Milos aus zu erreichen (10–25 min). Die Windmühle liegt 600 m vom Hafen entfernt auf einem Hügel* · **PREISE** *€–€€ (in der Hochsaison 3 Nächte Mindestaufenthalt)* · **ZIMMER** *5 Zimmer, darunter 1 Suite für bis zu 4 Gäste* · **KÜCHE** *In der „Windmill Café & Bar" werden Frühstück, Nachmittagstee und Snacks angeboten. Am Hafen und im Dorf gibt es mehrere Restaurants* · **GESCHICHTE** *Die Windmühle stammt aus dem Jahr 1852* · **X-FAKTOR** *Das letzte Glas am Abend unter einem mit Sternen übersäten Himmel*

SOUS LE SIGNE DU VENT

Aujourd'hui, ils sont les emblèmes des Cyclades et le motif photographique le plus apprécié des touristes. Autrefois, ils étaient le moteur de l'économie et de la communication sur les îles : les moulins à vent servaient à moudre le grain qu'apportaient les agriculteurs locaux et aussi de centre d'information et de station météorologique. Beaucoup sont vides aujourd'hui, mais certains ont été transformés en musées, restaurants ou hôtels – comme ce moulin à Kimolos. Construit il y a environ 170 ans, peint d'un blanc éclatant et restauré dans le style traditionnel, il propose cinq chambres d'hôtes. Celles-ci sont claires et lumineuses, aménagées habilement et sans fioritures dans des tons blancs et gris, et décorées d'accessoires maritimes. Chaque chambre a son plan particulier, qui suit les formes partiellement rondes du moulin, et sa propre terrasse ou un balcon. La suite duplex Strogilo avec sa terrasse de rêve, au premier étage, et la chambre double Agnantio avec balcon miniature au deuxième étage (attention, le vent souffle là-haut, les moulins à vent n'ont pas été construits dans des baies abritées) offrent la meilleure vue sur la côte et la mer. Pendant la journée, votre activité principale sera de laisser votre regard et vos pensées se perdre dans le bleu étincelant de la mer Égée et celui du ciel – Kimolos est une île tranquille et donc l'endroit parfait pour s'évader et se déconnecter. Des excursions courtes mènent aux plages voisines, au port de Psathi et au pittoresque village de Chorio, construit autour d'une forteresse, et qui possède des églises remarquables et un musée archéologique. ◆ À lire : « Offshore » par Petros Markaris

ACCÈS *Kimolos n'a pas d'aéroport. L'île volcanique peut être atteinte par ferry depuis le Pirée (de 4,5 h à 7,5 h, selon le trajet et le type de ferry) ou depuis l'île voisine de Milos (10–25 min). Le moulin à vent se dresse sur une colline, à 600 m du port* · **PRIX** *€–€€ (durant la haute saison, séjour minimum de 3 nuits)* · **CHAMBRES** *5 chambres, dont 1 suite pour 4 personnes maximum* · **RESTAURATION** *Le « Windmill Café & Bar » propose le petit-déjeuner, un goûter et des snacks. On trouve plusieurs restaurants sur le port et dans le village* · **HISTOIRE** *Le moulin à vent date de 1852* · **LES « PLUS »** *Le dernier verre sous un ciel constellé d'étoiles*

SKINOPI LODGE

MILOS

SKINOPI LODGE

Skinopi, 848 00 Milos
Tel. +30 2287 022 070 and +30 694 695 44 15 · info@skinopi.com
www.skinopi.com

WHAT A VIEW!

You need a good car and good means of finding the way to get to this lodge: a rental car with four-wheel drive and a map on paper to complement the sat nav are definitely recommended. But it is worth the effort, as the location of Skinopi Lodge is lonely and unique in equal measure: on the coast of Milos above a tiny fishing village, on a hillside full of wild flowers, herbs and olive trees, with a spectacular view across the bay. Nowhere on the island is sunset more beautiful than here. When the owner, Nausika Georgiadou, commissioned architects Maria Kokkinou and Andreas Kourkoulas to design three villas for the lodge, there were only two specifications: minimum intervention into the natural surroundings and maximum effect for the villas. They succeeded in both of these points. Built from local stone and simply fitted out in the tradition of the Cyclades, the bungalows simultaneously fit into their unspoiled environment and form a modern contrast. The gray surrounds of the windows and doors seem like picture frames that capture the wonderful scenery. Thanks to floor-to-ceiling windows and large terraces, the interior and exterior merge seamlessly. It was a wonderful design idea to place the kitchen outside. In every villa it is a fixed installation in the covered veranda, enabling residents to cook, eat and enjoy the panorama together. As Skinopi Lodge has no restaurant, all guests are self-caterers, doing their shopping in the neighboring villages: a rental car with four-wheel drive is definitely worthwhile! ◆ Book to pack: "A Poet's Journal" by Giorgos Seferis

DIRECTIONS *Milos is reached by air from Athens (45 min) or by ferry from Piraeus and Santorini (8 hrs/2 hrs). The self-catering lodge is 15 min by car from the airport, 5 min from the harbor and 10 min from the nearest food shops* · **RATES** *€€€–€€€€* · **ROOMS** *3 villas (60/645, 80/860 and 130/1,400 square meters/square feet, for 2–4 people). 2 villas can be combined. There are plans to add 4 more villas in 2021* · **FOOD** *The lodge does not have a restaurant, but a breakfast basket is provided if desired. Every villa has a small outside kitchen* · **HISTORY** *Opened in July 2016* · **X-FACTOR** *Sail in Nausika's own boat – viewing Milos from the water is a must*

SCHAU MAL!

Für die Anreise zu dieser Lodge braucht man ein gutes Auto und gute Orientierungshilfen: Ein Mietwagen mit Allradantrieb und eine Landkarte auf Papier als Ergänzung zum Navigationsgerät sind unbedingt empfehlenswert. Doch der Aufwand lohnt sich, denn die Skinopi Lodge ist so einsam wie einzigartig gelegen: an der Küste von Milos über einem winzigen Fischerdorf, an einem Hang voller Wildblumen, Kräuter und Olivenbäume und mit einem spektakulären Blick über die Bucht – schöner als hier ist der Blick in den Sonnenuntergang nirgendwo sonst auf der Insel. Als die Besitzerin Nausika Georgiadou die Architekten Maria Kokkinou und Andreas Kourkoulas mit dem Entwurf der drei Villen für die Lodge beauftragte, gab es nur zwei Prämissen: Minimal sollte der Eingriff in die Natur sein und maximal die Wirkung der Häuser. Beides ist gelungen. Aus einheimischem Stein errichtet und nach Kykladentradition schlicht ausgestattet, passen die Bungalows in die ursprüngliche Umgebung und setzen zugleich einen modernen Kontrast. Die grau eingefassten Fenster und Türen wirken wie Bilderrahmen, die die herrliche Szenerie einfangen, und dank raumhoher Glasfronten sowie großer Terrassen gehen Innen- und Außenwelt fast nahtlos ineinander über. Eine wunderbare Designidee war es, die Küche nach draußen zu verlegen – sie ist in jeder Villa fester Bestandteil der überdachten Veranda, sodass die Bewohner gemeinsam kochen, essen und das Panorama genießen können. Da die Skinopi Lodge kein Restaurant besitzt, versorgen sich alle Gäste selbst und erledigen ihre Einkäufe in den Nachbardörfern – der Mietwagen mit Allradantrieb bewährt sich über An- und Abreise hinaus! ◆ Buchtipp: „Ionische Reise“ von Giorgos Seferis

ANREISE *Milos ist mit dem Flugzeug von Athen aus (45 min) oder mit der Fähre ab Piräus und Santorin (8 bzw. 2 Std.) erreichbar. Die Selbstversorger-Lodge ist mit dem Auto 15 min vom Flughafen, 5 min vom Hafen sowie 10 min von den nächstgelegenen Lebensmittelläden entfernt* · **PREISE** *€€€–€€€€* · **ZIMMER** *3 Villen (60, 80 und 130 qm, für 2–4 Personen), 2 Villen können miteinander verbunden werden. 2021 sollen 4 weitere Villen dazukommen* · **KÜCHE** *Die Lodge hat kein Restaurant, auf Wunsch wird aber ein Frühstückskorb bereitgestellt. Jede Villa besitzt eine kleine Außenküche* · **GESCHICHTE** *Im Juli 2016 eröffnet* · **X-FAKTOR** *Ein Törn mit Nausikas eigenem Boot – Milos muss man auch vom Wasser aus erleben*

REGARDE !

Pour arriver ici, vous aurez besoin d'une bonne voiture et d'aide pour vous orienter : un quatre-quatre de location et une carte papier en plus du système de navigation sont fortement recommandés. Mais le jeu en vaut la chandelle, car le Skinopi Lodge est situé dans un endroit solitaire il est vrai, mais unique : sur la côte de Milos, au-dessus d'un minuscule village de pêcheurs, sur une pente couverte de fleurs, d'herbes sauvages et d'oliviers, qui offre une vue spectaculaire sur la baie – on peut assister ici au plus beau coucher de soleil sur l'île. Lorsque la propriétaire Nausicaa Georgiadou a chargé les architectes Maria Kokkinou et Andreas Kourkoulas de concevoir les trois villas du lodge, elle n'avait que deux exigences : l'impact environnemental devait être minime et les maisons produire l'effet maximum. Les deux ont été satisfaites. Construits en pierre locale et meublés simplement dans la tradition cycladique, les bungalows s'intègrent dans l'environnement originel tout en créant un contraste moderne. Les fenêtres et les portes encadrées de gris ressemblent à des cadres de photo dans lesquels apparaît le magnifique paysage, et, grâce aux vastes baies vitrées à hauteur de pièce et aux grandes terrasses, l'intérieur et l'extérieur se fondent presque parfaitement l'un dans l'autre. Une idée géniale a été de déplacer la cuisine à l'extérieur – dans chaque villa, elle fait partie de la véranda couverte, de sorte que les résidents peuvent cuisiner, manger et profiter ensemble du panorama. Comme le Skinopi Lodge n'a pas de restaurant, tous les clients préparent leurs repas sur place et font leurs courses dans les villages voisins – le quatre-quatre de location fait ici aussi ses preuves, au-delà de l'arrivée et du départ ! ◆ À lire : « Journal de bord » de Georges Séféris

ACCÈS *Milos est accessible en avion à partir d'Athènes (45 min) ou en ferry à partir du Pirée et de Santorin (8 h ou 2 h). Le lodge réservé à ceux qui préparent leurs repas eux-mêmes est à 15 min en voiture de l'aéroport, à 5 min du port et à 10 min des magasins d'alimentation les plus proches* · **PRIX** *€€€–€€€€* · **CHAMBRES** *3 villas (60, 80 et 130 m², pour 2–4 personnes), 2 villas peuvent être réunies. 4 autres villas supplémentaires sont prévues en 2021* · **RESTAURATION** *Le lodge ne possède pas de restaurant, un panier petit-déjeuner peut être mis à votre disposition si vous le souhaitez. Chaque villa possède une petite cuisine extérieure* · **HISTOIRE** *Ouvert en juillet 2016* · **LES « PLUS »** *Une croisière sur le bateau de Nausicaa – il faut avoir vu Milos de la mer*

ANEMOMILOS

FOLEGANDROS

ANEMOMILOS

840 11 Folegandros
Tel. +30 22860 413 09 · info@anemomiloshotel.com
www.anemomiloshotel.com

HIGH ON THE CLIFFS

Sometimes Folegandros is described as the "quiet Santorini": the houses are as brilliantly white here as on the island's big sister, the coast are just as steep, and the sunsets are no less spectacular – but Folegandros is calmer, more authentic and modest. It does not attract the party crowd and the round-the-islands trippers who visit seven islands in seven days. It is a destination for guests who appreciate a seven-day stay in the same hotel and feel more at home in a taverna alongside the locals than in an international cocktail bar. When Dimitris Patelis came to Folegandros for the first time, he immediately fell in love with this tranquil island, its residents and a plot of land on the cliffs of Chora. In a labor of love that lasted three years, he built Anemomilos, which takes its name from the windmill whose sails once turned on the site. The spacious, comfortable studio apartments of the hotel are decorated in classic Greek style in white, blue and green, and look out on the garden, the sea or Chora, which once won a prize as one of Europe's most beautiful villages. Some of the apartments have a view of the equally photogenic Panagia church, which stands majestically on the hillside above the village and can be approached on a zigzag path paved with light-colored stone. It is said to be the scene where a well-known tale of the island played out: according to popular belief, pirates long ago stole an icon of the Virgin Mary from the altar – but had not reckoned with the wrath of God. Their ship sank shortly afterwards in the depths of the Aegean, and by miraculous or divine means the precious looted icon found its way back to the church. ◆ Book to pack: "Mission Box" by Aris Alexandrou

DIRECTIONS *The island has no airport. Ferries come from Santorini (50 min), Milos (1 hr), Naxos (3 hrs 20 min) and Piraeus (4 hrs 40 min). The distance from the hotel to the harbor is 3.5 km/2 miles* · **RATES** *€€ (3–5 nights minimum stay in the high season)* · **ROOMS** *17 studios and family studios, each with a kitchenette* · **FOOD** *The restaurant next to the pool provides a superb panorama and Greek dishes with an international touch* · **HISTORY** *Opened in 1993* · **X-FACTOR** *Warm-hearted hosts who personally take care of every wish*

HOCH AUF DEN KLIPPEN

Manche bezeichnen Folegandros als das „stille Santorin“: Die Häuser sind hier ebenso strahlend weiß wie die der großen Schwester, die Küsten ebenso steil und die Sonnenuntergänge ebenso spektakulär – doch es ist ruhiger, authentischer und bescheidener. Folegandros lockt kein Partypublikum und keine Rundreisenden an, die sieben Kykladeninseln innerhalb von sieben Tagen besichtigen wollen. Hierher kommen Gäste, für die eine Woche im selben Hotel ein Geschenk ist und die sich in einer Taverne neben Einheimischen wohler fühlen als in einer internationalen Cocktailbar. Als Dimitris Patelis zum ersten Mal auf Folegandros war, verliebte er sich auf den ersten Blick in diese unaufgeregte Insel, in ihre Bewohner und in ein Grundstück auf den Klippen von Chora. Hier erbaute er in drei Jahren und mühevoller Kleinarbeit das Anemomilos, das seinen Namen von der Windmühle bekam, deren Flügel sich einst an derselben Stelle drehten. Die geräumigen und komfortablen Studios des Hotels sind im klassischen griechischen Stil in Weiß, Blau und Grün gehalten und schauen auf den Garten, aufs Meer oder auf Chora, das als eines der schönsten Dörfer Europas prämiert wurde. Von einigen Apartments sieht man auch die ebenso fotogene Panagia-Kirche, die majestätisch am Hang über dem Dorf steht und über einen mit hellen Steinen eingefassten Zickzackweg erreichbar ist. Sie soll Schauplatz einer bekannten Inselsage gewesen sein: Der Volksmund erzählt, dass vor langer Zeit Piraten eine Ikone der Jungfrau Maria aus dem Altarraum raubten – doch dabei nicht mit noch höherer Gewalt gerechnet hatten ... Ihr Schiff versank kurz darauf in den Fluten der Ägäis, und die wertvolle Beute fand ihren Weg wie durch Zauber- beziehungsweise Gotteshand zurück in die Kirche. ◆ Buchtipp: „Die Kiste“ von Aris Alexandrou

ANREISE *Die Insel hat keinen Flughafen, Fährverbindungen gibt es ab Santorin (50 min), Milos (1 Std.), Naxos (3 Std. 20 min) oder Piräus (4 Std. 40 min). Das Hotel ist 3,5 km vom Hafen entfernt* · **PREISE** *€€ (in der Hochsaison 3–5 Nächte Mindestaufenthalt)* · **ZIMMER** *17 Studios und Familienstudios, alle mit Kitchenette* · **KÜCHE** *Das Restaurant am Pool bietet ein traumhaftes Panorama und griechische Gerichte mit internationalen Akzenten* · **GESCHICHTE** *1993 eröffnet* · **X-FAKTOR** *Die herzlichen Gastgeber, die sich um jedes Anliegen persönlich kümmern*

LÀ-HAUT SUR LES FALAISES

Certains appellent Folégandros la « Santorin tranquille » : les maisons sont ici aussi blanches que celles de leur grande sœur, les côtes sont tout aussi escarpées et les couchers de soleil tout aussi spectaculaires – mais l'île est plus calme, plus authentique et plus modeste. Folégandros n'attire pas les fêtards ni les touristes qui veulent visiter sept îles des Cyclades en sept jours. Elle attire ceux pour qui passer une semaine dans le même hôtel est un cadeau et qui se sentent plus à l'aise dans une taverne à côté des gens du cru que dans un bar à cocktail international. Lorsque Dimitris Patelis a vu Folégandros pour la première fois, il a eu le coup de foudre pour cette île reposante, ses habitants et un terrain sur les falaises de Chora. C'est là qu'il a construit l'Anemomilos, qui doit son nom au moulin à vent dont les ailes tournaient autrefois au même endroit – le travail pénible et minutieux a duré trois ans. Les studios spacieux et confortables de l'hôtel sont décorés dans le style grec classique en blanc, bleu et vert et donnent sur le jardin, la mer ou sur Chora, qui a été récompensé comme l'un des plus beaux villages d'Europe. De certains appartements, on peut également voir l'église Panagia, tout aussi remarquable, qui se dresse majestueusement sur le flanc de la colline au-dessus du village et à laquelle on peut accéder par un chemin en zigzag bordé de pierres de couleur claire. On dit qu'elle a été le théâtre d'une célèbre légende insulaire : jadis, des pirates ont volé une icône de la Vierge Marie dans le sanctuaire – sans s'imaginer que des forces supérieures puissent en prendre ombrage... Leur navire a coulé un peu plus tard dans la mer Égée et le précieux butin a retrouvé son chemin vers l'église comme par magie ou par la toute-puissance divine. ◆ À lire : « La caisse » par Aris Alexandrou

ACCÈS *L'île n'a pas d'aéroport, des liaisons par ferry sont possibles depuis Santorin (50 min), Milos (1 h), Naxos (3 h 20) ou le Pirée (4 h 40). L'hôtel est situé à 3,5 km du port* · **PRIX** *€€ (durant la haute saison, séjour minimum de 3–5 nuits)* · **CHAMBRES** *17 studios et studios familiaux, tous avec kitchenette* · **RESTAURATION** *Le restaurant au bord de la piscine offre un panorama de rêve et sert des plats grecs aux accents internationaux* · **HISTOIRE** *Ouvert en 1993* · **LES « PLUS »** *Les hôtes chaleureux qui s'occupent de tout personnellement*

PERIVOLAS

OIA, SANTORINI

PERIVOLAS

Oia, 847 02 Santorini
Tel. +30 22860 713 08 · info@perivolas.gr
www.perivolas.gr

NEW HORIZONS

The sunset is the jewel in Santorini's crown. On clear summer evenings it delivers a show of superlatives, a play of colors in pink, violet and blue until the sun, an orange-red fireball, sinks into the shimmering Aegean and is extinguished. An unforgettable, cinematic, romantic spectacle – one that unfortunately must be shared with countless other admirers who stand shoulder to shoulder at the rim of the crater or queue in front of the bars that claim the "best view" on the island. But there is one exception: those lucky enough to be able to stay in Perivolas enjoy the sunset exclusively from their own private veranda. Once, fishermen and farmers lived in these cave-like houses, built into the vineyard slopes of soft lava rock. The hill encloses a central terrace like an amphitheater. In the late 1960s Manos Psychas, formerly a captain in the Greek navy, and his sister Nadia started to transform the caves into hideaways – with vaulted whitewashed ceilings, furniture manufactured on the island and radiantly colorful fabrics. Some suites even offer the luxury of their own pools; these are situated less spectacularly, however, than the infinity pool, whose water seems to flow directly over the cliffs into the sea. Right next to the pool is the restaurant, which serves Mediterranean menus for hotel guests only. They eat by candlelight – and naturally only after sunset, when Santorini's jewel has completed its performance. ◆ Book to pack: "Byron: A Portrait" by Leslie A. Marchand

DIRECTIONS *Located near Oía, 16 km/10 miles from the airport, 19 km/12 miles from Santorini harbor. The nearest beaches are 3 km/2 miles away* · **RATES** *€€€€* · **ROOMS** *20 studios and suites, each with a private patio* · **FOOD** *The restaurant is housed in a former wine cellar, and diners can also sit outside on the pool terrace* · **HISTORY** *The cave dwellings were built more than 300 years ago. The hotel originated in the 1960s and was completed in the middle of the first decade of this century* · **X-FACTOR** *Trips in the hotel's own boat*

NEUE HORIZONTE

Der Star von Santorin ist der Sonnenuntergang. Er liefert an klaren Sommerabenden eine Show der Superlative, ein Farbenspiel in Rosa, Violett und Blau, an dessen Ende die Sonne wie ein orangeroter Feuerball in die dunkel schimmernde Ägäis abtaucht und erlischt. Ein unvergessliches, leinwandtaugliches und romantisches Schauspiel – das man nur leider mit ungezählten anderen Bewunderern teilen muss, die am Kraterrand Schulter an Schulter stehen oder in langen Schlangen vor den Bars warten, die mit dem „besten Blick" der Insel werben. Eine Ausnahme gibt es jedoch: Wer das Glück hat, im Perivolas wohnen zu können, genießt den Sonnenuntergang exklusiv von seiner privaten Veranda aus. Einst lebten Fischer und Bauern in diesen höhlenartigen Häusern, die in den Weinberg aus weichem Lavagestein gebaut worden waren. Wie ein Amphitheater fasst der Berg eine zentrale Terrasse ein. Manos Psychas, ehemals Kapitän bei der griechischen Marine, und seine Frau Nadia begannen Ende der 1960er, die Höhlen in Hideaways zu verwandeln – mit gewölbten, weiß getünchten Decken, auf der Insel gefertigten Möbeln sowie leuchtend bunten Stoffen. Manche Suiten bieten heute sogar den Luxus eigener Pools; diese liegen aber nicht ganz so spektakulär wie der Infinitypool, dessen Wasser über die Klippen direkt ins Meer zu fließen scheint. Gleich neben dem Becken befindet sich das Restaurant, das ausschließlich für Hotelgäste mediterrane Menüs serviert. Gegessen wird im Kerzenschein – und natürlich erst nach Sonnenuntergang, nachdem der Star von Santorin seinen Auftritt hatte. ◆ Buchtipp: „Lord Byron. Briefe und Tagebücher", herausgegeben von Leslie A. Marchand

ANREISE *Bei Oia gelegen, 16 km vom Flughafen Santorin und 19 km vom Hafen entfernt. Die nächstgelegenen Strände sind 3 km entfernt* · **PREISE** *€€€€* · **ZIMMER** *20 Studios und Suiten, alle mit privater Terrasse* · **KÜCHE** *Das Restaurant entstand in einem ehemaligen Weinkeller. Man kann auch draußen auf der Poolterrasse sitzen* · **GESCHICHTE** *Die Höhlenwohnungen entstanden vor mehr als 300 Jahren. Die Anfänge des Hotels gehen in die 1960er-Jahre zurück, Mitte der 2000er-Jahre wurde es fertiggestellt* · **X-FAKTOR** *Die Ausflüge mit dem hoteleigenen Boot*

DE NOUVEAUX HORIZONS

À Santorin, le coucher de soleil est un rendez-vous à ne pas manquer. Par les claires soirées d'été, il offre un spectacle de superlatifs, un jeu de couleurs rose, violet et bleu, à la fin duquel le soleil, comme une boule de feu rouge orangé, plonge dans la mer Égée sombre et scintillante avant de s'éteindre. Un spectacle inoubliable et romantique qu'il faut malheureusement partager avec d'innombrables autres admirateurs qui se tiennent côte à côte au bord du cratère ou qui font la queue devant les bars annonçant la « meilleure vue » de l'île. Toutefois, il y a une exception : ceux qui ont la chance de séjourner à Perivolas peuvent profiter en exclusivité du coucher de soleil depuis leur véranda privée. Des pêcheurs et des agriculteurs vivaient autrefois dans ces logements aménagés dans des grottes creusées dans le basalte, au cœur du vignoble. Tel un amphithéâtre, la montagne entoure une terrasse centrale. À la fin des années 1960, Manos Psychas, un ancien capitaine de la marine grecque, et sa femme Nadia ont commencé à aménager dans les grottes des refuges aux plafonds voûtés et blanchis à la chaux, les dotant de meubles de fabrication locale et de tissus aux couleurs vives. Certaines suites offrent même aujourd'hui le luxe d'une piscine privée, mais celles-ci n'offrent pas une vue aussi spectaculaire que la piscine à débordement, dont l'eau semble couler directement dans la mer par-dessus les falaises. Juste à côté de la piscine se trouve le restaurant réservé aux clients de l'hôtel qui leur propose des menus méditerranéens. Le dîner est servi aux chandelles – et bien sûr à la nuit tombée, après que la star de Santorin a eu son moment de gloire. ◆ À lire : « Lord Byron. Selected letters and journals » édité par Leslie A. Marchand

ACCÈS *À proximité d'Oia, à 16 km de l'aéroport de Santorin et 19 km du port. Les plages les plus proches sont à 3 km* · **PRIX** *€€€€* · **CHAMBRES** *20 studios et suites, tous avec terrasse privée* · **RESTAURATION** *Le restaurant a été aménagé dans une ancienne cave à vins. On peut aussi s'asseoir à l'extérieur, sur la terrasse de la piscine* · **HISTOIRE** *Les habitations troglodytes ont été créées il y a plus de trois siècles. Les débuts de l'hôtel datent des années 1960, les travaux ont été terminés au milieu des années 2000* · **LES « PLUS »** *Les excursions avec le bateau de l'hôtel*

MYSTIQUE

OIA, SANTORINI

MYSTIQUE

Oia, 847 02 Santorini
Tel. +30 22860 711 14 · info@mystique.gr
www.mystique.gr

MYTH AND MAGIC

It is said to have been created from a lump of earth that was thrown into the sea from on board the "Argo." It was called Kalliste ("the most beautiful"), Thera ("spoils of the hunt") and Strongyle ("the round one") – until one of the biggest volcanic eruptions of all time gave it its crescent shape. It inspires archaeologists to speculate whether it was Minoan culture or the legendary Atlantis that perished here: Santorini really cannot lament any lack of history and stories. Many of them are told by the caldera – the crater whose rocky walls plunge a thousand feet down, deep into the Aegean, and which is best marveled at from the village of Oia. In its immediate vicinity, the Mystique has been built on a slope in the style typical of the country. However, only the shape of the suites and villas recalls the traditional cave dwellings of the island – everything else is light and luxurious. Architect Mary Kavagia and interior designer Frank Lefebvre have created rooms like a symphony in white and at the same time ensured that they do not make a cool or clinical impression: handmade furniture and items produced from driftwood such as mirror frames and lamp bases were designed exclusively for the hotel and bring nature inside – consciously plain and simple, unfinished and original. Outside every room, a terrace covered with a canvas canopy allows the interior and exterior worlds to merge almost imperceptibly. In the daytime guests look far out to sea from the veranda; at night they drink a glass of wine here by candlelight – and discover that Santorini is not merely myth, but also pure magic. ◆ Book to pack: "Secrets of Santorini" by Patricia Wilson

DIRECTIONS *Located in north Santorini, 15 km/9 miles from the airport and 19 km/12 miles from the harbor* · **RATES** *€€€€* · **ROOMS** *41 suites and villas, all with sea view, some with an outdoor Jacuzzi and/or a private pool* · **FOOD** *Diners enjoy modern Greek menus at the open-air restaurant "Charisma," sushi at "Asea" and dishes of the day at the casual "Captain's Lounge." There is also a pool bar and a first-class wine cellar* · **HISTORY** *Opened in May 2007, now a member of the Marriott Luxury Collection* · **X-FACTOR** *The two pools with a panoramic view*

MYTHOS UND MAGIE

Sie soll aus einem Klumpen Erde entstanden sein, der von Bord der „Argo" ins Meer geworfen wurde. Sie hieß Kalliste („die Schönste"), Thera („Jagdbeute") und Strongyle („die Runde") – so lange, bis ihr eine der gewaltigsten Vulkaneruptionen aller Zeiten ihre sichelförmige Gestalt gab. Sie lässt Archäologen spekulieren, ob hier die minoische Kultur unterging oder das sagenumwobene Atlantis: Santorin kann über einen Mangel an Geschichte und Geschichten wahrlich nicht klagen. Viele von ihnen erzählt die Caldera – der Krater, dessen Felswände bis zu 300 Meter tief in die Ägäis abfallen und den man am besten vom Dorf Oia aus bewundert. Ganz in der Nähe wurde das Mystique im landestypischen Stil an den Hang gebaut. An die traditionellen Höhlenwohnungen der Insel erinnert in den Suiten und Villen nur noch die Form – alles andere ist licht, leicht und luxuriös. Die Architektin Mary Kavagia und der Interiordesigner Frank Lefebvre haben die Räume wie eine Sinfonie in hellen Tönen gestaltet und zugleich dafür gesorgt, dass das Interieur nicht kühl oder aseptisch wirkt: Handgefertigte Holzmöbel sowie Objekte aus Treibholz wie Spiegelrahmen oder Lampenfüße wurden exklusiv für das Hotel entworfen und bringen die Natur ins Haus; bewusst schlicht, unvollkommen und ursprünglich. Die Terrassen vor allen Zimmern sind mit Segeltuch überspannt, das Innen- und Außenbereiche miteinander verschmelzen lässt. Von hier aus blickt man tagsüber weit übers Meer, und abends trinkt man hier ein Glas Wein im Kerzenschein – und entdeckt dabei, dass Santorin nicht nur ein Mythos ist, sondern auch pure Magie. ◆ Buchtipp: „Tagebuch einer Ewigkeit. Am Set mit Angelopoulos" von Petros Markaris

ANREISE *Im Norden Santorins gelegen, 15 km vom Flughafen der Insel und 19 km vom Hafen entfernt* · **PREISE** *€€€€* · **ZIMMER** *41 Villen und Suiten, alle mit Meerblick und zum Teil mit Außenjacuzzi und/oder Privatpool* · **KÜCHE** *Im Restaurant „Charisma" isst man unter freiem Himmel moderne griechische Menüs, im „Asea" Sushi und in der legeren „Captain's Lounge" Tagesgerichte. Zudem gibt es eine Poolbar und einen erstklassigen Weinkeller* · **GESCHICHTE** *Im Mai 2007 eröffnet und heute Mitglied der Luxury Collection von Marriott* · **X-FAKTOR** *Die zwei Panoramapools*

MYTHE ET MAGIE

Selon la légende, elle serait née d'une motte de terre que les marins de l'« Argo » aurait jetée dans la mer. Elle s'appela Kallisté (« la très belle »), Théra (« la sauvage ») et Strongylé (« la ronde »), jusqu'au jour où l'une des plus grandes éruptions volcaniques de tous les temps lui donna sa forme de faucille. Les archéologues pensent qu'elle aurait causé la disparition de la civilisation minoenne – ou celle de la légendaire Atlantide. Santorin peut donc s'enorgueillir de son histoire et de ses nombreuses légendes. Beaucoup sont racontées par la caldeira, ce cratère dont les parois sombrent dans la mer Egée jusqu'à 300 mètres de profondeur et que l'on peut le mieux admirer depuis le village d'Oia. Non loin de là, vous trouverez le Mystique construit à flanc de falaise dans le style typique de l'île. Ses suites n'ont gardé des logements troglodytiques traditionnels que la forme, le reste n'est que lumière, légèreté et luxe. L'architecte Mary Kavagia et le décorateur Frank Lefebvre ont aménagé ces pièces rondes dans une symphonie de blanc, tout en veillant à ce que l'intérieur ne paraisse pas froid ni aseptisé. Les meubles en bois faits à la main et les objets en bois flotté tels que les cadres de miroir et les pieds de lampe ont été conçus exclusivement pour l'hôtel et font entrer la nature dans la maison ; tout est délibérément simple, imparfait et authentique. De la toile à voile est tendue au-dessus des terrasses devant toutes les chambres, ce qui permet de faire fusionner l'intérieur et l'extérieur. D'ici, vous aurez dans la journée une vue imprenable sur la mer. Le soir, vous y prendrez un verre à la lueur de bougies et vous découvrirez que Santorin n'est pas seulement un mythe, mais aussi pure magie. ◆ À lire : « Journal de la nuit » par Petros Markaris

ACCÈS *Au nord de Santorin, à 15 km de l'aéroport de l'île et à 19 km du port* · **PRIX** *€€€€* · **CHAMBRES** *41 suites et villas, toutes avec vue sur la mer, en partie avec jacuzzi extérieur et/ou piscine privée* · **RESTAURATION** *Le restaurant « Charisma » sert en plein air une cuisine grecque moderne, l'« Asea » des sushis, et le bar sans chichis « Captain' Lounge » propose des plats du jour. Il y a aussi un pool bar et une cave exceptionnelle* · **HISTOIRE** *L'hôtel a ouvert ses portes en 2007 et est aujourd'hui membre de la Luxury Collection du Marriot* · **LES « PLUS »** *Les deux piscines panoramiques*

HOTEL ARCHONTIKO ANGELOU

ALINDA, LEROS

HOTEL ARCHONTIKO ANGELOU

Alinda, 854 00 Leros
Tel. +30 22470 227 49 and +30 694 490 81 82 · marianna.angelou@gmail.com
www.hotel-angelou-leros.com

QUIET LEROS

This villa is a Mediterranean bed & breakfast taken straight from a picture postcard: set in an enchanted garden, with a mansion-like façade painted in a dark red peony shade that Farrow & Ball could not have blended more tastefully, the rooms filled with antiques, floral fabrics and lace covers (but deliberately without TV sets!). It is romantic and a little bit old-fashioned, it has charm and just enough patina to be a home and not a hotel – and it is one of those places from which you would rather write a postcard than send snapshots from a smartphone. Since the mid-1970s, the family of Marianna Angelou has been sharing its home with travelers who would like to experience rural, tranquil Leros. As the recent history of the island has not always been untroubled, and as it is not a typical destination with the wide sandy beaches that attract package tours, tourism has arrived here in a relatively gentle way – Leros can still be explored at a slow pace and in the manner of the locals. Marianna is pleased to reveal her favorite excursions for visitors, and sets them up in the morning with a healthy breakfast that is vegetarian, largely vegan, and gluten-free as well. The hostess is famous for her homemade jams, using fruit that she grows herself, and for the bread and cake that she bakes. For guests who cannot get enough of her delicious treats, she prepares a midday picnic basket with sandwiches and salads. On request she even serves a snack in the evening, so that there is no need to leave this wonderful bed & breakfast for dinner. ◆ Book to pack: "The Greek Vegetarian Cookbook" by Heather Thomas

DIRECTIONS *Leros lies in the southern Aegean Sea. The island can be reached from Athens by air (45 min) or by ferry: the neighboring islands are Kalymnos (45 min) and Kos (1 hr 30 min to 2 hrs 30 min, depending on the ferry). The villa is situated in the northeast of Leros, 5 km/3 miles from the airport and 7 km/4 miles from the harbor* · **RATES** *€* · **ROOMS** *6 rooms and 2 suites (the latter for up to 4 guests) in the villa. 1 room in an adjacent building that was previously used for pressing and storing wine, now the home of the owner* · **FOOD** *Breakfast is served wherever guests wish: on the veranda, in the garden, on the private balconies that belong to several of the rooms, or even in bed* · **HISTORY** *The villa was built in 1895 and has always been owned by the Angelou family. It was renovated thoroughly in 2005–2006* · **X-FACTOR** *The beach at Alinda is only a few minutes' walk away*

DAS LEISE LEROS

Diese Villa ist ein mediterranes Bed & Breakfast wie aus dem Bilderbuch: in einem verwunschenen Garten gelegen, mit einer schlösschenartigen Fassade in einem dunklen Pfingstrosenton, den Farrow & Ball nicht hätte schöner mischen können, und Zimmern voller Antiquitäten, Blümchenstoffen und Spitzendecken (und bewusst ohne Fernseher!). Sie ist romantisch und ein bisschen altmodisch, hat Charme und gerade so viel Patina, dass sie ein Heim ist und kein Hotel – sie ist noch einer jener Orte, von denen man lieber Postkarten als Smartphone-Schnappschüsse verschicken möchte. Schon seit Mitte der 1970er-Jahre teilt die Familie von Marianna Angelou ihr Anwesen mit Reisenden, die das ländliche und zurückgezogene Leros kennenlernen möchten. Da die jüngere Geschichte der Insel nicht immer einfach war und sie nicht zu den typischen Pauschalreisezielen mit breiten Sandstränden gehört, hat der Tourismus hier vergleichsweise sanft eingesetzt – Leros lässt sich noch in langsamem Tempo und nach Art der Einheimischen erleben. Marianna verrät ihren Besuchern gerne ihre liebsten Ausflugsziele und stärkt sie morgens mit einem gesunden Frühstück, das vegetarisch und weitgehend vegan sowie glutenfrei ist. Für ihre hausgemachten Marmeladen mit Obst aus eigenem Anbau und für ihre selbst gebackenen Brote und Kuchen ist die Hausherrin berühmt. Gästen, die von ihren Köstlichkeiten nicht genug bekommen können, stellt sie mittags einen Picknickkorb mit Sandwiches und Salaten zusammen. Auf besonderen Wunsch serviert sie sogar abends eine Kleinigkeit, sodass man das wunderbare Bed & Breakfast zum Dinner nicht verlassen muss. ◆ Buchtipp: „Tante Poppis Küche. Griechische vegetarische Familienrezepte“ von Nikoletta Bousdoukou und Theopoula Kechagia

ANREISE *Leros liegt in der südlichen Ägäis. Die Insel ist per Flug von Athen aus erreichbar (45 min) oder per Fähre: Die nächsten Inseln sind Kalymnos (45 min) und Kos (1,5–2,5 Std., je nach Fähre). Die Villa im Nordosten von Leros ist 5 km vom Flughafen und 7 km vom Hafen entfernt* · **PREISE** *€* · **ZIMMER** *6 Zimmer und 2 Suiten (diese für bis zu 4 Gäste) in der Villa. 1 Zimmer in einem Nebenhaus, das früher als Weinpresse sowie -lager diente und in dem heute auch die Besitzerin wohnt* · **KÜCHE** *Frühstück wird serviert, wo man will: auf der Veranda, im Garten, auf den privaten Balkonen, die einige Zimmer haben, und sogar im Bett* · **GESCHICHTE** *Die Villa stammt aus dem Jahr 1895 und gehört seit jeher der Familie Angelou. 2005/2006 wurde sie grundlegend renoviert* · **X-FAKTOR** *Der Strand von Alinda ist nur wenige Gehminuten entfernt*

LEROS LA LÉGÈRE

Cette villa est un Bed & Breakfast méditerranéen qui semble tout droit sorti d'un livre d'images. Elle est située dans un jardin enchanteur, avec une façade évoquant celle d'un château dans un ton rose pivoine poudré que Farrow & Ball n'aurait pas pu mieux mélanger, et abritant des pièces remplies d'antiquités, de tissus fleuris et de nappes en dentelle (et délibérément sans télévision !). Romantique et un peu désuète, la villa a du charme et juste assez de patine pour être une maison où on se sent bien et non un hôtel – c'est encore un de ces endroits où l'on préfère envoyer des cartes postales que des photos de smartphones. Depuis le milieu des années 1970, la famille de Marianna Angelou partage sa propriété avec des voyageurs qui veulent découvrir Leros, une région rurale et isolée. Comme l'histoire récente de l'île n'a pas toujours été facile et qu'elle ne fait pas partie des destinations de vacances à forfait typiques offrant de vastes plages de sable, le tourisme y a été introduit en douceur – Leros peut encore être vécue à un rythme lent et en suivant le mode de vie de ses habitants. Marianna révèle volontiers ses destinations préférées à ses visiteurs et leur donne des forces le matin en préparant un petit-déjeuner végétarien, largement végétalien, et sans gluten. La propriétaire est célèbre pour ses confitures maison faites avec les fruits du verger et pour son pain et sa pâtisserie. Pour les clients qui ne peuvent pas se passer de ses délicatesses, elle prépare un panier de pique-nique avec des sandwiches et des salades pour le déjeuner. Elle sert même sur demande une collation le soir, afin que vous n'ayez pas à quitter le merveilleux Bed & Breakfast pour dîner. ◆ À lire : « La cuisine grecque végétarienne » par Heather Thomas

ACCÈS *Leros est située dans le sud de la mer Égée. L'île est accessible par avion depuis Athènes (45 min) ou par ferry : les îles les plus proches sont Kalymnos (45 min) et Kos (1,5 h à 2,5 h, selon le ferry). La villa au nord-est de Leros se trouve à 5 km de l'aéroport et à 7 km du port* · **PRIX** *€* · **CHAMBRES** *6 chambres et 2 suites (pour 4 personnes maximum) dans la villa. 1 chambre dans une maison annexe, qui servait autrefois de pressoir et de dépôt et dans laquelle la propriétaire habite aussi aujourd'hui* · **RESTAURATION** *Le petit-déjeuner est servi où on veut : sur la véranda, au jardin, sur les balcons privés que possèdent quelques chambres et même au lit* · **HISTOIRE** *La villa date de 1895 et appartient depuis à la famille Angelou. Elle a été entièrement rénovée en 2005/2006* · **LES « PLUS »** *La plage d'Alinda est à quelques minutes de marche seulement*

OKU KOS

MARMARI, KOS

OKU KOS

Sikamini, Marmari, 853 00 Kos
Tel. +30 2242 440 380 · info.kos@okuhotels.com
www.okuhotels.com

LUXURIOUS AND LAID-BACK

A long time ago, the good reputation of Kos was based primarily on medicine: Hippocrates, the most famous doctor of the ancient world, was born on the island in about 460 BCE. Kos had the world's best schools of medicine and one of the foremost places of healing and hospitals, the Asclepieion, dedicated to Asclepius, the god of healing. Its ruins can still be admired. Today, fortunately, more sun seekers and active vacationers than doctors and patients travel to Kos. The attractions in the interior of the island are varied routes for walkers and cyclists, the summer wind Meltemi blows surfers and sailors across the water off the coast, and the sandy beaches are among the finest in all of Greece. On one of these stunning beaches – one that is, moreover, private and thus undisturbed – lies the Oku Kos. The Athens architectural firm Mastrominas has laid it out on the model of a typical island village, while giving a modern interpretation to this old theme and a thoroughly minimalistic design to the one- and two-story white cubes. The buildings are linked by quiet paths, lined by olive trees, palms and lavender bushes, and lead past many a surprising detail, whether hidden outdoor stairs or a bench for a contemplative break. The interior design of the rooms, bungalows, suites and pool villas is the work of Lambs and Lions from Berlin, who achieved a skillful balancing act between the luxurious and the laid-back, using natural materials such as stone and untreated wood as well as subdued earthy colors. Greek herbal oils and Aegean sea salt are used in the equally stylish spa. Its wellness menu features a whole-body massage according to Hippocrates – the master himself would surely have felt relaxed from head to toe! ◆ Book to pack: "Mythos, the Greek Myths Retold" by Stephen Fry

DIRECTIONS *The hotel is located on the north coast, about 11 km/7 miles from Kos international airport* · **RATES** *€€–€€€€* · **ROOMS** *44 rooms, 47 suites, 6 bungalows, 3 villas (all with a terrace, some with a shared or private pool); adults only* · **FOOD** *"To Kima" is a restaurant, bar and beach club all in one, serving Greek dishes based on island recipes using fresh, local ingredients* · **HISTORY** *Built in 2017 and operated by Oku Hotels since 2020* · **X-FACTOR** *The yoga classes in the beach pavilion*

LUXURIÖS UND LÄSSIG

Vor langer Zeit verdankte Kos seinen guten Ruf vor allem der Medizin: Auf der Insel wurde um 460 v. Chr. Hippokrates geboren, der berühmteste Arzt des Altertums. Hier gab es eine der besten Ärzteschulen der Welt und eines der bedeutendsten Kur- und Krankenhäuser – das dem Heilgott Asklepios geweihte Asklepieion, dessen Ruinen man heute noch bewundern kann. Inzwischen reisen nach Kos aber glücklicherweise mehr Aktivurlauber und Sonnenanbeter als Ärzte und Patienten. Im Landesinneren locken abwechslungsreiche Wander- und Radrouten, vor der Küste lassen sich Surfer und Segler vom Sommerwind Meltemi übers Wasser wehen, und die Sandstrände gehören zu den schönsten, die Griechenland zu bieten hat. An einem dieser traumhaften Strände – der noch dazu privat und somit ungestört ist – liegt das Oku Kos. Das Athener Architekturbüro Mastrominas hat es nach dem Vorbild eines typischen Inseldorfs angelegt, dabei das alte Thema jedoch modern interpretiert und die ein- und zweistöckigen weißen Kuben ganz minimalistisch entworfen. Verbunden sind die Gebäude durch stille Wege, die von Olivenbäumen, Palmen und Lavendelbüschen gesäumt werden und immer wieder an überraschenden Details vorbeiführen, sei es eine versteckte Außentreppe oder eine Bank zum Innehalten. Das Interiordesign der Zimmer, Bungalows, Suiten und Poolvillen stammt von Lambs and Lions (Berlin), die mit Naturmaterialien wie Stein und unbehandeltem Holz sowie gedeckten Erdtönen gekonnt zwischen Luxus und Lässigkeit balancieren. Ebenso stilvoll ist das Spa gehalten, in dem griechische Kräuteröle und Meersalz aus der Ägäis verwendet werden und sogar eine Ganzkörpermassage nach Art des Hippokrates auf dem Wellness-Menü steht – sie hätte bestimmt auch den Meister selbst rundum entspannt! ◆ Buchtipp: „Mythos“ von Stephen Fry

ANREISE *Das Hotel liegt an der Nordküste, ca. 11 km vom internationalen Flughafen Kos entfernt* · **PREISE** *€€–€€€€* · **ZIMMER** *44 Zimmer, 47 Suiten, 6 Bungalows, 3 Villen (alle mit Terrasse, einige mit gemeinsamem oder privatem Pool); nur für Erwachsene* · **KÜCHE** *Das „To Kima“ ist Restaurant, Bar und Beachklub in einem und serviert griechische Gerichte nach Rezepten der Insel und mit frischen, lokalen Zutaten* · **GESCHICHTE** *2017 erbaut und seit 2020 von Oku Hotels betrieben* · **X-FAKTOR** *Die Yogaklassen im Strandpavillon*

LUXE ET NONCHALANCE

C'est surtout à la médecine que Kos devait jadis sa bonne réputation – il faut dire qu'Hippocrate, le plus célèbre médecin de l'Antiquité, est né sur l'île vers 460 avant J.-C. Il y avait ici l'une des meilleures écoles de médecine du monde et l'un des plus importants sanctuaires de guérison, l'Asclépiéon, dédié à Asclépios, le dieu de la médecine, dont on peut encore admirer les ruines. Heureusement, les vacanciers actifs et les amoureux du soleil sont désormais plus nombreux à se rendre à Kos que les médecins et les patients. À l'intérieur du pays, il existe de nombreux itinéraires de randonnée et de cyclisme, tandis qu'au large des côtes, les surfeurs et les plaisanciers peuvent profiter du vent d'été Meltemi, et les plages de sable sont parmi les plus belles que la Grèce puisse offrir. L'Oku Kos se dresse sur l'une de ces plages – privée et donc paisible. Le cabinet d'architectes athénien Mastrominas s'est inspiré du village insulaire typique en proposant une interprétation moderne du thème ancien et une conception très minimaliste des cubes blancs à un et deux étages. Les bâtiments sont reliés par des chemins tranquilles bordés d'oliviers, de palmiers et de buissons de lavande, qui mènent sans cesse à des détails surprenants, que ce soit un escalier extérieur caché ou un banc pour s'arrêter un instant. L'aménagement intérieur des chambres, bungalows, suites et villas avec piscine est l'œuvre de Lambs and Lions (Berlin), qui utilisent habilement des matériaux naturels tels que la pierre et le bois non traité ainsi que des tons de terre atténués, trouvant un équilibre entre le luxe et la nonchalance. Dans le spa tout aussi élégant on utilise des huiles à base de plantes grecques et du sel de la mer Égée. Même un massage complet du corps dans le style d'Hippocrate figure au programme du bien-être – le « père de la médecine » n'y trouverait rien à redire. ◆ À lire : « Le feuilleton d'Hermès. La mythologie grecque en cent épisodes » par Murielle Szac

ACCÈS *L'hôtel est situé sur la côte septentrionale, à environ 11 km de l'aéroport international de Kos* · **PRIX** *€€–€€€€* · **CHAMBRES** *44 chambres, 47 suites, 6 bungalows, 3 villas (tous dotés d'une terrasse, certains avec piscine commune ou privée); pour adultes seulement* · **RESTAURATION** *Le « To Kima » est à la fois restaurant, bar et club de plage. Il propose des plats de la cuisine grecque préparés d'après des recettes de l'île avec des produits frais de la région* · **HISTOIRE** *Construite en 2017 et dirigée par Oku Hotels depuis 2020* · **LES « PLUS »** *Les cours de yoga dans le pavillon de la plage*

THEY PASS AWAY
JIMMY NELSON

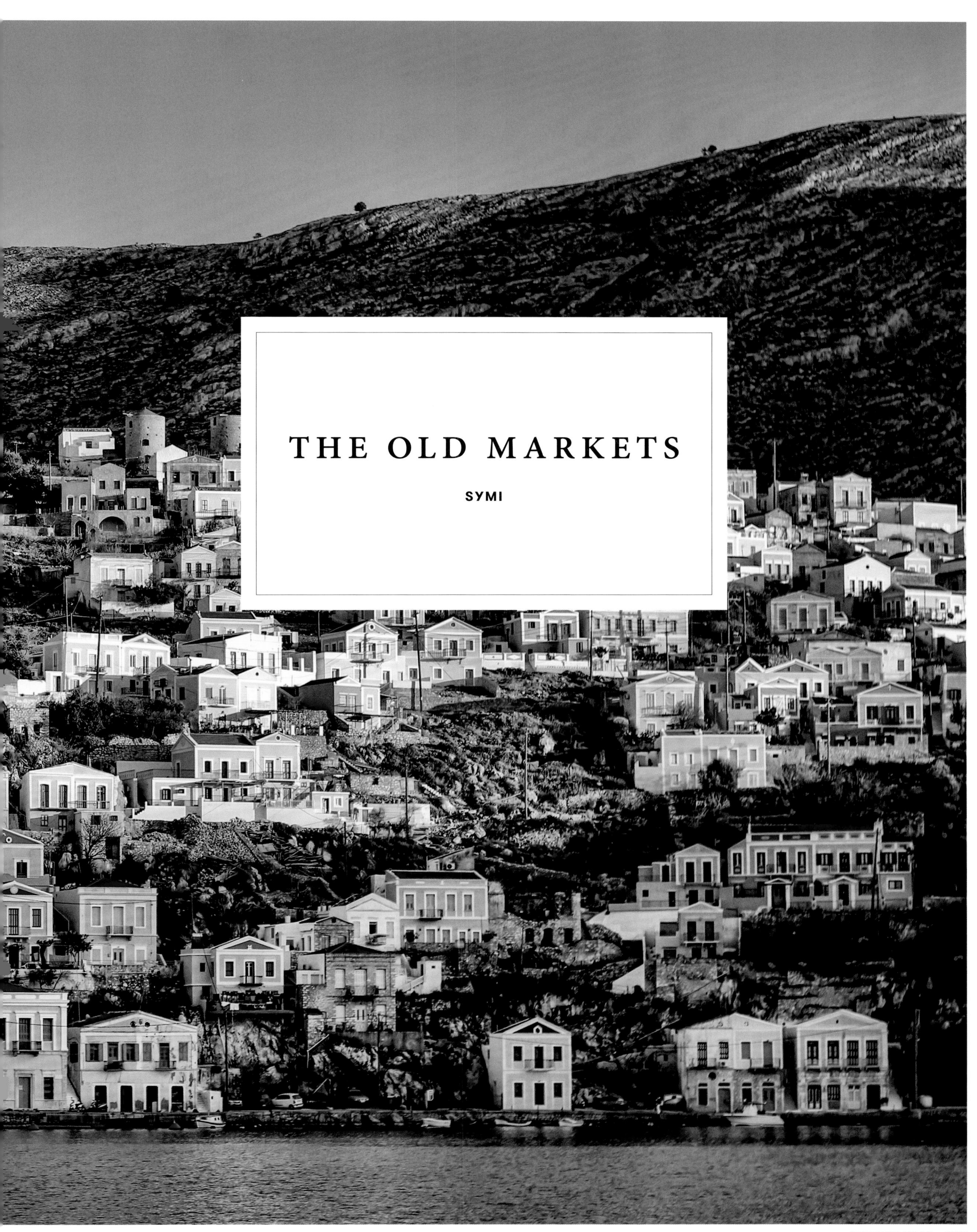

THE OLD MARKETS

SYMI

THE OLD MARKETS

Kali Strata, 856 00 Symi
Tel. +30 22460 714 40 and +30 695 730 25 65 · info@theoldmarkets.com
www.theoldmarkets.com

MARKET SCENES

Symi was once well-known primarily for the trade in sponges and spices. Merchants and locals met at the agora near the harbor – the central marketplace, for chatting, for buying and selling. Today the old market is a protected heritage building, home to this unique boutique hotel, opened by Andrew Davies from Britain. Nine former shops with walls, floors and vaults of rough-hewn stone were turned into guest bedrooms that are named after the destinations of legendary trade routes – including the Ottoman Room in the old bakery, which has a hammam-style bathroom, and the Venetian Room, where Italian antiques and paintings tell of bygone days. All of these rooms emanate great charm and historical atmosphere, but are not generously sized, as space was at a premium on Symi. Those who would like more room for maneuver find large, elegant accommodation in the Captain's House, which is also part of the complex. The Ouranos Suite ("Heaven") on the top floor looks out onto a perfect panorama from its private balconies, the Aegean Suite on two levels has a view of the picturesque harbor, and the beauty of the Symi Suite is revealed in pastel shades and a hand-painted ceiling. The restaurant on the roof terrace, too, is a treat for the eyes – complemented by treats for the palate, as a champagne breakfast for late risers is served here every day until noon. ◆ Book to pack: "Circe" by Madeline Miller

DIRECTIONS *Symi is just under 1 hr by ferry from Rhodes. The hotel is situated on Kali Strata, steps that lead from the harbor to the upper town; porters help to carry suitcases up the 40 steps* · **RATES** *€€–€€€€* · **ROOMS** *7 rooms and 3 suites in the ancient shops and the Captain's House* · **FOOD** *A fine Mediterranean dinner is served three times per week; on the other evenings guests can dine in the Emporio sister hotel or nearby restaurants* · **HISTORY** *The restored agora was opened in 2011, the Captain's House in 2016* · **X-FACTOR** *Relaxing spa treatments after a walk through town up and down all the steps*

MARKTSZENEN

Symi war früher vor allem für den Handel mit Schwämmen und Gewürzen bekannt. Kaufleute und Einheimische trafen sich auf der Agora in der Nähe des Hafens – dem zentralen Marktplatz, auf dem man plauderte, kaufte und verkaufte. Heute steht der alte Markt unter Denkmalschutz und beherbergt dieses einmalige Boutiquehotel, das der Brite Andrew Davies eröffnet hat. In neun ehemaligen Ladenlokalen mit Wänden, Böden und Gewölben aus grob behauenen Steinen entstanden Gästezimmer, die nach den Zielen legendärer Handelsrouten getauft sind – darunter das osmanische Zimmer in der einstigen Bäckerei, das ein Bad im Hammam-Stil hat, sowie das venezianische Zimmer, in dem italienische Antiquitäten und Bilder von vergangenen Zeiten erzählen. All diese Räume verströmen viel Charme und historisches Flair, bieten jedoch nicht ganz so viel Platz, denn auf Symi wurde auf kleinem Raum gearbeitet. Wer sich mehr Bewegungsfreiheit wünscht, findet im Kapitänshaus, das ebenfalls zum Komplex gehört, großzügige und elegante Unterkünfte. Die Ouranos Suite („Himmel") im obersten Stock eröffnet von Privatbalkonen aus ein perfektes Panorama, die Aegean Suite liegt auf zwei Ebenen und schaut auf den pittoresken Hafen, und die Symi Suite entpuppt sich als Schönheit in Pastelltönen mit handbemalter Decke. Ebenfalls ein Augenschmaus ist das Restaurant auf der Dachterrasse – den Gaumenschmaus gibt es noch dazu, denn hier wird täglich bis 12 Uhr ein Champagnerfrühstück für Langschläfer serviert. ◆ Buchtipp: „Ich bin Circe" von Madeline Miller

ANREISE *Symi ist in knapp 1 Std. per Fähre von Rhodos aus zu erreichen. Das Hotel liegt an der Treppe Kali Strata, die vom Hafen zur Oberstadt führt; Gepäckträger helfen auf den ca. 40 Stufen mit den Koffern* · **PREISE** *€€–€€€€* · **ZIMMER** *7 Zimmer und 3 Suiten in den antiken Ladenlokalen und dem Kapitänshaus* · **KÜCHE** *Dreimal pro Woche wird ein delikates mediterranes Dinner serviert; an den anderen Abenden kann man im Schwesterhotel Emporio oder in nahen Lokalen essen* · **GESCHICHTE** *Der sanierte Agora-Bereich wurde 2011 eröffnet, das Kapitänshaus 2016* · **X-FAKTOR** *Nach einem Stadtspaziergang über viele Treppen entspannen Spa-Anwendungen*

SCÈNES DE MARCHÉ

Symi était autrefois surtout connue pour le commerce des éponges et des épices. Les commerçants et les habitants se retrouvaient près du port sur l'agora, la place centrale du marché, où les gens discutaient, achetaient et vendaient. Aujourd'hui, le vieux marché est un monument classé et abrite cet hôtel-boutique unique en son genre, qui a été ouvert par le Britannique Andrew Davies. Dans neuf anciennes boutiques dont les murs, les sols et les voûtes sont en pierre de taille, on a créé des chambres d'hôtes qui portent le nom de destinations de routes de commerce légendaires – parmi lesquelles la chambre ottomane dans l'ancienne boulangerie, qui possède une salle de bains de style hammam, et la chambre vénitienne, dans laquelle des antiquités et des tableaux italiens évoquent les temps passés. Toutes ces pièces ont beaucoup de charme et une atmosphère historique, mais leurs dimensions sont modestes : à Symi on travaillait dans des espaces restreints. Ceux qui souhaitent avoir plus de liberté de mouvement trouveront des logements spacieux et élégants dans la Maison du Capitaine, qui fait également partie du complexe. La suite Ouranos (« Ciel »), au dernier étage, offre une vue imprenable depuis des balcons privés, la suite Aegean s'étend sur deux niveaux et donne sur le port pittoresque, et la suite Symi s'avère être une beauté dans des tons pastel avec un plafond peint à la main. Le restaurant situé sur le toit en terrasse est également un régal pour les yeux – et pour les papilles, car un petit-déjeuner au champagne pour les lève-tard y est servi tous les jours jusqu'à midi. ◆ À lire : « Circé » par Madeline Miller

ACCÈS *Symi est joignable en moins d'une heure par le ferry de Rhodes. L'hôtel est situé près des escaliers de la Kali Strata qui mènent du port à la ville haute; des porteurs aident à porter les bagages sur la quarantaine de marches* · **PRIX** *€€–€€€€* · **CHAMBRES** *7 chambres et 3 suites dans les anciennes boutiques et la maison du capitaine* · **RESTAURATION** *Un savoureux dîner méditerranéen est servi trois fois par semaine; les autres soirs on peut prendre son repas à l'hôtel Emporio ou dans des restaurants voisins* · **HISTOIRE** *La zone restaurée de l'Agora a été ouverte en 2011, la maison du capitaine en 2016* · **LES « PLUS »** *Après vous être promené en ville en empruntant de nombreux escaliers, les soins du spa vous détendront*

MARCO POLO MANSION

OLD TOWN, RHODES

MARCO POLO MANSION

Agiou Fanouriou 40–42, 851 00 Rhodes (Old Town)
Tel. +30 22410 255 62 and +30 694 488 91 39 · marcopolomansion@hotmail.com
www.marcopolomansion.gr

A FAVORITE PLACE

In the labyrinthine alleys of Rhodes Town, this address is not easy to find, but it is worth making the effort of looking: Marco Polo Mansion is a picture-perfect bed & breakfast in the Turkish quarter, surrounded by mosques with their slender minarets, rows of shops with a bazaar atmosphere and splashing fountains. What was once an Ottoman mansion was turned into a "house for friends" by a Greek woman, Efi Dede, commissioned by the Italian artist and collector Giuseppe Sala, who had opened a gallery nearby; being a historian, Efi wanted to retain the character of the building, so she used traditional methods to paint the walls in the loveliest shades of rose and terracotta, aubergine and cobalt blue, sunshine yellow and golden orange. In front of them she placed antique accessories, four-poster beds, oriental carpets and colorful fabrics. Every room has its own exotic style and narrates a chapter from the eventful history of the house, the town or the island. As her first visitors liked to take a look around the kitchen, poking their noses longingly in the refrigerator and cooking pots, Efi decided without further ado to open a restaurant, which is now one of the best on Rhodes. The ambience alone, in an idyllic courtyard that Efi's green-thumbed husband Spiros tends lovingly, is a delight. The creative Greek and Mediterranean menu never ceases to tempt, while the clientele is a colorful mix of people who are nevertheless on the same wavelength. ◆ Book to pack: "Reflections on a Marine Venus" by Lawrence Durrell

DIRECTIONS *In the historic center of Rhodes Town, about 20 km/13 miles from the island airport* · **RATES** *€* · **ROOMS** *12 rooms* · **FOOD** *Greek and superb – from breakfast to dinner* · **HISTORY** *The mansion dates from the Ottoman period and opened as a bed & breakfast in the 1990s* · **X-FACTOR** *Artistic and restored in bohemian chic style*

EINE LIEBLINGSADRESSE

Im Gewirr der labyrinthartigen Gassen von Rhodos-Stadt ist diese Adresse nicht ganz leicht zu finden, doch die Suche lohnt sich: Die Marco Polo Mansion ist ein bildschönes Bed & Breakfast im türkischen Viertel, umgeben von Moscheen mit schlanken Minaretten, Ladenzeilen mit dem Flair eines Basars und plätschernden Brunnen. Aus dem einstigen osmanischen Herrensitz machte die Griechin Efi Dede im Auftrag des italienischen Künstlers und Sammlers Giuseppe Sala, der in der Nähe eine Galerie eröffnet hatte, ein „Haus für Freunde"; ein Hotel sollte es bewusst nicht werden. Als Historikerin wollte sie den Charakter des Gebäudes erhalten – so strich sie die Wände nach alter Technik in den schönsten Rosé- und Terrakottatönen, in Aubergine und Kobaltblau, Sonnengelb und Goldorange und platzierte davor antike Accessoires, Himmelbetten, orientalische Teppiche sowie farbenfrohe Stoffe. Jeder Raum hat seinen eigenen exotischen Stil und erzählt ein Kapitel der abwechslungsreichen Geschichte von Haus, Stadt oder Insel. Da ihre ersten Besucher gerne mal in ihrer Küche vorbeischauten und ihre Nasen sehnsüchtig in Kühlschrank und Kochtöpfe steckten, eröffnete Efi kurzerhand auch noch ein Restaurant, das inzwischen zu den besten Lokalen auf Rhodos zählt. Schon das Ambiente im idyllischen Innenhof, den Efis Mann Spiros mit grünem Daumen hegt und pflegt, ist ein Genuss, die kreative griechisch-mediterrane Karte immer wieder verlockend und das Publikum bunt gemischt und dennoch auf einer Wellenlänge. ◆ Buchtipp: „Leuchtende Orangen" von Lawrence Durrell

ANREISE *Im historischen Zentrum von Rhodos-Stadt gelegen, ca. 20 km vom Flughafen der Insel entfernt* · **PREISE** *€* · **ZIMMER** *12 Zimmer* · **KÜCHE** *Griechisch und großartig – vom Frühstück bis zum Abendessen* · **GESCHICHTE** *Das Haus stammt aus osmanischer Zeit. Ende der 1990er wurde es als Bed & Breakfast eröffnet* · **X-FAKTOR** *Kunstvoll und mit Boho-Chic restauriert*

UNE ADRESSE DE RÊVE

Cette adresse n'est pas facile à trouver dans le labyrinthe des ruelles enchevêtrées de la ville de Rhodes, mais la chercher en vaut la peine : le Marco Polo Mansion est un magnifique Bed & Breakfast situé dans le quartier turc, entouré de mosquées aux minarets élancés, de rangées de boutiques ayant l'ambiance d'un bazar et de fontaines clapotantes. À la demande de l'artiste et collectionneur italien Giuseppe Sala, qui avait ouvert une galerie à proximité, la Grecque Efi Dede a transformé l'ancienne demeure seigneuriale ottomane en « maison d'amis » ; il ne voulait en aucun cas d'un hôtel. Historienne de formation, elle a voulu préserver le caractère du bâtiment. Elle a donc peint les murs en utilisant des techniques anciennes dans les plus belles nuances de rose et de terre cuite, d'aubergine et de bleu cobalt, de jaune soleil et d'orange doré, et a placé devant eux des antiquités, des lits à baldaquin, des tapis orientaux et des étoffes aux couleurs vives. Chaque chambre a son propre style exotique et raconte son propre chapitre de l'histoire riche en événements de la maison, de la ville ou de l'île. Comme les premiers visiteurs aimaient regarder ce qui se passait dans sa cuisine et mettre leur nez dans le réfrigérateur et les casseroles, Efi a également ouvert sans plus attendre un restaurant qui est aujourd'hui l'un des meilleurs de Rhodes. Rien que l'ambiance de la cour intérieure verte et fleurie, que Spiros, le mari d'Efi, chérit et dont il prend soin – il a la main verte –, est idyllique, le menu créatif gréco-méditerranéen toujours tentant et le public cosmopolite, et pourtant sur la même longueur d'onde, fascinant. ◆ À lire : « Vénus et la mer » de Lawrence Durrell

ACCÈS *Dans le centre de la cité historique de Rhodes, à environ 20 km de l'aéroport de l'île* · **PRIX** *€* · **CHAMBRES** *12 chambres* · **RESTAURATION** *Sublime cuisine grecque – du petit-déjeuner au dîner* · **HISTOIRE** *La maison date de l'époque ottomane. Convertie en Bed & Breakfast à la fin des années 1990* · **LES « PLUS »** *Artistement restaurée avec des touches de chic bohème*

MEDITERRANEO KASTELORIZO

KASTELLORIZO

MEDITERRANEO KASTELORIZO

851 11 Megisti (Kastellorizo)
Tel. +30 22460 490 07 and +30 697 367 60 38 · bookings@mediterraneo-kastelorizo.com
www.mediterraneo-megisti.com

WHERE CULTURES MEET

On Kastellorizo, Marie Rivalant fell in love no less than three times: with the island itself, to which she first traveled as a young student of architecture from Paris, then with a restaurant-owner named Giorgios, who later became her husband, and finally with this old building by the water, which she turned into the Mediterraneo. Just like the island, which lies on the border between Greece and Turkey – a place where Europe ends and Asia begins – the hotel brings different cultures together. With its colorful walls, window frames and doors, its diverse mix of furniture and oriental accessories, it feels like the villa of a likeable artist. An air of creativity and a bohemian touch pervade the seven rooms. Each of them has its own style and little extras. The suite on the ground floor is even blessed with a sunny terrace from which guests can leap straight into the sea. For those who would like to take a piece of this exotic atmosphere home with them, items are sold in the owner's shop: decorative objects, fabrics and clothes from Greece, Turkey, France and India. To stay with Marie is to understand why Kastellorizo has inspired many a famous visitor. Italian film director Gabriele Salvatores, for example, set his movie "Mediterraneo" here and won the Oscar for the best foreign-language film in 1992. Pink Floyd guitarist Dave Gilmour dedicated the opening song of one of his solo albums to the island – and "Castellorizon" was nominated for a Grammy in 2006. ◆ Film to watch: "Mediterraneo" (1991) by Gabriele Salvatores

DIRECTIONS *Kastellorizo (officially called Megisti) is the easternmost inhabited Greek island. It lies just over 2 km/1 mile from the Turkish coast. The island has an airport for domestic flights (3 km/2 miles from the hotel) and can be reached by ferry from Rhodes (2 hrs 30 min to 3 hrs 45 min, depending on the type of ferry) and Kaş in Turkey (20 min, during the main season)* · **RATES** *€ (3 nights minimum stay)* · **ROOMS** *7 rooms* · **FOOD** *Breakfast in the hotel is a mix of Greek, Turkish and French. For lunch and dinner, guests go to the nearby harbor, e.g. for fresh seafood to Giorgios' restaurant "Lazarakis"* · **HISTORY** *Marie Rivalant visited the island for the first time in 1983. In 2000 she opened Mediterraneo* · **X-FACTOR** *Yoga retreats are held at the start and end of the season*

TREFFPUNKT DER KULTUREN

Auf Kastelorizo verliebte sich Marie Rivalant gleich dreimal: in die Insel selbst, die sie zum ersten Mal als junge Architekturstudentin aus Paris bereiste, in den Wirt Giorgios, der später ihr Ehemann wurde, und in dieses alte Gebäude am Wasser, aus dem sie das Mediterraneo machte. Wie das Eiland, das an der Grenze zwischen Griechenland und der Türkei liegt – also dort, wo Europa aufhört und Asien beginnt –, verbindet auch das Haus unterschiedliche Kulturen. Mit seinen farbenfrohen Wänden, Fenster- und Türrahmen, bunt zusammengewürfelten Möbeln und orientalischen Accessoires wirkt es wie die Villa eines sympathischen Künstlers. In den sieben Zimmern liegen Kreativität und ein Hauch Boheme in der Luft – alle Räume haben ihren eigenen Stil und kleine Extras (zur Suite im Erdgeschoss gehört sogar eine Sonnenterrasse, von der aus man direkt ins Meer springen kann). An Gäste, die ein Stück der exotischen Atmosphäre mit nach Hause nehmen möchten, verkauft die Besitzerin Deko-Objekte, Stoffe und Mode aus Griechenland, der Türkei, Frankreich und Indien im eigenen Shop. Wer bei Marie wohnt, kann verstehen, warum Kastelorizo schon so manchen berühmten Besucher inspiriert hat. Der italienische Regisseur Gabriele Salvatores beispielsweise ließ seinen Film „Mediterraneo" hier spielen, der 1992 den Oscar als bester fremdsprachiger Film bekam. Und der Pink-Floyd-Gitarrist Dave Gilmour widmete der Insel den Eröffnungssong eines seiner Soloalben – „Castellorizon" wurde 2006 für einen Grammy nominiert. ◆ Filmtipp: „Mediterraneo" (1991) von Gabriele Salvatores

ANREISE *Kastelorizo (offizielle Bezeichnung: Megisti) ist die östlichste bewohnte Insel Griechenlands. Sie liegt 2 km vor dem türkischen Festland. Die Insel hat einen nationalen Flughafen (3 km vom Hotel entfernt) und ist per Fähre ab Rhodos (2,5 Std. bis 3 Std. 45 min, je nach Fährtyp) und dem türkischen Kaş (20 min, während der Saison) erreichbar* · **PREISE** *€ (3 Nächte Mindestaufenthalt)* · **ZIMMER** *7 Zimmer* · **KÜCHE** *Das Frühstück im Hotel ist griechisch-türkisch-französisch. Mittags und abends isst man am nahen Hafen, z. B. frische Meeresfrüchte in Giorgios Restaurant „Lazarakis"* · **GESCHICHTE** *Marie Rivalant kam 1983 zum ersten Mal auf die Insel. 2000 eröffnete sie das Mediterraneo* · **X-FAKTOR** *Am Beginn und Ende der Saison werden Yoga-Retreats angeboten*

LE RENDEZ-VOUS DES CULTURES

À Kastellorizo, Marie Rivalant est tombée amoureuse à trois reprises : de l'île elle-même, qu'elle a visitée pour la première fois alors qu'elle était jeune étudiante en architecture à Paris, du restaurateur Giorgios, qui est devenu plus tard son mari, et de ce vieux bâtiment au bord de l'eau, dont elle a fait le Mediterraneo. À l'image de l'île qui se trouve à la frontière entre la Grèce et la Turquie – là où l'Europe se termine et l'Asie commence – la maison fait le lien entre différentes cultures. Avec ses murs, ses encadrements de fenêtres et de portes aux couleurs vives, son mobilier joyeusement hétéroclite et ses accessoires orientaux, elle ressemble à la villa d'un artiste sympathique. Les sept chambres respirent la créativité et une touche de bohème – chaque chambre a son style propre et de petits extras (la suite du rez-de-chaussée a même une terrasse ensoleillée d'où l'on peut plonger directement dans la mer). Si des clients veulent emporter chez eux un peu de cette atmosphère exotique, la propriétaire leur vend dans sa boutique des objets décoratifs, des tissus et des articles de mode venus de Grèce, de Turquie, de France et d'Inde. Ceux qui séjournent chez Marie comprennent aisément pourquoi Kastellorizo a éveillé l'inspiration de nombreux visiteurs célèbres. Le réalisateur italien Gabriele Salvatores, par exemple, y a tourné son film « Mediterraneo », Oscar du meilleur film étranger en 1992. Et le guitariste de Pink Floyd, Dave Gilmour, a dédié la chanson d'ouverture d'un de ses albums solo à l'île – « Castellorizon » a été nominé pour un Grammy en 2006. ◆ À voir : « Mediterraneo » (1991) de Gabriele Salvatores

ACCÈS *Kastellorizo (nom officiel : Megisti) est l'île habitée la plus orientale de la Grèce. Elle est située à 2 km du continent turc. L'île dispose d'un aéroport national (à 3 km de l'hôtel) et est accessible par ferry depuis Rhodes (2,5 h à 3 h 45 min, selon le type de ferry) et de Kaş en Turquie (20 min, en saison)* · **PRIX** *€ (séjour minimum 3 nuits)* · **CHAMBRES** *7 chambres* · **RESTAURATION** *Le petit-déjeuner servi à l'hôtel est gréco-turco-français. Le midi et le soir on peut se restaurer dans le port tout proche, savourer par exemple des fruits de mer au restaurant « Lazarakis » de Giorgios* · **HISTOIRE** *Marie Rivalant est arrivée sur l'île en 1983. Elle a ouvert le Mediterraneo en 2000* · **LES « PLUS »** *Des retraites de yoga sont proposées en début et en fin de saison*

THE ROU ESTATE

NEAR SINIES, CORFU

THE ROU ESTATE

Rou, near Sinies, 490 81 Corfu
Tel. +44 208 392 58 58 · sales@simpsontravel.com
www.simpsontravel.com/the-rou-estate

MY ISLAND, MY VILLAGE

Even as a child, Dominic Skinner found architecture fascinating – and loved Corfu, where his family regularly spent their vacations: at the tender age of thirteen he helped to design his parents' beach villa in Kalamaki. As a young architect he worked with Lord Norman Foster in Britain before returning to Corfu. With his wife Claire, an interior designer, he founded his own company and bought a deserted hamlet more than 200 years old in the northeast of the island. The historic houses were restored from top to bottom, while retaining their Corfiot architecture as far as possible. A few new buildings were added, but designed so faithfully in the existing style that they blend seamlessly into the ensemble. Today this picturesque village with its heavenly tranquility consists of fourteen stunningly lovely houses, which are either old or at least look old, have built-in verandas or panorama terraces, are furnished in an elegant country-house style and are equipped with every modern luxury. From the kitchen to the air conditioning, from the WiFi to the washing machine, they leave nothing to be desired (and if a wish should remain unfulfilled after all, the team, operating almost invisibly, will do the job in the twinkling of an eye: the service lives up to the standards of a five-star hotel). The elevated east-west location of Rou is a further privilege. In the morning, guests see the sun rise in the east over the Albanian mountains, and in the evening they can watch it go down in the west behind Corfu's highest peak. During the day they can admire the wonderful Mediterranean gardens, which were expertly laid out and are permeated with the scents of lavender, rosemary and jasmine.
◆ Book to pack: "Prospero's Cell" by Lawrence Durrell

DIRECTIONS *In the northeast of Corfu, almost 30 km/20 miles from the airport (a little under 1 hour's drive). The distance to the beach at Agni is about 6 km/4 miles* · **RATES** *€€€* · **ROOMS** *14 houses, each with 2 to 5 bedrooms, kitchen, garden and pool* · **FOOD** *The estate restaurant, "The Garden Terrace," serves local dishes four evenings each week. Guests can have breakfast, meals and groceries delivered or hire a private chef* · **HISTORY** *The Skinners bought the Rou Estate in 2005 and opened it in 2008* · **X-FACTOR** *The spa and the private yoga, Pilates, cookery and painting courses that can be arranged on request*

MEINE INSEL, MEIN DORF

Schon als Kind war Dominic Skinner von der Architektur fasziniert – und liebte die Insel Korfu, wo seine Familie regelmäßig die Ferien verbrachte: Mit gerade einmal 13 Jahren half er begeistert mit, die Strandvilla seiner Eltern in Kalamaki zu entwerfen. Als junger Architekt arbeitete er mit Sir Norman Foster in Großbritannien, ehe es ihn zurück nach Korfu zog. Gemeinsam mit seiner Frau Claire, einer Interiordesignerin, gründete er eine eigene Firma und kaufte im Nordosten der Insel einen verlassenen, mehr als 200 Jahre alten Weiler. Die historischen Häuser wurden von Grund auf saniert, wobei ihre korfiotische Architektur so weit wie möglich erhalten blieb. Einige wenige Gebäude kamen neu hinzu – sie wurden aber so stilgetreu designt, dass sie sich nahtlos ins Ensemble einfügen. Heute umfasst das pittoreske und paradiesisch ruhige Dorf 14 traumhafte Häuser, die alt sind oder zumindest alt aussehen, eingewachsene Verandas oder Panoramaterrassen besitzen, im eleganten Landhausstil eingerichtet und mit allem modernen Luxus ausgestattet sind. Von der Küche bis zur Klimaanlage und vom WiFi bis zur Waschmaschine bleibt kein Wunsch offen (und falls doch, erfüllt ihn das fast unsichtbar agierende Team im Handumdrehen – der Service kann sich mit dem eines Fünfsternehotels messen). Ein weiteres Privileg ist die erhöhte Ost-West-Lage von Rou. Morgens sieht man die Sonne im Osten über den Bergen Albaniens aufund abends im Westen hinter Korfus höchstem Gipfel untergehen. Und tagsüber bewundert man die herrlichen mediterranen Gärten dazwischen, die fachkundig angelegt wurden und nach Lavendel, Rosmarin und Jasmin duften. ◆ Buchtipp: „Schwarze Oliven. Korfu, Insel der Phäaken“ von Lawrence Durrell

ANREISE *Im Nordosten von Korfu gelegen, ca. 30 km vom Flughafen der Insel entfernt (knapp 1 Std. Fahrtzeit). Der Agni-Strand ist ca. 6 km entfernt* · **PREISE** *€€€* · **ZIMMER** *14 Häuser mit je 2–5 Schlafzimmern sowie Küche, Garten und Pool* · **KÜCHE** *Das gutseigene Restaurant „The Garden Terrace“ serviert an vier Abenden pro Woche lokale Gerichte. Gäste können sich Frühstück sowie Speisen und Lebensmittel ins Haus liefern lassen oder einen Privatkoch engagieren* · **GESCHICHTE** *2005 erwarben die Skinners das Grundstück. The Rou Estate eröffnete 2008* · **X-FAKTOR** *Das Spa und die privaten Yoga-, Pilates-, Koch- und Malkurse, die auf Anfrage arrangiert werden*

MON ÎLE, MON VILLAGE

Enfant, Dominic Skinner était déjà fasciné par l'architecture et il aimait l'île de Corfou, où sa famille passait régulièrement ses vacances. À 13 ans seulement, il a participé avec enthousiasme à la conception de la villa de plage de ses parents à Kalamaki. Jeune architecte, il a travaillé avec Sir Norman Foster en Grande-Bretagne avant de retourner à Corfou. Il a fondé sa propre entreprise avec sa femme Claire, décoratrice d'intérieur, et acheté un hameau abandonné datant de plus de deux siècles dans le nord-est de l'île. Les maisons historiques ont été entièrement rénovées, en préservant autant que possible leur architecture corfiote. Quelques nouveaux bâtiments ont été ajoutés, mais conçus avec un tel respect du modèle qu'ils s'intègrent parfaitement à l'ensemble. Aujourd'hui, le village pittoresque où règne un calme paradisiaque comprend 14 maisons de rêve, des maisons anciennes ou qui en ont l'air, dotées de vérandas ou de terrasses panoramiques, élégamment meublées dans le style campagnard et équipées de tout le luxe moderne. De la cuisine à la climatisation et de la WiFi au lave-linge, aucun souhait n'est laissé insatisfait (et si c'est le cas, l'équipe presque invisible le réalisera en un rien de temps – le service peut rivaliser avec celui d'un hôtel cinq étoiles). Un autre privilège est l'emplacement élevé de Rou, d'est en ouest. Le matin, vous pouvez voir le soleil se lever à l'est au-dessus des montagnes d'Albanie et le soir, se coucher à l'ouest derrière le plus haut sommet de Corfou. Pendant la journée, vous admirerez les magnifiques jardins méditerranéens, savamment aménagés et embaumant la lavande, le romarin et le jasmin. ◆ À lire : « L'île de Prospero » par Lawrence Durrell

ACCÈS *Au nord-est de Corfou, à environ 30 km de l'aéroport de l'île (moins d'une heure de route). La plage d'Agni est à environ 6 km* · **PRIX** *€€€* · **CHAMBRES** *14 maisons abritant 2 à 5 chambres à coucher avec une cuisine, un jardin et une piscine* · **RESTAURATION** *« The Garden Terrace », le restaurant du domaine, propose des plats de la cuisine régionale quatre soirs par semaine. Les hôtes peuvent se faire livrer leur petit-déjeuner, leurs repas et de l'alimentation ou engager un cuisinier privé* · **HISTOIRE** *Les Skinner ont acheté le terrain en 2005. The Rou Estate a ouvert ses portes en 2008* · **LES « PLUS »** *Le spa et les cours privés de yoga, de Pilates, de cuisine et de peinture, qui sont organisés sur demande*

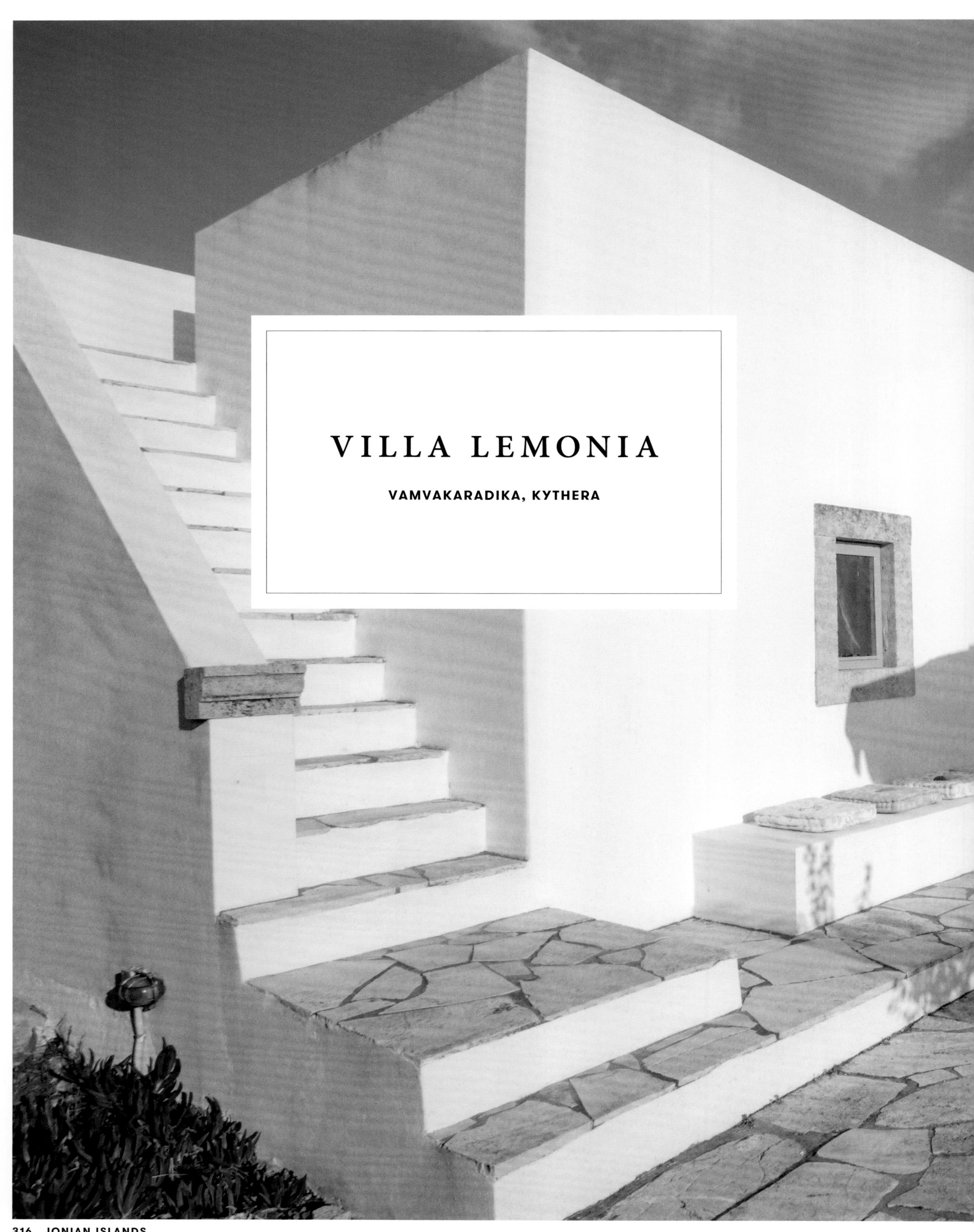

VILLA LEMONIA

VAMVAKARADIKA, KYTHERA

τα Τραγανά
του Καραβά
ΠΑΞΙΜΑΔΙΑ ΟΛΙΚΗΣ
ΑΛΕΣΕΩΣ

VILLA LEMONIA

Vamvakaradika, 802 00 Kythera
Tel. +30 697 240 66 98 · info@villalemonia.gr
www.villalemonia.gr

SIMPLY LOVELY

According to the myth, her birth was preceded by a bitter family conflict in which Gaia cut off Uranos' genitals and threw them into the sea off Kythera. Aphrodite emerged from the semen, blood and water. Although the goddess of love, beauty and sensuality was blown away to Cyprus in a shell, her connection to her place of birth endured. Poets mentioned her in their verses about Kythera, artists took inspiration for great paintings, and a beach was dedicated to Aphrodite in the Bay of Paleopoli. Despite its divine history, the island has remained down-to-earth and natural. It is not beautiful in the classical sense everywhere, but always likeable, and is a place of activity: on Kythera archaeological sites await the curious, deep gorges delight walkers, and waterfalls attract swimmers (if they are not too sensitive to cold). The island's products – fresh goat cheese, golden olive oil and honey scented with thyme – are simple and good. And the local population welcomes strangers with open arms. You can stop for a chat with them everywhere, and ideally even stay with them – as in the case of Ellie and Vassilis. In the island interior they converted an old stone building into an enchanting guesthouse which, with its green window frames and doors, yellow cornices and red roof tiles, emanates a cheerful mood. The three spotless rooms for guests were furnished in rustic style by the hosts themselves with beds of their own design and loving details. Every room has a veranda with a view across the countryside and a kitchen where a basket containing homemade treats, coffee, tea and a bottle of wine welcomes new arrivals. Ellie and Vassilis are also generous with their helpful tips. They know every beach, every village and every restaurant on Kythera, and are always ready to help in planning a route. If Aphrodite only knew what she missed out on when she left the island! ◆ Film to watch: "Voyage to Kythera" (1984) by Theo Angelopoulos

DIRECTIONS *Kythera lies off the southern tip of the Peloponnese and is reached by air from Athens or by ferry. The most frequent ferry connections are from Neapoli on the Peloponnese (1 hr 15 min), but boats also cross from Gythio (2 hrs) and Piraeus (6 hrs 30 min)* · **RATES** *€* · **ROOMS** *2 double rooms and 1 apartment for up to 3 persons, all with a kitchenette and veranda* · **FOOD** *For self-caterers* · **HISTORY** *Opened in 2004* · **X-FACTOR** *Ellie's homemade jam brightens up every morning and is a popular souvenir to take home*

EINFACH SCHÖN

Der Sage nach ging ihrer Geburt ein erbitterter Familienstreit voraus, bei dem Gaia Uranos die Genitalien abschneiden und ins Meer vor Kythera werfen ließ – aus den Samen, dem Blut und Wasser entstand Aphrodite. Obwohl sie in einer Muschel weiter nach Zypern getrieben wurde, blieb die Göttin der Liebe, Schönheit und Sinnlichkeit immer auch mit ihrem Geburtsort verbunden. Poeten erwähnten sie in ihren Gedichten über Kythera, Maler ließen sich von ihr zu großen Gemälden inspirieren, und in der Bucht von Paleopoli wurde Aphrodite ein Strand gewidmet. Trotz ihrer göttlichen Geschichte ist die Insel jedoch bodenständig und natürlich geblieben. Sie ist nicht immer schön im klassischen Sinn, aber immer sympathisch – und immer aktiv: Auf Kythera warten archäologische Stätten auf Entdecker, tiefe Schluchten auf Wanderer und Wasserfälle auf (kälteunempfindliche) Schwimmer. Die Produkte der Insel, frischer Ziegenkäse, goldenes Olivenöl sowie nach Thymian duftender Honig, sind so einfach wie gut. Und ihre Bewohner empfangen Fremde mit offenen Armen. Man kann überall einen Plausch mit ihnen halten und im Idealfall sogar bei ihnen wohnen, wie bei Ellie und Vassilis. Sie haben im Landesinneren ein altes Steinhaus in ein bezauberndes Gästehaus umgebaut, das mit seinen grünen Fensterrahmen und Türen, gelben Gesimsen und roten Dachziegeln gute Laune ausstrahlt. Die drei blitzblanken Gästezimmer sind mit von den Besitzern selbst entworfenen Betten und liebevollen Details rustikal ausgestattet. Zu jedem Raum gehören eine Veranda mit Blick übers Land sowie eine Küche, in der ein Willkommenskorb mit hausgemachten Köstlichkeiten, Kaffee, Tee sowie einer Flasche Wein wartet. Großzügig sind Ellie und Vassilis auch mit guten Tipps – sie kennen jeden Strand, jedes Dorf und jedes Restaurant auf Kythera und sind bei der Routenplanung immer behilflich. Wenn Aphrodite wüsste, was sie auf dieser Insel alles verpasst hat! ◆ Filmtipp: „Die Reise nach Kythera" (1984) von Theo Angelopoulos

ANREISE *Kythera liegt vor der Südspitze des Peloponnes und ist per Flugzeug von Athen oder per Fähre erreichbar: Die meisten Fährverbindungen bestehen ab Neapoli auf dem Peloponnes (1 Std. 15 min), man kann aber auch ab Gythio (2 Std.) und Piräus (6,5 Std.) reisen* · **PREISE** *€* · **ZIMMER** *2 Doppelzimmer und 1 Apartment für bis zu 3 Personen, alle mit Küchenzeile und Veranda* · **KÜCHE** *Für Selbstversorger* · **GESCHICHTE** *2004 eröffnet* · **X-FAKTOR** *Ellies selbst gemachte Marmelade verschönt jeden Morgen und ist ein begehrtes Mitbringsel*

LA BEAUTÉ, C'EST TOUT

Selon la légende, une querelle familiale acharnée a précédé la naissance de la déesse, au cours de laquelle Gaïa a fait couper les organes génitaux d'Ouranos et les a jetés dans la mer au large de Cythère – Aphrodite serait née de « l'écume », du mélange de sperme, de sang et d'eau. Bien qu'elle ait été emmenée plus loin à Chypre dans un coquillage, la déesse de l'amour, de la beauté et de la sensualité est toujours restée liée à son lieu de naissance. Les poètes la mentionnent dans leurs odes à Cythère, les peintres se sont inspirés d'elle pour créer de célèbres tableaux, et une plage de la baie de Paleopoli lui a été dédiée. Malgré son histoire divine, l'île est restée rustique et naturelle. Elle n'est pas toujours belle au sens classique, mais toujours avenante – et toujours active : sur Cythère, des sites archéologiques attendent les explorateurs, des gouffres profonds attendent les randonneurs, et des cascades attendent les nageurs (ne craignant pas le froid). Les produits de l'île, le fromage de chèvre frais, l'huile d'olive dorée et le miel parfumé au thym, sont aussi simples que délicieux. Et ses habitants accueillent les étrangers à bras ouverts. Vous pouvez discuter avec eux partout et même habiter chez eux, comme c'est le cas chez Ellie et Vassilis. À l'intérieur des terres, ils ont transformé une vieille maison de pierre en une charmante maison d'hôtes qui rayonne de bonne humeur avec ses cadres de fenêtres et ses portes verts, ses corniches jaunes et ses tuiles rouges. Les trois chambres étincelantes de propreté sont meublées dans un style rustique avec des lits conçus par les propriétaires eux-mêmes et des détails soignés. Chaque chambre dispose d'une véranda avec vue sur la campagne et d'une cuisine où vous attend un panier de bienvenue rempli de délices faits maison, avec du café, du thé et une bouteille de vin. Ellie et Vassilis sont également prodigues de bons conseils – ils connaissent toutes les plages, tous les villages et tous les restaurants de Cythère et sont toujours disposés à vous aider à préparer vos sorties. Si Aphrodite avait su tout cela, elle serait sûrement restée ici ! ◆ À voir : « Voyage à Cythère » (1984) de Theo Angelopoulos

ACCÈS *Cythère est située à l'extrémité sud du Péloponnèse et est accessible par avion depuis Athènes ou par ferry. La plupart des liaisons par ferry partent de Neapoli dans le Péloponnèse (1 h 15), mais vous pouvez également partir de Gythio (2 h) et du Pirée (6,5 h)* · **PRIX** *€* · **CHAMBRES** *2 chambres doubles et 1 appartement pour 3 personnes max., tous avec cuisine et véranda* · **RESTAURATION** *Pour ceux qui préparent eux-mêmes leurs repas* · **HISTOIRE** *Ouvert en 2004* · **LES « PLUS »** *La confiture maison d'Ellie vous réjouit tous les matins et est un cadeau très apprécié*

NOSTOS

CHORA, KYTHERA

NOSTOS

Chora, 801 00 Kythera
Tel. +30 27360 310 56 and +30 27306 318 34 · info@nostos-kythera.gr
www.nostos-kythera.gr

VENETIAN ATMOSPHERE

The Venetian fort that stands high above Chora and puts its stamp on the principal town on Kythera was once known as the "eye of Crete": from there, the inhabitants and rulers of the island could look far out across the Ionian, the Aegean and the Cretan Sea to trace the course of their own ships, and above all to track hostile vessels. Right by the entrance to the old fort stands a mansion, now a heritage monument, that was built in the Venetian style in the nineteenth century as the home of a respected man of the church. Today's owners have restored it carefully and fitted it out with hand-picked antiques. They welcome their guests in a family atmosphere. The seven rooms are named after the winds that regularly sweep across Kythera according to their compass orientation. Thus Maistros recalls the fresh northwest breeze that cools the island on hot summer days, Zefiros represents the gentle sea wind from the west that caresses guests' faces on the room's private roof terrace, and Levantes stands for the easterly that blows in spring and autumn. These seasons are, by the way, the host's favorite time of year, because the light is then especially soft on Kythera and the temperature ideal for excursions and for the olive harvest. Anyone who wishes to join in can help to gather them in October for production of the hotel's own cold-pressed oil. It can be sampled and bought in the cozy café at Nostos, which serves delicious local snacks, including crunchy Greek crispbread, tsipouro spirit made from grape must, and fatourada liqueur with cinnamon and cloves. ◆ Book to pack: "The Venetian Empire, A Sea Voyage" by Jan Morris

DIRECTIONS *Kythera can be reached by air from Athens and by ferry from various ports. The best connections are from Neapoli (1 hr 15 min), but boats also cross from Gythio (2 hrs) and Piraeus (6 hrs 30 min)* · **RATES** *€* · **ROOMS** *7 rooms, one of them with a roof terrace* · **FOOD** *The in-house café serves breakfast and Greek snacks. For lunch and dinner the restaurants of Chora are close at hand* · **HISTORY** *Opened as a guesthouse about 20 years ago* · **X-FACTOR** *The central location in the Old Town – ideal for exploring the fort and strolling through the alleys*

VENEZIANISCHES FLAIR

Die venezianische Burg, die hoch über Chora thront und die Silhouette von Kytheras Hauptort bestimmt, wurde früher auch das „Auge von Kreta" genannt: Von hier aus sahen die Bewohner und Beherrscher der Insel weit über das Ionische, Ägäische sowie Kretische Meer und konnten die Fahrt eigener und vor allem feindlicher Schiffe verfolgen. Direkt am Eingang zur alten Festungsanlage steht dieses denkmalgeschützte Herrenhaus, das im 19. Jahrhundert ebenfalls im venezianischen Stil erbaut wurde und in dem damals ein angesehener Kirchenmann lebte. Die heutigen Besitzer haben es sorgfältig saniert und mit handverlesenen Antiquitäten eingerichtet. Sie heißen ihre Gäste in familiärem Ambiente willkommen. Die sieben Zimmer sind ihrer Ausrichtung entsprechend nach den Winden getauft, die regelmäßig über Kythera hinwegwehen. So erinnert Maistros an die frische Nordwestbrise, die an heißen Sommertagen Kühlung bringt, Zefiros an den leichten Meerwind von Westen, der einem auf der privaten Dachterrasse des Zimmers um die Nase streicht, und Levantes an den Ostwind, der im Frühjahr und Herbst bläst. Diese Jahreszeiten sind übrigens die Lieblingszeiten des Gastgebers, denn dann ist das Licht auf Kythera besonders weich und die Temperatur perfekt für Ausflüge oder für die Olivenlese – wer mag, kann im Oktober bei der Ernte für das hauseigene kalt gepresste Öl helfen. Verkostet und verkauft wird es im behaglichen Café des Nostos, das köstliche lokale Kleinigkeiten anbietet, darunter knuspriges griechisches Trockenbrot, der Tresterbrand Tsipouro und der Likör Fatourada mit Zimt und Nelken. ◆ Buchtipp: „Taube unter Falken" von Katherine Allfrey

ANREISE *Kythera ist per Flug aus Athen sowie per Fähre von verschiedenen Orten erreichbar. Die meisten Verbindungen bestehen ab Neapoli (1 Std. 15 min), man kann aber auch ab Gythio (2 Std.) und Piräus (6,5 Std.) fahren* · **PREISE** *€* · **ZIMMER** *7 Zimmer, eines davon mit Dachterrasse* · **KÜCHE** *Frühstück und griechische Snacks gibt es im hauseigenen Café. Mittags und abends isst man in den nahen Lokalen von Chora* · **GESCHICHTE** *Vor rund 20 Jahren als Gasthaus eröffnet* · **X-FAKTOR** *Die zentrale Lage in der Altstadt – ideal, um die Festung zu erkunden und durch die Gassen zu schlendern*

VENISE EN GRÈCE

Le château vénitien qui domine Chora et donne à la capitale de Cythère sa silhouette particulière, était autrefois appelé « l'œil de la Crète » : d'ici, les habitants et les dirigeants de l'île avaient une vue imprenable sur la mer Ionienne, la mer Egée et la mer de Crète et pouvaient observer leurs navires et surtout le mouvement des navires ennemis. À l'entrée de l'ancienne citadelle se dresse ce manoir classé, construit au XIXe siècle, lui aussi dans le style vénitien, et dans lequel vivait un ecclésiastique respecté à l'époque. Les propriétaires actuels l'ont soigneusement rénové et meublé et décoré avec des antiquités minutieusement sélectionnées. Ils accueillent leurs hôtes dans une ambiance familiale. Les sept chambres portent, selon leur orientation, le nom des vents qui soufflent régulièrement sur Cythère. Ainsi, Maistros rappelle la fraîcheur de la brise du nord-ouest qui rend les chaudes journées d'été plus supportables, Zefiros le vent marin léger venu de l'ouest qui caresse votre visage sur le toit-terrasse privé de la chambre, et Levantes le vent d'est qui souffle au printemps et en automne. D'ailleurs, ces saisons sont les préférées de l'hôte, quand la lumière sur Cythère est particulièrement douce et la température idéale pour faire des excursions ou pour récolter les olives – ceux qui le souhaitent peuvent en octobre aider à récolter les fruits qui donneront l'huile pressée à froid de la maison. Elle est dégustée et vendue dans le confortable café du Nostos, qui propose de délicieuses spécialités locales, notamment du pain sec grec croustillant, du tsipouro, une eau-de-vie de marc, et de la fatourada, la liqueur traditionnelle à la cannelle et aux clous de girofle. ◆ À lire : « Entre la vague et le vent » par Georges Séféris

ACCÈS *Cythère est accessible par avion depuis Athènes ainsi que par ferry depuis divers endroits. La plupart des liaisons se font depuis Naples (1 h 15), mais vous pouvez aussi partir de Gythio (2 h) et du Pirée (6,5 h)* · **PRIX** *€* · **CHAMBRES** *7 chambres, une avec toit-terrasse* · **RESTAURATION** *Petit-déjeuner et collations grecques proposés dans le café de la maison. On peut déjeuner et dîner dans les restaurants de Chora, tout proches* · **HISTOIRE** *La maison d'hôtes a ouvert ses portes il y a une vingtaine d'années* · **LES « PLUS »** *Au centre de la cité historique, l'emplacement idéal pour explorer la citadelle et déambuler dans les ruelles*

HOTEL DOMA

CHANIA, CRETE

ΔΩ
ΜΑ

HOTEL DOMA

Venizelos Street 124, Chania, 731 33 Crete
Tel. +30 28210 517 723 · info@hotel-doma.gr
www.hotel-doma.gr

THE SISTERS' HOUSE

This villa on Crete was originally a diplomatic residence: in the late nineteenth century, the consul of the Austro-Hungarian Empire resided here. In 1933 the grandmother of the present owners bought the building and turned it into a private house, as it was the perfect place for a family thanks to its idyllic site in Chalepa, a suburb of Chania, right by the sea with vines at the back of the house. In the Second World War and the following years, the residents had to hand over their home to German occupying forces, then to British diplomats, and it was not officially returned to them until 1955. Since Christmas 1971 two sisters, Irene (Rena) Valyraki and Ioanna Koutsoudaki, have run it as a hotel, and they give a joyful and sensitive account of the turbulent history of their family and their island. They were able to preserve valuable antiques, faded photos and original works of art with which they have furnished the reception and lounge areas as well as the private rooms – the glass case with exotic headgear and magnificent hats that Ioanna has collected on her travels are a sight for sore eyes. The guest rooms, all individually furnished and with a view of the Mediterranean garden with its marble fountain or out into the blue, are somewhat simpler. The finest prospect is to be had from the roof terrace of the suite on the top floor. To book this panorama, it is necessary to reserve the room in good time, as Doma has many regular guests who come one summer after another to see the house and hosts again. Even now, though advanced in years, Rena and Ioanna insist on being present in person for their guests. ◆ Book to pack and film to watch: "Maintaining Pereira" by Antonio Tabucchi (the Italian author was a frequent guest and friend of the hotel owners), filmed by Roberto Faenza (1995), with Marcello Mastroianni

DIRECTIONS *On the seaside promenade of Chania, 1 km/0.5 miles from the Venetian harbor and 13.5 km/8 miles from Chania international airport* · **RATES** *€–€€€* · **ROOMS** *20 rooms and suites* · **FOOD** *A hearty Cretan breakfast is served in the dining room with its picture windows and many memorabilia from the island* · **HISTORY** *A marble plaque at the entrance commemorates the history of the house as the consulate of the Austro-Hungarian Empire, and in the hall the sign from the former British consulate hangs on the wall* · **X-FACTOR** *The discreet and personal service*

DAS HAUS DER SCHWESTERN

Ursprünglich war diese Villa auf Kreta eine diplomatische Vertretung: Hier residierte Ende des 19. Jahrhunderts der Konsul von Österreich-Ungarn. 1933 kaufte die Großmutter der heutigen Besitzerinnen das Gebäude und machte aus ihm ein Privathaus, denn dank der idyllischen Lage in Chanias Vorort Chalepa, direkt am Meer und mit Weinreben auf der Rückseite des Hauses, war es der perfekte Platz für eine Familie. Im Zweiten Weltkrieg und in den Jahren danach mussten die Bewohner ihr Heim erst deutschen Besatzern, dann britischen Diplomaten überlassen, bis sie es 1955 offiziell zurückbekamen. Seit Weihnachten 1971 führen es die Schwestern Irene (Rena) Valyraki und Ioanna Koutsoudaki als Hotel und erzählen hier feinsinnig und lebensfroh von der bewegten Geschichte ihrer Familie und ihrer Insel. Sie konnten wertvolle Antiquitäten, verblichene Fotos sowie originale Kunstwerke bewahren und haben damit die Empfangs- und Loungebereiche sowie die Privaträume eingerichtet (eine Augenweide ist die Vitrine mit exotischem Kopfschmuck und prächtigen Hüten, die Ioanna auf ihren Reisen gesammelt hat). Etwas schlichter zeigen sich die Gästezimmer, die alle individuell gestaltet sind und auf den mediterranen Garten mit Marmorbrunnen oder ins Blaue blicken: Die schönste Sicht eröffnet die Suite im obersten Stockwerk von ihrer Dachterrasse. Damit man dieses Panorama genießen kann, muss man rechtzeitig reservieren, denn das Doma hat viele Stammgäste, die Sommer für Sommer anreisen, um das Haus und seine Hausherrinnen wiederzusehen. Auch im hohen Alter lassen Rena und Ioanna es sich nicht nehmen, höchstpersönlich für ihre Besucher da zu sein. ◆ Buch- und Filmtipp: „Erklärt Pereira“ von Antonio Tabucchi (der italienische Autor war ein regelmäßiger Gast und Freund der Hotelbesitzerinnen), verfilmt von Roberto Faenza (1995), mit Marcello Mastroianni

ANREISE *An der Seepromenade von Chania gelegen, 1 km vom venezianischen Hafen und 13,5 km vom internationalen Flughafen Chania entfernt* · **PREISE** *€–€€€* · **ZIMMER** *20 Zimmer und Suiten* · **KÜCHE** *Im Speisesaal mit Panoramafenstern und vielen Inselmemorabilien wird ein reichhaltiges kretisches Frühstück serviert* · **GESCHICHTE** *Eine Marmortafel am Eingang erinnert an die Vergangenheit des Hauses als österreichisch-ungarisches Konsulat, und in der Halle hängt das einstige britische Konsulatsschild an der Wand* · **X-FAKTOR** *Der diskrete und persönliche Service*

LA MAISON DES SŒURS

À la fin du XIXe siècle, cette villa abritait le consulat austro-hongrois en Crète. La grand-mère des propriétaires actuelles a acheté le bâtiment en 1933 et l'a transformé en résidence privée – sa situation idyllique dans la banlieue de La Canée, à Chalepa, au bord de la mer et avec des vignes à l'arrière de la maison en faisait l'endroit idéal pour une famille. Pendant la Seconde Guerre mondiale et dans les années qui ont suivi, les habitants ont dû laisser leur maison aux occupants allemands, puis aux diplomates britanniques avant de pouvoir la récupérer officiellement en 1955. Depuis Noël 1971, les sœurs Irene (Rena) Valyraki et Ioanna Koutsoudaki la gèrent comme un hôtel et racontent l'histoire de leur famille et de leur île avec animation et joie de vivre. Elles ont pu conserver des antiquités de valeur, des photographies pâlies par le temps et des œuvres d'art et les ont utilisées pour meubler la réception et le salon ainsi que les pièces privées (la vitrine abritant les coiffes exotiques et les magnifiques chapeaux qu'Ioanna a collectionnés lors de ses voyages est un plaisir pour les yeux). Les chambres sont un peu plus simples, toutes décorées individuellement, et donnent sur le jardin méditerranéen avec sa fontaine en marbre ou sur l'immensité bleue : depuis son toit-terrasse, la suite au dernier étage offre la plus belle vue. Pour profiter de ce panorama, il faut réserver à temps, car le Doma compte de nombreux hôtes réguliers qui arrivent été après été pour revoir la maison et ses propriétaires. Même à leur âge avancé, Rena et Ioanna aiment s'occuper personnellement de leurs visiteurs. ◆ À lire et à voir : « Pereira prétend » par Antonio Tabucchi (l'écrivain italien était un habitué et un ami des propriétaires de l'hôtel), porté à l'écran par Roberto Faenza (1995), avec Marcello Mastroianni

ACCÈS *Situé sur le bord de mer de La Canée, à 1 km du port vénitien et à 13,5 km de l'aéroport international de La Canée* · **PRIX** *€–€€€* · **CHAMBRES** *20 chambres et suites* · **RESTAURATION** *Un opulent petit-déjeuner crétois est servi dans la salle à manger dotée de fenêtres panoramiques et qui abrite de nombreux souvenirs de l'île* · **HISTOIRE** *Une plaque de marbre à l'entrée évoque le passé de la maison, autrefois consulat austro-hongrois, et l'ancienne plaque consulaire britannique est suspendue au mur du hall* · **LES « PLUS »** *Le personnel discret et prévenant*

DILETTA

AMMOS

CHANIA, CRETE

AMMOS

Irakli Avgoula Street, Chania, 731 00 Crete
Tel. +30 28210 330 03 and in winter: +30 694 600 96 86 · info@ammoshotel.com
www.ammoshotel.com

A SUMMER HOUSE

Thanks to its picturesque Venetian harbor guarded by an Egyptian lighthouse, its picture-postcard promenade with cafés and restaurants and the winding alleys of the Old Town lined by boutiques selling craft products, Chania is regarded as the most beautiful town in Crete, if not in the whole of Greece. Every bit as photogenic as the historic town center but in a wholly modern style, Ammos stands right by the beach and owes its name to its wonderful location: the Greek word "ammos" means "sand." Though it has a plain exterior in the white and sky-blue typical of the island, the hotel is a blaze of color inside. In collaboration with architect Elisa Manola, owner Nikos Tsepetis has fitted out the rooms so playfully and joyfully that guests immediately get a boost of energy and an elevated mood when they enter. The designer chairs for the lobby, lounge and restaurant have been assembled with a passion for collecting and a sense of style – no two pieces of furniture are identical, and new items are added every year. The guest rooms have no television, but wonderful terrazzo floors, beds by the Greek ecological brand Coco-Mat and chic extras such as colorful stools by Moroso and curtains by Kvadrat. With a keen and demanding eye for art and design, Nikos also combines works by Jean Prouvé and Ilmari Tapiovaara, Odd Matter and Pierre Yovanovitch, Christodoulos Panayiotou and Konstantin Kakanias. Kitchenettes are also a standard feature, but are not really necessary – the food, from the sumptuous breakfast for late risers to the exquisite dessert after dinner, is first-class and just as laid-back as the rest of the hotel. ◆ Book to pack: "Zorba the Greek" by Nikos Kazantzakis (there is a copy in every room); film to watch: "Zorba the Greek" (1964) by Michael Cacoyannis with Anthony Quinn, which is screened in the restaurant every Sunday after dark

DIRECTIONS *5 km/3 miles from the Old Town of Chania, 20 km/13 miles from Chania airport, 140 km/90 miles from Heraklion airport* · **RATES** *€–€€€* · **ROOMS** *33 rooms with a garden or sea view. Several are rather small, and it is worth booking a room with a balcony or terrace* · **FOOD** *Breakfast is served until 11:30 am. For lunch and dinner, classic Greek dishes get a modern interpretation, best enjoyed on the veranda* · **HISTORY** *The hotel was opened in 1996 and redesigned from 2005 to 2008* · **X-FACTOR** *The exceptionally family-friendly, personal service*

EIN SOMMERHAUS

Dank des malerischen venezianischen Hafens, über den ein ägyptischer Leuchtturm wacht, der Postkartenpromenade mit Cafés und Restaurants sowie der verwinkelten Altstadtgassen, in denen sich Boutiquen mit Kunsthandwerk Tür an Tür reihen, gilt Chania als schönste Stadt Kretas, wenn nicht sogar Griechenlands. Ebenso fotogen wie das historische Zentrum, aber in ganz modernem Stil zeigt sich das Hotel Ammos, das direkt am Strand liegt und dieser herrlichen Lage seinen Namen verdankt – das griechische Wort „ammos" bedeutet „Sand". Außen schlicht in inseltypischem Weiß und Himmelblau gehalten, ist das Haus innen ein Farbenspiel. Gemeinsam mit der Architektin Elisa Manola hat der Besitzer Nikos Tsepetis die Räume so fröhlich und unbeschwert gestaltet, dass man beim Eintreten sofort gute Laune und neue Energie bekommt. Mit Sammlerleidenschaft und Stilsicherheit wurden die Designerstühle für Lobby, Lounge und Restaurant zusammengetragen – kein Möbel gleicht dem anderen, und jedes Jahr kommen neue Modelle hinzu. In den Gästezimmern gibt es keine Fernseher, doch dafür wunderschöne Terrazzoböden, Betten der griechischen Ökomarke Coco-Mat und schicke Extras wie bunte Hocker von Moroso sowie Vorhänge von Kvadrat. Mit gutem – und anspruchsvollem – Auge für Kunst und Design kombiniert Nikos zudem Werke von Jean Prouvé und Ilmari Tapiovaara, Odd Matter und Pierre Yovanovitch, Christodoulos Panayiotou und Konstantin Kakanias. Auch eine Kitchenette gehört zur Standardausstattung der Zimmer – wäre aber eigentlich nicht nötig, denn die Küche des Ammos ist vom üppigen Langschläferfrühstück bis zum feinen Dessert nach dem Dinner erstklassig und genauso entspannt wie der Rest des Hotels. ◆ Buchtipp: „Alexis Sorbas" von Nikos Kazantzakis (liegt in jedem Zimmer bereit!); Filmtipp: „Alexis Sorbas" (1964) von Michael Cacoyannis, mit Anthony Quinn, der jeden Sonntag nach Einbruch der Dunkelheit im Restaurant gezeigt wird

ANREISE *5 km von der Altstadt Chanias, 20 km vom Flughafen Chania, 140 km vom Flughafen Heraklion entfernt* · **PREISE** *€–€€€* · **ZIMMER** *33 Zimmer mit Garten- oder Meerblick. Einige sind recht klein, es lohnt sich, ein Zimmer mit Balkon oder Terrasse zu buchen* · **KÜCHE** *Frühstück bis 11:30 Uhr. Mittags und abends genießt man griechische Klassiker modern interpretiert – am schönsten auf der Veranda* · **GESCHICHTE** *Das Hotel wurde 1996 eröffnet und von 2005 bis 2008 neu designt* · **X-FAKTOR** *Der außergewöhnlich (familien-)freundliche, persönliche Service*

UN PAVILLON D'ÉTÉ

Son pittoresque port vénitien surveillé par un phare égyptien, sa promenade de carte postale avec cafés et restaurants et le labyrinthe de ruelles de la vieille ville, où les boutiques artisanales se suivent, font de La Canée la plus belle ville de Crète, sinon de Grèce. Tout aussi photogénique que le centre historique, mais dans un style très moderne, l'hôtel Ammos s'élève directement sur la plage et doit son nom à cet emplacement magnifique – en grec « ammos » signifie « sable ». L'extérieur est sobre, blanc et bleu ciel, ce qui est caractéristique de l'île, tandis que les espaces intérieurs jouent avec les couleurs. Avec l'architecte Elisa Manola, le propriétaire Nikos Tsepetis a aménagé les chambres de manière si joyeuse et ludique qu'elles dispensent immédiatement de la bonne humeur et un regain d'énergie. Les chaises design qui se trouvent dans le hall d'entrée, le salon et le restaurant ont été assemblées par un collectionneur passionné amoureux de l'élégance – aucun meuble ne ressemble à l'autre, et chaque année voit de nouveaux modèles arriver. Pas de télévision dans les chambres, mais de magnifiques sols en terrazzo, des lits de la marque grecque écologique Coco-Mat et des extras chics tels des tabourets multicolores de Moroco ainsi que des rideaux de Kvadrat. Avec son œil averti, Nikos combine également des œuvres de Jean Prouvé et Ilmari Tapiovaara, Odd Matter et Pierre Yovanovitch, Christodoulos Panayiotou et Konstantin Kakanias. Les chambres possèdent toutes une kitchenette, ce qui ne serait pas nécessaire, car la cuisine de l'Ammos, de l'opulent petit-déjeuner des amateurs de grasse matinée au dessert raffiné proposé après dîner, est aussi remarquable et décontractée que le reste de l'hôtel. ◆ À lire : « Alexis Zorba » de Nikos Kazantzakis (on le trouve dans toutes les chambres !) ; à voir : le film « Zorba le Grec » (1964) de Michael Cacoyannis, avec Anthony Quinn, qui est montré tous les dimanches au restaurant à la nuit tombée

ACCÈS *À 5 km de la ville historique de La Canée. À 20 km de l'aéroport de La Canée, à 140 km de celui d'Héraklion* · **PRIX** *€–€€€* · **CHAMBRES** *33 chambres avec vue sur le jardin ou la mer. Certaines sont très petites, réserver une chambre avec balcon ou terrasse vaut la peine* · **RESTAURATION** *Le petit-déjeuner est servi jusqu'à 11 h 30. On peut savourer le midi et le soir des plats classiques grecs interprétés de manière moderne – la véranda est l'endroit idéal* · **HISTOIRE** *Ouvert en 1996, le design a été repensé de 2005 à 2008* · **LES « PLUS »** *Le service exceptionnellement aimable (les enfants sont les bienvenus) et soucieux du bien-être de chacun*

METOHI KINDELIS

CHANIA, CRETE

METOHI KINDELIS

Chania, 731 00 Crete
Tel. +30 28210 413 21 and +30 694 472 42 96 · info@metohi-kindelis.gr
www.metohi-kindelis.gr

RURAL LIFE

It is not known when exactly this picturesque estate was established – it is assumed that it was founded in about 1580 as the summer residence of wealthy Venetians. Today the Kindelis family lives here, cultivating fruit and vegetables on one of the first organic farms not only on Crete but in the whole of Greece. In order to share their ideal of a sustainable life in the country and also to share discreet, intelligent luxury with more people, they converted three areas of the historic farm to holiday cottages using natural materials and Venetian artisan methods. Beneath original stone arches and dark wooden ceilings, protected by thick walls, they created rustic retreats of extraordinary charm: Danae in simple country-house style, Kynthia with antiques and a bathroom in watery mint green, and Kyriakos with an elegant, relaxed atmosphere. Each of these houses has a private patio, a saltwater pool and a blooming garden. The host Danai Kindeli welcomes her guests with unexpected personal gestures: they find a guidebook to Chania, a list of local wines to sample and even a selection of music await them on arrival. Every morning the refrigerator is filled with regional breakfast goodies, while in the evening, on request, a basket with a recipe and ingredients for a healthy Cretan dinner is placed at the door. Danai's uncle Manolis himself is pleased to guide his guests around the farm and teach them the basics of organic agriculture. The lovingly tended natural surroundings of Metohi Kindelis make for a perfect picnic – just heavenly!
◆ Book to pack: "The Cretan Runner" by George Psychoundakis

DIRECTIONS *In the northwest of Crete, 3 km/2 miles from the center of Chania and about 20 km/13 miles from Chania airport or 140 km/86 miles from Heraklion airport* · **RATES** *€–€€* · **ROOMS** *3 apartments, each for up to 2 adults and 2 children, all with a kitchen* · **FOOD** *For self-caterers. Meals can be delivered on request* · **HISTORY** *The Kindelis family has owned the farm for more than 100 years. The three holiday apartments were converted in 1995, 2001 and 2007* · **X-FACTOR** *Massages, yoga, qi gong and tai chi in the garden are on offer*

LANDLEBEN

Wann genau der Grundstein für dieses malerische Anwesen gelegt wurde, ist unbekannt – man nimmt an, dass es 1580 als Sommerresidenz wohlhabender Venezianer entstand. Heute wohnt hier die Familie Kindelis, die auf einem der ersten Biohöfe Kretas, ja sogar Griechenlands organischen Obst- und Gemüseanbau betreibt. Um ihr Ideal vom nachhaltigen Leben auf dem Land sowie von leisem und intelligentem Luxus mit mehr Menschen zu teilen, baute sie drei Bereiche der historischen Farm mit natürlichen Materialien und venezianischen Handwerkstechniken zu Ferienwohnungen um. Unter originalen Steinbögen und dunklen Holzdecken sowie geschützt von dicken Mauern sind rustikale Refugien mit außergewöhnlich viel Charme entstanden – Danae im schlichten Landhausstil, Kynthia mit Antiquitäten und einem Bad in verwaschenem Mintgrün sowie Kyriakos mit elegant-entspannter Atmosphäre. Zu jeder Unterkunft gehören ein privater Patio, ein Salzwasserpool und ein blühender Garten – die Gastgeberin Danai Kindeli überrascht mit ganz persönlichen Gesten: So liegen bei der Ankunft ein Reiseführer für Chania, eine Liste mit lokalen Weinen, die man probieren sollte, und sogar eine Musikauswahl bereit. Jeden Morgen wird der Kühlschrank mit Frühstücksleckereien aus der Region gefüllt, und abends steht auf Wunsch ein Korb mit Rezept und Zutaten für ein gesundes kretisches Abendessen vor der Tür. Danais Onkel Manolis führt seine Besucher gerne übers Gelände und gibt ihnen dabei einen Grundkurs in organischer Landwirtschaft. Die liebevoll gepflegte Natur rund um Metohi Kindelis kann man auch bei einem Picknick im Grünen genießen – himmlisch! ◆ Buchtipp: „Die Frauen der Familie Ftenoudos" von Lily Zografou

ANREISE *Im Nordwesten von Kreta gelegen, 3 km vom Zentrum Chanias entfernt und ca. 20 km vom Flughafen Chania, 140 km vom Flughafen Heraklion* · **PREISE** *€–€€* · **ZIMMER** *3 Wohnungen, alle mit Küche und für bis zu 2 Erwachsene und 2 Kinder* · **KÜCHE** *Für Selbstversorger. Auf Anfrage werden Speisen geliefert* · **GESCHICHTE** *Die Familie Kindelis besitzt den Hof seit mehr als 100 Jahren. Die drei Ferienwohnungen entstanden 1995, 2001 und 2007* · **X-FAKTOR** *Im Garten werden Massagen, Yoga, Qigong und Tai-Chi angeboten*

VIVRE À LA CAMPAGNE

On ne sait pas exactement quand la première pierre de ce pittoresque domaine a été posée – on suppose qu'il a été construit vers 1580 pour servir de résidence d'été à de riches Vénitiens. Aujourd'hui, la famille Kindelis vit ici et cultive des fruits et légumes biologiques – dans l'une des premières fermes biologiques de Crète, et même de Grèce. Afin de partager plus largement son idéal de mode de vie rural durable et de luxe tranquille et intelligent, elle a converti trois espaces de la ferme historique en appartements de vacances, utilisant pour ce faire des matériaux naturels et des techniques artisanales vénitiennes. Sous des arcs en pierre d'origine et des plafonds en bois sombre, protégés par des murs épais, des refuges rustiques au charme extraordinaire ont été créés – Danaé dans un style sobre de maison de campagne, Kynthia qui abrite des antiquités et une salle de bains aux nuances de vert menthe à l'eau, et Kyriakos dont l'atmosphère est élégante et détendue. Chaque logement dispose d'un patio privé, d'une piscine d'eau salée et d'un jardin fleuri – et l'hôtesse Danai Kindeli vous surprend par des gestes très personnels : à votre arrivée, un guide de La Canée, une liste de vins locaux à déguster et même une sélection de musique vous sont fournis. Chaque matin, le frigo est rempli de savoureuses spécialités locales et, le soir, si vous le souhaitez, un panier contenant la recette et les ingrédients d'un dîner crétois frais et léger vous attend devant la porte. Manolis, l'oncle de Danai, aime guider les visiteurs à travers le site, en leur dévoilant les principes généraux de l'agriculture biologique. On peut aussi apprécier la nature amoureusement entretenue autour de Metohi Kindelis en pique-niquant dans la verdure – on se croirait au paradis ! ◆ À lire : « Les élégies d'Oxopetra » par Odysséas Elytis

ACCÈS *Au nord-ouest de la Crète, à 3 km du centre de La Canée et environ 20 km de l'aéroport de La Canée ; à 140 km de l'aéroport d'Héraklion* · **PRIX** *€–€€* · **CHAMBRES** *3 appartements avec cuisine pour 2 adultes et 2 enfants* · **RESTAURATION** *Pour ceux qui préparent leurs repas eux-mêmes. Des plats sont livrés sur demande* · **HISTOIRE** *La famille Kindelis est propriétaire de la ferme depuis plus d'un siècle. Les trois appartements de vacances ont vu le jour en 1995, 2001 et 2007* · **LES « PLUS »** *Des cours de yoga, Qi Gong, Tai Chi et des massages sont proposés dans le jardin*

KAPSALIANA VILLAGE HOTEL

RETHYMNON, CRETE

KAPSALIANA VILLAGE HOTEL

Rethymnon, 741 00 Crete
Tel. +30 28310 834 00 · info@kapsalianavillage.gr
www.kapsalianavillage.gr

THE OLIVE FARMERS' VILLAGE

The olive tree used to be held sacred: its fruit was prized for nutrition, while its oil burned in lamps and had healing properties. The tree also provided work, as here in the north of Crete, where the abbot of the Arkadi monastery had an oil mill constructed in 1763. Farmers who moved into the area built the village of Kapsaliana, which had fifty inhabitants at its peak. In the mid-twentieth century the monks abandoned the mill, however. The families left their homes and Kapsaliana fell into decay – until Myron Toupoyannis came along. Born on Crete and working in Paris as an architect, he discovered the ruins in the 1970s, then bought and restored them little by little – until, some thirty years later, he opened Kapsaliana as a hotel village. The houses, restored using local materials such as wood, stone and terracotta following old craft techniques, today accommodate twenty-two rooms and suites for up to fifty guests – because the new old village is not intended to grow larger than it used to be. Characteristic features such as arches, unplastered walls, open fireplaces and stone ovens and basins are still visible. The decommissioned mill has now become a museum of olive oil, where the huge millstone and corkscrew press can still be admired; and oil tastings are held in the restaurant. It goes without saying that the aromatic oil is used in the kitchen, where meals are cooked according to traditional Cretan recipes. For guests from all over the world, Kapsaliana is a journey back into the past; for its employees it is a present and future project close to their hearts: they are evidently proud of their village and maintain it passionately. It could almost be said that Kapsaliana is as sacred to them as the olive tree once was ... ◆ Book to pack: "The Elements" by Harry Mulisch

DIRECTIONS *Kapsaliana is located in the interior of Crete in the north, 18 km/11 miles from Rethymnon and 75 km/45 miles from Heraklion airport* · **RATES** *€€–€€€€* · **ROOMS** *22 rooms and suites named after stars and constellations, some of them with a terrace. The Borealis suite has a pool and a kitchen* · **FOOD** *The Cretan restaurant is run according to the principles of the Slow Food movement. There is also a bar by the communal pool* · **HISTORY** *Opened in 2008 as a hotel village* · **X-FACTOR** *Guided excursions in the region*

DAS DORF DER OLIVENBAUERN

Früher galt der Olivenbaum als heilig – seine Früchte waren wertvolle Nahrung, sein Öl brachte Lampen zum Brennen und hatte heilende Wirkung. Zudem gab der Baum Arbeit, wie hier im Norden Kretas, wo der Abt des Klosters Arkadi 1763 eine Ölmühle errichten ließ. Die Bauern, die in die Gegend zogen, bauten das Dorf Kapsaliana, das zu seinen besten Zeiten 50 Einwohner zählte. Mitte des 20. Jahrhunderts gaben die Mönche die Mühle jedoch auf, die Familien verließen ihre Häuser, und Kapsaliana verfiel. Bis Myron Toupoyannis kam. Der gebürtige Kreter, der in Paris als Architekt lebte, entdeckte die Ruinen in den 1970ern, kaufte und restaurierte sie nach und nach – bis er rund 30 Jahre später Kapsaliana als Hoteldorf eröffnete. Mit lokalen Materialien wie Holz, Stein sowie Terrakotta und nach alter Handwerkskunst saniert, beherbergen die Häuser heute 22 Zimmer und Suiten für maximal 50 Gäste, denn größer als damals sollte das neue alte Dorf nicht werden. In den Räumen sind noch charakteristische Elemente wie Bögen, unverputzte Wände, offene Kamine oder steinerne Öfen und Becken zu sehen. Die stillgelegte Mühle ist inzwischen ein Olivenölmuseum, in dem man den mächtigen Mühlstein und die Schraubpresse bestaunen kann; und im Restaurant werden Ölverkostungen angeboten. Selbstverständlich kommt das aromatische Öl auch in der Küche zum Einsatz, wo nach überlieferten kretischen Rezepten gekocht wird. Für seine Gäste aus aller Welt ist Kapsaliana eine Reise in die Vergangenheit und für seine Mitarbeiter ein Herzensprojekt der Gegenwart und Zukunft: Sie sind erkennbar stolz auf ihr Dorf und bewahren es mit Leidenschaft. Fast könnte man sagen, es ist ihnen so heilig wie es einst der Olivenbaum war … ◆ Buchtipp: „Die Elemente" von Harry Mulisch

ANREISE *Kapsaliana liegt im Inselinneren im Norden von Kreta, 18 km von der Stadt Rethymnon und 75 km vom Flughafen Heraklion entfernt* · **PREISE** *€€–€€€€* · **ZIMMER** *22 nach Sternen und Sternbildern benannte Zimmer und Suiten, teilweise mit Terrasse. Die Suite Borealis hat einen Pool und eine Küche* · **KÜCHE** *Das kretische Restaurant folgt der Slow-Food-Philosophie. Zudem gibt es eine Bar am Gemeinschaftspool* · **GESCHICHTE** *2008 als Hoteldorf eröffnet* · **X-FAKTOR** *Die geführten Ausflüge durch die Region*

LE VILLAGE DES OLÉICULTEURS

L'olivier était autrefois un arbre sacré – ses fruits étaient précieux, son huile servait à tous les usages culinaires, fournissait de la lumière dans les lampes et avait des vertus curatives. Et cultiver l'olivier demandait de la main-d'œuvre, comme ici dans le nord de la Crète, où l'abbé du monastère Arkadi a fait construire un moulin à huile en 1763. Les agriculteurs qui se sont installés dans la région ont construit le village de Kapsaliana, qui comptait 50 habitants à l'époque où il était florissant. Au milieu du XXe siècle, les moines ont renoncé à exploiter le moulin, les familles ont abandonné le village et Kapsaliana est tombé en ruine. Et puis Myron Toupoyannis est arrivé. Originaire de Crète et ayant vécu à Paris où il était architecte, il a découvert les ruines dans les années 1970, les a achetées et les a progressivement restaurées – avant d'ouvrir le village hôtelier de Kapsaliana une trentaine d'années plus tard. Aujourd'hui, les maisons restaurées avec des matériaux locaux tels que le bois, la pierre et la terre cuite en mettant à profit un savoir-faire artisanal ancien, abritent 22 chambres et suites pour un maximum de 50 personnes, car le village ne doit pas devenir plus grand qu'il l'était autrefois. Dans les chambres, on peut encore voir des éléments caractéristiques comme des arcs, des murs non crépis, des cheminées ouvertes ou des poêles et des bassins en pierre. Le pressoir désaffecté a été transformé en musée de l'olive, où l'on peut admirer la puissante meule de pierre et le pressoir à vis, et des dégustations d'huile sont proposées au restaurant. Bien sûr, l'huile aromatique est également utilisée en cuisine, pour préparer des recettes crétoises traditionnelles. Pour ses hôtes du monde entier, Kapsaliana est un voyage dans le passé, et pour ses employés, un projet porteur d'avenir : ils sont visiblement fiers de leur village et le préservent avec passion. On pourrait presque dire qu'il est aussi sacré pour eux que l'olivier l'était pour leurs ancêtres…
◆ À lire : « Les éléments » par Harry Mulisch

ACCÈS *Kapsaliana est situé à l'intérieur des terres, au nord de la Crète, à 18 km de la ville de Réthymnon et à 75 km de l'aéroport d'Héraklion* · **PRIX** *€€–€€€€* · **CHAMBRES** *22 chambres et suites portant les noms d'étoiles et de constellations, dotées en partie d'une terrasse. La suite Borealis dispose d'une piscine et d'une cuisine* · **RESTAURATION** *Le restaurant grec suit les préceptes de la philosophie Slow-Food. Il y a également un bar près de la piscine commune* · **HISTOIRE** *Le village hôtelier est ouvert depuis 2008* · **LES « PLUS »** *Les excursions guidées à travers la région*

PHOTO CREDITS

8 **Apeiros Chora**
Supplied by the hotel

18 **Astra Inn**
Supplied by the hotel (pp. 18–20, 23, 28 above right, 28 below left: Stratos Chatzigiannakis; pp. 24–27, 28 below right, 29: Alexandros Malapetsas)

30 **Chatzigakis Manor**
Supplied by the hotel (pp. 30-35: Julia Klimi; pp. 36/37: Oliver Emil Mauthe)

38 **Nymfaio Retreats**
Supplied by the hotel

48 **Imaret**
Supplied by the hotel

58 **Eagles Palace**
Supplied by the hotel

64 **Elivi Skiathos**
Supplied by the hotel

70 **Euphoria Retreat**
George Sfakianakis, supplied by the hotel

80 **Mazaraki Guesthouse**
Supplied by the hotel

86 **Amanzoe**
Courtesy of Aman

94 **Kinsterna Hotel**
Supplied by the hotel

102 **Tainaron Blue Retreat**
Supplied by the hotel

110 **Kyrimai Hotel**
Supplied by the hotel (pp. 110/111, 116: Giorgos Vitsaropoulos)

118 **Pirgos Mavromichali**
Supplied by the hotel

124 **The Patrick & Joan Leigh Fermor House**
Supplied by the hotel

132 **Dexamenes**
Supplied by the hotel

138 **Orloff Boutique Hotel**
Supplied by the hotel

146 **Four Seasons Hydra**
Supplied by the hotel (pp. 146–148, 151: George Anastasakis; pp. 152–153: Julia Klimi)

154 **Poseidonion Grand Hotel**
Supplied by the hotel

162 **Onar**
Supplied by the hotel

168 **Mèlisses**
pp. 6, 168–183, 359: supplied by the hotel (pp. 168–170: Nicole Franzen; pp. 175, 177: Issy Croker; p. 176: Ingrid Hofstra; pp. 179, 182/183: Renée Kemps)

184 **The Wild Hotel by Interni**
Supplied by the hotel

192 **Soho Roc House**
Supplied by SOHO house

198 **Boutique Hotel Ploes**
pp. 2–3, 198–209
Gianni Basso/Vega MG

210 **Coco-Mat Eco Residences**
Supplied by the hotel

218 **Beachhouse Antiparos**
Supplied by the hotel

224 **Verina Astra**
Supplied by the hotel

232 **The Windmill Kimolos**
Supplied by Studioreskos

240 **Skinopi Lodge**
Supplied by the hotel (pp. 240–242, 247: Louis A. W. Sheridan; p. 245 above: Erieta Attali; pp. 245 below, 246: Ioanna Nikolareizi)

248 **Anemomilos**
Supplied by the hotel

258 **Perivolas**
Supplied by the hotel (pp. 258/259, 263 above: Enrique Menossi; pp. 260, 263 below: William Abranowicz)

264 **Mystique**
Supplied by the hotel

270 **Hotel Archontiko Angelou**
Yuki Sugiura

276 **Oku Kos**
Georg Roske, supplied by the hotel

286 **The Old Markets**
Supplied by the hotel

292 **Marco Polo Mansion**
Gianni Basso/Vega MG

304 **Mediterraneo Kastelorizo**
Julia Klimi, supplied by the hotel

310 **The Rou Estate**
Supplied by Simpson Travel

316 **Villa Lemonia**
Supplied by the hotel

322 **Nostos**
Supplied by the hotel

328 **Hotel Doma**
Giorgos Vitsaropoulos, supplied by the hotel

336 **Ammos**
James Bedford, supplied by the hotel

344 **Metohi Kindelis**
Danai and Kynhtia Kindeli

352 **Kapsaliana Village Hotel**
Supplied by the hotel

IMPRINT

EACH AND EVERY TASCHEN BOOK PLANTS A SEED!
TASCHEN is a carbon-neutral publisher. Each year, we offset our annual carbon emissions with carbon credits at the Instituto Terra, a reforestation program in Minas Gerais, Brazil, founded by Lélia and Sebastião Salgado. To find out more about this ecological partnership, please check: www.taschen.com/zerocarbon
Inspiration: unlimited. Carbon footprint: zero.

To stay informed about TASCHEN and our upcoming titles, please subscribe to our free magazine at www.taschen.com/magazine, follow us on Instagram and Facebook, or e-mail your questions to contact@taschen.com.

Hohenzollernring 53, D-50672 Köln
www.taschen.com

Printed in Slovakia
ISBN 978-3-8365-8520-0

EDITING, ART DIRECTION AND LAYOUT
Angelika Taschen, Berlin

PROJECT MANAGER
Stephanie Paas, Cologne

DESIGN
Maximiliane Hüls, Cologne

TEXTS
Christiane Reiter, Brussels

ENGLISH TRANSLATION
John Sykes, Cologne

FRENCH TRANSLATION
Michèle Schreyer, Cologne

THE EDITOR
Angelika Taschen studied art history and German literature in Heidelberg, gaining her doctorate in 1986. Working for TASCHEN from 1987, she has published numerous titles on art, architecture, photography, design, travel and lifestyle.

With special thanks to Nikos Tsepetis.

THE AUTHOR
Christiane Reiter is a freelance author based in Brussels. She studied journalism at the University of Eichstätt and worked as a travel editor for Ringier Publishing in Munich and Zurich. Later, she established the travel section of the *Frankfurter Allgemeine Sonntagszeitung.*

FRONT COVER
Skinopi Lodge, Milos
Photo: Frank Adrian Barron/supplied by the hotel

BACK COVER
Mêlisses, Andros
Photo: Renée Kemps/supplied by the hotel

ENDPAPERS
Kyrimai Hotel, Gerolimenas, East Mani
Photo: Supplied by the hotel

PRICE CATEGORIES
€ up to 150 € · **€€** up to 250 € ·
€€€ up to 450 € · **€€€€** over 450 €